1001 WAYS TO IMPROVE YOUR CHILD'S SCHOOLWORK

An Easy-to-Use Reference Book of Common School Problems and Practical Solutions

LAWRENCE J. GREENE

A Dell Trade Paperback

A DELL TRADE PAPERBACK

Published by
Dell Publishing
a division of
Bantam Doubleday Dell Publishing Group, Inc.
666 Fifth Avenue
New York, New York 10103

The trademark Dell® is registered in the U.S. Patent and Trademark Office.

ISBN: 0–440–50265–9

Book design by Robin Arzt

Illustrations by Artfolio

Photo by David Bassett

Printed in the United States of America

Published simultaneously in Canada

December 1991

10 9 8 7 6 5 4 3 2 1

RRH

This book is for Adelaide and Harold.
You were always there.

ACKNOWLEDGMENTS

There are many wonderful people whom I want to thank for their assistance and support. Foremost are Katie Andrade and Melissa Havercroft, my able research assistants. Others who have helped me include Pamela Wilding, Alison Lucas, Monroe Gross, M.D., Mark Steinberg, Ph.D., Estella Lacey, M.F.C.C., Anne Henshall, and Alison Freeman, Ph.D. And then, of course, there are my four exceptional colleagues: Robbie Dunton, Elizabeth Gustafson, Joan Belford, and Helen Waugh. You are the consummately talented educational therapists who demonstrate every day how to help children achieve their full potential.

CONTENTS

INTRODUCTION

What should you do when your son doesn't complete his homework or neglects to write down his assignments? Can you realistically be expected to help him with a reading, spelling, or math problem? How should you react when your daughter leaves her book reports to the last minute and invariably runs out of time? What should you do if she seems perfectly content to hand in sloppy, illegible assignments or reports with run-on sentences? And how should you respond when she studies diligently, appears to know the material, and then does poorly on the test? Should you commiserate with her, admonish her, or roll up your sleeves and become her tutor?

If you have wrestled with any of these issues, you know the frustration of wanting to help and not knowing what to do. Perhaps, in exasperation, you have felt like exclaiming "I'm not a teacher! I haven't been trained to deal with these problems." And perhaps, in desperation, you resorted to the classic weapons that parents use to "motivate" their children: nagging, threats, punishment, and denial of privileges.

You wouldn't be reading this book if you weren't a concerned, responsible parent. You recognize the importance of good academic and problem-solving skills in an increasingly technological world. You want your child to have the tools to be academically and vocationally successful. You want him to establish goals, make his best effort, acquire self-confidence, and be proud of his talents and accomplishments. You want him to develop the intellectual, emotional, and academic resources to prevail over challenges, analyze problems, evaluate opportunities, learn from mistakes, and bounce back from setbacks. These are the legitimate and universal desires of every parent.

Each year millions of potentially capable students fail to acquire the skills they need to win in a highly competitive world. Some are inadequately educated. Some struggle because of learning problems. Others have acquired a pattern of self-defeating habits. They procrastinate, hand in sloppy work, and do not pay attention to important details. Many underachieving children simply do not know how to study effectively. They haven't a clue about how to identify important information, remember key facts, budget study time, or anticipate what is likely to be asked on the next test.

The battle to survive academically can exact a terrible toll on children's self-confidence, expectations, attitude, effort, behavior, and pride. To protect themselves, struggling children often begin to avoid challenges. But rather than provide a shield against feelings of inadequacy, the counterproductive behaviors they adopt as defense mechanisms simply guarantee continued marginal performance and continued deterioration of self-confidence. Children enmeshed in an underachievement loop, of course, do not recognize this obvious irony. Convinced, either consciously or unconsciously, that effort is futile, they choose the path of least resistance: they deny, blame, rationalize, resist, complain, give up, turn off, and shut down.

Achieving youngsters respond very differently to obstacles and challenges. They establish personal performance goals and develop strategies for achieving their goals. They persevere despite roadblocks and setbacks. They are motivated because they are convinced they can control their destiny and because they enjoy the payoffs their efforts produce.

If you have concluded that you cannot necessarily count on your child's public or private school to correct all of your child's academic problems, you are not alone. Each year thousands of parents come to the same painful realization. Our educational system often does not even provide help for children with relatively serious learning problems. Students with subtle problems almost invariably fall through the cracks. Left to fend for themselves, they flail and flounder while their parents watch helplessly. That their untreated "insignificant" problems often become academically and emotionally debilitating is an unpleasant reality that many poorly funded, myopic school systems choose to overlook.

Whether your child has relatively "minor," nonspecific learning deficits or significant, specific learning disabilities, you no longer have to stand powerlessly on the sideline. This book, the distillation of more than twenty-one years of experience in treating more than 8,000 underachieving youngsters, will show you how to help your child succeed in school.

By becoming informed and by understanding the educational and psychological issues that affect your child's schoolwork, you can play a key role in making sure your child develops his full academic and intellectual potential. You will be able to identify deficits, resolve problems, respond to crises, evaluate options, monitor progress, assess programs, and communicate effectively with school personnel. Because you are informed, you will be able to ask penetrating, incisive questions that require meaningful, substantive answers from school personnel. If conflicts or inequities occur, you will also be able to serve as your child's advocate. This parental activism sends an unequivocal message to the educational system: "My child *deserves* a first-rate education, and I am here to see that he gets it. I promise to be reasonable and do my share at home. You must also be reasonable and do your share in school."

HOW TO USE THIS BOOK

Designed as a reference guide, this book is structured like an alphabetized home medical dictionary. Each symptom, behavior, attitude, or problem is briefly described, then followed by a wide range of practical, easy-to-implement techniques designed to help your child succeed in school.

Ideally, your child's academic problems can be solved in school. To facilitate this, each entry includes specific suggestions and strategies for enlisting the help of your child's teacher. Each entry also outlines practical methods for helping your child at home and for supplementing school-provided learning assistance. The objective is not to transform you into a teacher or therapist, but rather to show how you can participate productively in helping your child improve his schoolwork. *You do not need to be a teacher to use these strategies.* The only requirements are that you be concerned about your child's learning and willing to assist in a constructive, supportive, patient, and loving way.

Certain learning difficulties, of course, do not lend themselves to easy solutions. Problems such as attention deficit disorder (difficulty concentrating), dyslexia (letter and number reversals), spelling problems, and chronic self-sabotaging behavior are complex and often involve overlapping educational, physiological, and psychological factors. Checklists have been included under certain entries to help you, your child, and your child's teacher identify specific deficits that may be causing academic inefficiency. Although identified deficits may not be easily remedied, there are positive, practical steps you can take to assist your child. While children with significant learning problems require the assistance of trained professionals in the public or private sector, these youngsters can usually make quicker progress when they receive effective help and guidance at home.

You do not need to read this book from cover to cover. Use it as you would a dictionary. Look up a specific problem or issue and experiment with the suggested strategies. If you want more information, examine the many cross-referenced entries. Select a strategy consistent with your parenting style and temperament. If your first choice doesn't work, try another.

HOW TO HELP YOUR CHILD

Here are some guidelines to keep in mind whenever you work with your child:

■ Your child will be more receptive and will do better work when you communicate optimism and positive expectations, when you are supportive and patient, and when you affirm his or her progress.

■ Be creative and make the time you spend with your child as interesting and engaging as possible. Having fun and enjoying the process is not only permissible; it is ideal! Encourage your child's active involvement in the learning process. Use examples and analogies your child can understand and appreciate. (For example: "If you were playing a video game and ten alien spaceships attacked you and you destroyed half of them, how many would be left?" "If your team needs to gain eight yards for a touchdown and on the first down the fullback carries the ball for 25 percent of the distance, how many yards would still need to be gained for the touchdown?")

■ Keep the sessions relatively short. Your child's attention span is shorter than yours. As a general rule sessions with younger children (grades 1–3) should last no longer than fifteen minutes (unless of course, you and your child are having so much fun that neither of you wants to quit!). Children in grades 4–6 can generally be expected to work for fifteen to thirty minutes at a time. Children in junior and senior high school should be able to work for twenty-five to forty minutes without a break.

■ Provide reasonably spaced breaks when your child is becoming mentally fatigued. Children who are struggling with schoolwork will tire more quickly than those who find the work easy.

■ Don't hesitate to stop for the day when you've worked for the allotted time, even if your child hasn't achieved your objective and is still confused. The alternative, to plow ahead and disregard the fatigue factor, is certain to trigger counterproductive resistance and resentment.

■ If your child is highly resistant to your help, consider hiring an educational therapist or a private tutor. Some children may also require counseling.

■ Involve your child in the entire process. Discuss academic or behavioral problems with him in understandable terms. Urge him to participate in the process of establishing goals, rather than imposing an inflexible agenda on him.

■ Set aside a specific time for the assistance sessions. This doesn't mean you must work with your child *every* evening, but it does mean that you both agree the sessions should take place, for example, between 7:00 and 7:30 P.M. If your child has a specific problem with his homework (e.g., "What is a participle?"), you can, of course, provide "crisis intervention." Be succinct. Children who want a quick fix to a minor problem resent long-winded, comprehensive explanations.

What to Expect from Your Child

Some problems can be resolved relatively quickly. Others may require months or even years of educational assistance. Even highly trained and competent educational therapists often have difficulty predicting how much time will be required to remedy learning problems.

If your child has several learning deficits, you must decide whether to work on these issues concurrently or to establish priorities. A child who has both handwriting and spelling problems could work on correcting both problems. In some cases, however, it is advisable to work exclusively on one problem before beginning to work on another. Consult with your child's teacher and trust your intuition. Don't be afraid to change your strategy if your judgment call was wrong and the plan is not working.

You should always match the activities you choose to help your child with your child's age, skill level, emotional maturity, and attitude. The suggested corrective strategies for junior and senior high school students have been combined because individual subjects are taught in forty- to sixty-minute periods by different teachers who spend less time with their students than do elementary school teachers. Be aware, however, that seventh-graders generally have a shorter attention span than tenth-graders. And know that there will be exceptions. A tenth-grader with a long history of learning problems may be resistant to help and may have developed an elaborate system of emotional defense mechanisms to insulate himself from failure, frustration, and feelings of inadequacy. His attention span may actually be shorter than a seventh-grader's. If you encounter resistance, you may need to limit the duration and frequency of the assistance sessions and make creative adjustments in your expectations, approach, and techniques. You may also need to seek professional help.

Parents and educators have become justifiably alarmed about the quality of American education. With increasing frequency we are bombarded by the media with depressing stories that chronicle the deterioration of our children's academic skills.

You no longer need to be a spectator who stands passively on the sideline watching your child struggle. You can now assume a significant, active, and constructive role in helping your child remove the barriers impeding his or her progress and success in school. This book will provide you with the information and tools you need to get your child back on track.

NOTE ABOUT CODES USED IN THIS BOOK

The suggested corrective strategies within each entry are sometimes preceded by the code **ES** or **J/HS**. **ES** means that strategy applies to elementary school students. **J/HS** means the strategy applies to junior high and high school students. A strategy without a code applies to all students, regardless of grade level.

1001 WAYS TO IMPROVE YOUR CHILD'S SCHOOLWORK

ANGER AND FRUSTRATION

Frustration is a natural response to mistakes, setbacks, and unyielding problems. The intensity and duration of the upset usually reflect the nature of the impediment. When minor obstacles trigger rage or depression, the child's reaction signals unresolved emotional and self-esteem issues that are defeating his coping mechanisms. Children who cannot handle their anger and frustration may become emotionally and academically dysfunctional.

The effects of chronic frustration and anger are cumulative and psychologically corrosive. Children who consciously or unconsciously conclude their situation is hopeless often compensate by becoming withdrawn, defensive, irresponsible, aggressive, or academically immobilized. They latch on to these behaviors to protect themselves. As the defeats and the real or imagined humiliations take their toll, their self-confidence inexorably erodes. Pain begins to warp their perceptions about themselves and their abilities.

Some children respond to setbacks immediately and openly express their upset and frustration. They decide to resolve the problem, put it aside, or move on to the next challenge. Other children warehouse their anger and frustration, and in time the walls of the containment structure usually begin to leak or crumble. The suppressed emotions detonate in rage, seep out in the form of teasing, sarcasm, or cruelty, or implode in the form of depression.

The conscientious student who becomes frustrated upon receiving a poor test grade is reacting normally. If his self-esteem and confidence are secure, he will be able to cope with the setback. He will analyze the situation, make the appropriate adjustments, and tell himself he will do better next time (see **Smart Thinking,** page 275, and **Bouncing Back from Setbacks and Learning from Mistakes,** page 30). If, however, he continues to do poorly despite diligent studying, his rationalizations and coping mechanisms will become increasingly strained, and he will probably be tempted to give up. To hide his feelings of inadequacy, he may acquire an elaborate set of compensatory behaviors (see

Psychological Problems and Psychological Overlay, page 239). He may act out, become the class clown, or focus his energy exclusively in areas where he can excel, such as sports or art. He may retreat into a shell or become aggressive and hostile. He may cry, scream at his mother, have a temper tantrum, or hit his little brother. His anger may subside quickly or continue for hours.

For some children an explosion of fury is cathartic, and after a brief cooling-off period they are ready to move ahead. If, however, the source of the difficulty is not resolved after a series of setbacks, the internal pressure will build.

Children in the grip of such anger may become withdrawn, depressed, and emotionally isolated. Some will sulk, daydream, or escape into a fantasy world that is a peaceful oasis or an angry and violent battleground. Others will express their frustration and unhappiness by striking out at others in nonobvious or camouflaged ways. Children who repress their anger can become so adept at denying and hiding their feelings that adults—even mental health professionals—may not perceive the extent of their inner turmoil.

Negative emotions can be very frightening and difficult for children to recognize and acknowledge, and most unhappy children are not consciously aware that they are hiding their feelings. Perceiving themselves as "bad," they will often try to disown their unpleasant feelings (see **Guilt,** page 101). The guilt they feel can be especially intense when they are angry at their parents.

Chronic anger rarely disappears of its own accord. Although the anger may assume different forms as a child matures—hitting, bullying, self-sabotage, vandalism, sadism, violent fantasies, stealing, cutting school, lying—it will continue to manifest itself until the underlying feelings and issues have been examined and resolved. The sooner he is provided with such help, the better.

The chronically angry child requires professional help in the form of counseling or psychotherapy. He must begin to make peace with himself, his parents, and the world around him before school and social problems can be productively addressed and resolved.

Learning problems and family problems can be primary sources of frustration and anger. The family whose interaction is characterized by poor communication, resentment, manipulation, double messages, inconsistently enforced family rules, unrealistic expectations, and sibling competition is going to produce dysfunctional children.

In some instances anger and frustration may be attributable to several overlapping conditions. A child who is depressed primarily because of a personal trauma or a dysfunctional family situation may also be dyslexic (see page

58). Treating one problem without addressing the other will be ineffective. To resolve these problems the child will require both psychological and academic intervention and therapy (see **Psychological Problems and Psychological Overlay,** page 239).

Although prolonged frustration can cause emotional damage, some types of frustration can actually have a positive effect. Children thwarted by challenges and problems must discover how to mobilize their emotional and intellectual resources. These children must learn how to cope with frustration, solve problems, and prevail over challenges if they are to acquire self-confidence and self-esteem (see **Bouncing Back from Setbacks and Learning from Mistakes,** page 30, and **Self-Esteem and Self-Confidence,** page 266). A vital distinction, however, must be made between frustration that mobilizes a child's resources and chronic, hopeless frustration that produces futility and despair.

SUGGESTED CORRECTIVE STRATEGIES

In School

1. If the teacher informs you that your child is experiencing a great deal of frustration and is angry or hostile in school, you and the teacher must identify the sources of the frustration and brainstorm ways to reduce the child's unhappiness and stress.

2. If your child is having social problems, explore ways in which he might better handle teasing or rejection. Encourage him to eliminate specific behaviors that alienate him from other children, such as telling on other children or acting silly. Also encourage him to develop talents that would improve his self-confidence (e.g., karate or gymnastics) and make him more appealing or acceptable to other children. Enrolling him in after-school programs that develop confidence-building talents can reduce his frustration and nonadaptive social behaviors.

3. If your child is frustrated because of academic difficulties, ask his teacher whether reducing the work load or providing tutorial support is advisable. Next, ask his teacher to identify specific learning deficits and work with the teacher to develop a strategy for resolving these deficits. A diagnostic evaluation by the school psychologist, assistance from the resource specialist, placement in a special day class (a full-time learning assistance program), and/or private educational therapy may be components of this strategy. Refer to relevant entries in this book for specific strategies to correct the learning deficits you and the teacher identify.

4. If you or the teacher observe explosive rage or depression and are concerned about your child's mental health, request that he be evaluated by the school psychologist. If symptoms of an emotional problem are detected, ask for a referral to a mental health professional. (Some enlightened school districts have social workers and therapists on staff or on call.)

At Home

1. Make note of the specific behaviors that concern your child's teacher. Select appropriate issues to examine with your child. For example, you might say: "When I met with your teacher today, she told me that you are hitting other children. This concerns me. Tell me what you think might be causing the problem." Allow time for your child to respond. If he does not respond, you might ask the following questions to help your child get in touch with his underlying feelings and to examine alternatives for expressing these feelings: "Could the fact that you are having difficulty with reading be causing you to get angry? How could this problem of becoming frustrated and angry and then hitting other children be solved? Do you think a tutor might help you with your reading?

What could you do when you sense yourself becoming angry or frustrated? Could you talk to the teacher about what is upsetting you? Could you hang on to your anger until you get home and discuss it with me? Would it help to hang a punching bag in the garage that you could hit to let off some of the steam? If you feel you are about to hit or tease someone, could you walk away and take some time to get yourself under control? Could you count slowly in your head to fifteen before responding? Would it help to have someone besides us or your teacher to talk to about what is making you upset? Let's make a list of things you could do when you are feeling upset. The first step could be to identify what it is that is making you upset. What could you do next?"

2. Consult a mental health professional if you conclude that you cannot identify the source of your child's problems or help him resolve the issues that are causing his frustration and anger. Admitting that your child or your family requires counseling is not an admission of inadequacies but rather a testimony to your honesty and concern. Responsible parents admit when they need help. Irresponsible parents put their head in the sand and naively hope serious problems will magically disappear.

ATTENTION DEFICIT DISORDER

Children who have difficulty filtering out distractions, staying on track, inhibiting impulses, focusing their attention, and controlling their body rarely function in school at a level commensurate with their potential. For many years physicians, psychologists, and educators described these children as hyperactive (manifesting chronic, frenetic, and often purposeless activity) because they believed the inattentiveness frequently observed in these youngsters was caused by their hyperactivity. Extensive observations of distractible children have, however, revealed that this cause-and-effect link was flawed. Although most hyperactive children are indeed inattentive, all inattentive children are *not* necessarily hyperactive. The terms *attention deficit disorder* with *hyperactivity* (*ADHD*) and *attention deficit disorder* without *hyperactivity* (*ADD*) were created to underscore this important distinction and to permit a more precise diagnosis.

ADD and ADHD are usually associated with a perceptual dysfunction (the inefficient processing of sensory data) and are often compounded by specific learning disabilities (see **Learning Disabilities,** page 157). In some cases ADD or ADHD can undermine academic performance in all subjects but in others may manifest itself exclusively in one or two specific areas; for example, a child may be able to concentrate when doing math but not when studying spelling or history.

It is estimated that 2–4 percent of all children have ADHD. That means there are approximately two million hyperactive children in American classrooms at any given time. Although estimates about the size of the nonhyperactive ADD population vary depending on the diagnostic criteria, many additional millions of children clearly fall into this category.

The counterproductive behaviors associated with ADD and ADHD include impulsiveness, inattention to details (see page 12), disorganization (see page 46), improperly recorded assignments (see page 258), missed deadlines (see **Time Management**, page 308), and sloppy, incomplete, inaccurate work (see page 121).

These behaviors can sabotage the work of children with learning disabilities *and* children with good academic skills.

Concentration deficits can be especially debilitating when children are required to do work they find uninteresting or difficult. Keeping a distractible, impulsive child on task while he completes a page of math problems or diagrams sentences can be a formidable task. Ironically, many parents report that ADD children who can concentrate on schoolwork for only a few moments can concentrate for hours while building a model airplane or playing a video game. This selective capacity to concentrate suggests that high-interest activities can sometimes offset the effects of ADD.

ADD children generally have difficulty handling challenging, repetitive, or boring academic tasks that require sustained effort and self-discipline. The traditional "prescription" for dealing with ADD in the classroom is to impose additional structure and external control and to create an environment with few distractions. A teacher might, for example, place the highly distractible child near the teacher's desk or designate a "quiet place" where the child is sent when he becomes excessively hyperactive or unmanageable.

Children with concentration deficits often function best with controlled stimulation, clearly defined behavior guidelines and performance standards, immediate feedback, affirmation for improved behavior, and individualized teaching strategies. However, some distractible students respond best to a highly stimulating, interactive, and creative classroom environment that is not tightly controlled. These youngsters, who are often very bright, pay attention because their brains are actively engaged, and they have difficulty when they are expected do repetitive and mindless work.

Chronic inattentiveness and hyperactivity can create stress for everyone affected by the behavior. In a class of thirty students each child should theoretically receive approximately 3 percent of the teacher's time and energy. A hyperactive or highly distractible child who demands 10 percent of the teacher's energy undermines this equation. Teachers who must continually monitor and control ADD or ADHD children are thrust into the role of police officers. Realizing they are depriving other students of their fair share of instructional time, many of these teachers become frustrated, resentful, demoralized, and weary.

Because ADD children often act out in class, fidget, distract other students, disregard instructions, and "forget" to do assigned work, they usually receive much negative feedback, which undermines their self-confidence and often encourages them to fulfill the perception that they are "bad."

Limited funds, inadequate teacher training, too few specialists, insufficient parental support and involvement, and a production line mentality have forced some school districts to adopt simplistic solutions to the problem of ADD. When students who cannot concentrate do not conform to demands and standards that may be reasonable for other children but are not for them, they are often isolated, punished, resented, disregarded, or targeted for drug therapy.

Recent research (*New England Journal of Medicine,* November 1990) has pinpointed a brain abnormality that could explain why children develop ADD and ADHD. The report indicates that the brains of hyperactive adults (50 percent of hyperactive children become hyperactive adults!) use 8 percent less glucose than normal. (Glucose is the brain's main source of energy.) The research suggests that hyperactivity results when specific regions of the brain that control attention, handwriting, motor coordination, and inhibited responses function improperly. The new findings, when combined with previous research that found that approximately 30 percent of all children with ADHD have at least one parent with ADHD, confirm that hyperactivity is genetically and biologically based and pave the way for the development of a precise diagnostic test for ADHD.

Some physicians who treat ADD and ADHD children regularly prescribe stimulants or antihistamines such as Dexedrine, Ritalin, Cyalert, or Benadryl to control the symptoms. (For complex neurological reasons stimulants have a *calming* effect on many children with ADD and ADHD.) Although these drugs have demonstrated their effectiveness in treating concentration disorders and neurologically based learning disabilities, some professionals are concerned about the potential long-term physical and emotional consequences of extended stimulant use and particularly about possible depression after children stop using the drug, as well as sleeplessness, inhibited growth, reduced appetite, accelerated heart rate, and drug dependency. In rebuttal other physicians argue that drugs such as Ritalin have been used safely and effectively for more than twenty years with no conclusive, documented serious side effects. (Some physicians are now using a new drug program to control neurotransmitter functions and treat ADD. These doctors claim that antidepressant drugs such as Norpramin, Prozac, and Desyrel act for more extended time periods and do not produce many of the negative side effects of stimulants and antihistamines. See *Helping Your Hyperactive Child,* included in the Resource List ("Learning Disabilities") at the back of this book, for more information about medication.

Parents who have concerns about drug therapy should question their child's pediatrician, neurologist, or psychiatrist closely about the pluses and minuses of the treatment. If their concerns are not allayed, they should seek a second opinion and/or explore alternative strategies (see the following suggestions).

Although hyperactivity usually diminishes with the onset of puberty, the distractibility and impulsivity may persist in less overt forms. A teenager who no longer appears hyperactive may still have difficulty staying on track, following instructions, and filtering out distractions in class and when studying. Unless the underlying perceptual processing problems are resolved, the deficits will continue to create academic barriers in junior and senior high school. Because stimulants often do not produce the same calming effect after puberty, this medication is less frequently prescribed for teenagers and adults.

Other means besides medication have also proven effective in treating ADD. Behavior modification, counseling, diets that eliminate food additives, creative teaching strategies, disciplined athletic training, and consistent and firm parenting and teaching have proven beneficial in helping ADD and ADHD children control their impulsivity and inhibit their inattentiveness and distractibility.

SUGGESTED CORRECTIVE STRATEGIES

In School

1. (ES) If your child is manifesting ADD behaviors, consult with his teacher. (She is undoubtedly already aware of the problem!) If she concurs that your child is struggling to pay attention and keep his body under control, discuss the matter with the school psychologist and your pediatrician. If the concentration deficits and hyperactivity also involve specific learning problems, your child should be tested to determine if he qualifies for learning assistance (see **Parents' Rights,** page 201).

2. (ES) A well-conceived behavior modification strategy can be an important teacher resource for controlling ADD. Children who are expected to modify their behavior must be helped to identify specific problem areas, taught methods for achieving specific objectives, and given incentives for making changes (see the daily self-control checklist on page 9). The teacher and your child have a vested interest in working together to solve the distractibility problem. Once your child gains greater control over himself, everyone's life will be easier. Daily feedback is vital. Ask the teacher to fill out the following evaluation of your child, which will take only a few moments at the end of the day.

3. (ES) An alternative to the daily checklist is to provide your child with more immediate feedback. With

DAILY SELF-CONTROL CHECKLIST

Code: *1 = difficulty*   *2 = average*   *3 = good*   *4 = excellent*

	MON.	TUES.	WED.	THURS.	FRI.
You paid attention in class.	___	___	___	___	___
You didn't disturb other students.	___	___	___	___	___
You worked independently.	___	___	___	___	___
You completed your assignments.	___	___	___	___	___
You handed in your work on time.	___	___	___	___	___
You followed instructions.	___	___	___	___	___
Your work was neat.	___	___	___	___	___
Your work was complete.	___	___	___	___	___

Encourage your child to aim for a minimum daily score, which you can increase as his self-control and self-discipline increase. The teacher might establish a symbolic reward such as a gold star for achieving daily and weekly targets. You can reinforce this incentive system by providing additional rewards for good behavior at home (see page 10). Ideally, the teacher will also provide a great deal of verbal encouragement. Affirmation for effort and progress, positive expectations, and patience are essential. Ultimately your child should make the transition from working diligently for extrinsic payoffs (gold stars, free time, reduced homework, etc.) to working for the intrinsic satisfaction of doing a good job.

younger children (grades K–4), the teacher might affix a wide piece of masking tape to the upper corner of your child's desk. A "sad face" should be drawn on the top left-hand side of the tape and a "happy face" on the top right, creating two columns. When the teacher is conscious of your child's paying attention and getting his work done, she could signal your child with a raised index finger. Your child would then put a check in the "happy face" column. When he is distracted or inattentive, the teacher could call his name and signal him with two fingers. He would then put a check in the "sad face" column. Your child should be encouraged to aim for a specific number of "happy face" checks each day (or period), and a reward for improvement should be established in school and at home (e.g., a minimum of ten "happy face" checks in one day can be used for an extra half hour of TV or an ice cream cone). Keep in mind, however, that a reward is an acknowledgment for effort or positive performance, while a bribe is an instrument of manipulation that demeans the person who accepts it. Treats, toys, and excursions are examples of motivating rewards for children. Do not hesitate to use extrinsic rewards as incentives until your child is motivated to do a first-rate job for his own intrinsic satisfaction. And be prepared for periodic "bad days." Even when their self-control has been improving, children with ADD can be easily "set off" by a wide range of stimuli, causing temporary regression.

At Home

1. (ES) Enroll your child in an athletic program that stresses self-discipline and control, preferably an individual versus group sport such as gymnastics, karate, judo, tennis, or swimming.

2. Establish reasonable homework periods during which there will be no interruptions. Encourage your child to concentrate intensely for these agreed-on time segments. For younger children (grades 1–5) these segments initially might last for five minutes and be followed by a short break. Gradually increase the periods to ten minutes, aiming to condition your child as an athlete is conditioned to develop endurance. Structure, practice, and repetition are essential. Establish a point system to reward your child when he attains the targeted goal for the day.

3. When your child realizes he is becoming agitated or distracted, relaxation techniques may help him control his inattentiveness and hyperactivity. At first you will need to provide feedback: "You are becoming overactive (or inattentive). Do you realize that you've gotten out of your chair seven times and dropped your pencil four times during the last three minutes? This is interfering with your concentration on your homework. I would like you to close your eyes and take a slow, deep breath. Take another breath, keeping your eyes closed. Now take another. Now I want you to do three more math problems calmly, without getting up or dropping your pencil. If you sense you're becoming distracted, do the breathing technique again." By providing nondemeaning feedback ("John, I can see you are not paying attention right now"), helping your child recognize his counterproductive behavior without causing embarrassment, and encouraging him to relax and become "centered," you (and the teacher if she uses this method in class) are helping your child take responsibility for his own behavior. You'll know this technique is working when he begins to use it without having to be told that he is out of control.

4. (ES) Select academically oriented games—Junior Scrabble, chess, pickup sticks—that you and your child can play together to improve his concentration skills. Choose games that your child will enjoy and make the sessions fun. Establish a specific time each week for playing them and know when to quit for the day—your goal is to develop your child's concentration skills in increments. If the games involve competition, give your child a handicap. For example, you might say "I've had sixteen years of education, and you've had four years. I'll give you a handicap of ten points for every additional year of education I've had. Let's do the math together and figure out your handicap." When your child reaches the point where he prefers to play the game with friends or siblings, by all means urge him to do so. Affirm him for improving his concentration span. Once your child realizes that he *can* control his attention and focus for sustained periods, his self-concept will begin to change, and this in turn will reinforce continued positive behavioral changes.

ATTENTION
TO DETAILS

Successful students pay attention to details, carefully proofreading reports to find spelling and grammar mistakes, rechecking math problems, and rewriting essays to make them legible and accurate. They take pride in their work and covet the payoffs for doing a first-rate job.

Children who do not pay attention to details are at the other end of the achievement spectrum. Because their primary objective is to complete their assignments as quickly as possible, the outcome is of secondary importance. The effect of their failure to proofread essays or check over math computations is predictable: a potential A or B paper receives a C–, a D, or an F.

Inattention to details is habit-forming. Self-monitoring demands time and effort, and children who are in the habit of not paying attention to details are rarely willing to make this investment. Checking over an assignment simply requires too much work. This attitude is consistent with another trait of inattentive children. They are usually *passive* learners who manifest many of the following behaviors:

■ They do not establish personal goals.

■ They do not establish personal performance standards.

■ They are not motivated by the payoffs for diligence.

■ They have not internalized the basic principles of cause and effect (see **Disregard of Consequences,** page 50).

Children who are inattentive to details rarely connect their decision not to check their work carefully with the foreseeable consequences of this decision. When their parents or teachers point out the implications of their behavior, they typically disregard the warning. Their attitude guarantees marginal performance, and they soon begin to accept errors and sloppy work as an inescapable fact of life. To protect themselves from feeling inadequate, they often rationalize: "I can't spell no matter what I do!" "The teacher is unfair." "Well, *I* can read what I write!" "I don't care!"

Chronic inattentiveness to details may be symptomatic of a condition called *attention deficit disorder* (see page 5). Children with concentration problems have difficulty staying on task, filtering out distractions, and monitoring themselves. They rush through projects because they lack internal impulse control. The result is substandard work that is replete with mistakes.

Most children who habitually disregard important details can be taught to be more attentive. You must be prepared, however, for some resistance. Like his adult counterparts, your child may be very reluctant to relinquish his entrenched habits.

SUGGESTED CORRECTIVE STRATEGIES

In School

1. (ES) If your child is not paying attention to details, ask his teacher to specify those details that are chronically neglected. Ask her if she would be willing to provide daily feedback. You might want to have the following rubber stamp made up at an office supply store. The teacher could stamp each assignment and pinpoint specific problems *and* accomplishments for one

---

DAILY PERFORMANCE

Work Completed	_____	Work Not Completed	_____
Work Neat	_____	Work Sloppy	_____
Spelling Correct	_____	Spelling Mistakes	_____
Good Handwriting	_____	Poor Handwriting	_____

By indicating accomplishments as well as deficits, the teacher can provide your child with vital positive feedback. Positive reinforcement is generally far more effective than negative reinforcement in promoting effort and improvement.

month. (Do *not* make a stamp for older students as this would embarrass them and probably trigger resentment.)

2. To identify the details your child is overlooking or neglecting, request that your child's teacher(s) complete the following checklist. Ask the teacher to complete the same checklist one month later so that you can determine whether your child is making progress. Only those teachers in whose subjects your child is having difficulty need complete the checklist. (It may be more practical to have your child's school counselor distribute the checklists.) Explain to your child why you are requesting this information: "If you are going to improve your schoolwork and your grades, you need to know what the problem areas are. This checklist will provide this information, and we can then discuss a plan for making improvements."

At Home

1. (ES) Use the feedback on the stamped daily performance checklist (page 13) to create a reward system, perhaps giving points for each accomplishment. Your child might use the points to get a desired toy or perhaps a

ATTENTION TO DETAILS CHECKLIST

This student:	YES	NO
Submits neat work	____	____
Adequately proofreads assignments	____	____
Writes legibly	____	____
Hands in assigned work	____	____
Hands in complete assignments	____	____
Hands in assignments on time	____	____
Follows instructions carefully	____	____
Avoids careless mistakes	____	____

trophy. Do not subtract points for negative checks. *Resist any temptation to lecture or sermonize.* Help your child figure out why the teacher found problem areas; identify specific sloppy sections or spelling mistakes. Show your child how to proofread and edit. Make these sessions short.

2. Brainstorm with your child about how he could correct the deficiencies noted on the checklist. Develop a plan with specific behavior and performance goals. He might create his own checklist for each assignment, including categories such as "read twice," "checked spelling," and so on. When your child is convinced his work is legible, he checks the appropriate column. He then does the same after carefully proofreading the assignment. You might both agree that initially you will check over his work. Once he demonstrates he is taking responsibility for the details, you will no longer need to monitor.

3. **(ES)** Write a simple paragraph with basic, easy-to-identify spelling, grammar, and punctuation errors. Make a game of finding the errors, encouraging your child to locate as many as possible on his own. Then write a paragraph that is sloppy and hard to read. Examine the work together, then brainstorm how to improve the legibility, and finally rewrite the paragraph together. Perhaps you could write one sentence and your child the next. Keep the sessions short. Use your discretion in determining when to discontinue the procedure. Some children will make significant improvement in only five sessions. Others will require more extended help.

4. **(ES)** Follow the same procedure with math problems.

ATYPICAL
LEARNING PROBLEMS

Some learning deficits puzzle everyone—parents, teachers, resource specialists, and school psychologists. Everyone recognizes that a child is not learning efficiently, but no one understands *why* she is struggling. Unfortunately, children with enigmatic and hard-to-identify academic problems often slip through the safety net, because schools generally reserve their assistance programs for students with specific learning deficits. Subtle or intermittent learning deficits are rarely properly diagnosed and even more rarely treated. Children afflicted with these problems typically muddle through school and are usually described as unmotivated or lacking in ability. Those who are intelligent are labeled underachievers.

Perplexed teachers who cannot define a child's learning problems frequently attribute the difficulties to irresponsibility, immaturity, laziness, and poor attitude. These convenient but inadequate explanations are the teacher's way of saying "I don't really know what's wrong."

Parents and teachers also may erroneously conclude that children with enigmatic problems are intellectually deficient. Unfortunately, the children themselves often arrive at the same conclusion. Although some children intuitively figure out how to overcome or compensate for their atypical learning problems, many others are psychologically and academically defeated by their painful experiences in school and continue to perform below their potential throughout their education and, in many instances, throughout their lives. Children whose repeated negative experiences convince them that effort will produce few if any tangible rewards will be very tempted to turn off, shut down, and run away from challenges. To deflect their parents' and teachers' expectations and to insulate themselves from frustration, disappointment, and feelings of inadequacy, many of these children often begin to act irresponsibly. Some may direct their energies to sports, others may spend hours cerebrally anesthetized in front of the TV, and still others will experiment with drugs. Although these nonadaptive behaviors may appear to cause the academic problems, they are actually *symptoms*.

The difficulty in identifying and treating atypical learning problems is compounded by the fact that some children do well in certain subjects and poorly in others. In second grade a child may excel in math and struggle in reading. The following year he may do well in reading and struggle in math. In high school he may pay attention and be conscientious in history class but may be distracted and unmotivated in science class. He may be inspired by his art teacher and unresponsive to his English teacher. He may study diligently during the first semester and shut down during the second semester. These erratic patterns can perplex and test the patience and fortitude of even the most dedicated parents and teachers.

Identifying nonspecific learning problems involves a degree of subjectivity. A school psychologist locked into narrow diagnostic criteria and relying exclusively on standardized tests (a minimum of two years below grade level, a significant discrepancy between the subsections on the IQ test, or a significant discrepancy between standardized test performance and classroom performance) may overlook, disregard, or misdiagnose atypical learning patterns. (See **Performance on Standardized Tests,** page 212, and **IQ Test Scores,** page 130.) Children who do not work up to their potential but who deviate only slightly from the norms often slip through the diagnostic screen. To assess these children properly, professionals must examine many complex, overlapping factors that include family dynamics, peer pressures, individual learning styles, teaching methods, perceptual decoding skills, and psychological issues.

Once the underlying issues are identified, help must be provided. Appropriate assistance may involve teaching children how to regulate themselves (see **Attention Deficit Disorder,** page 5), organize their ideas (see **Critical Thinking,** page 42, and **Disorganization,** page 46), budget their time (see **Time Management,** page 308), prepare for exams (see **Preparing for Tests,** page 225), memorize information (see **Memorizing Information,** page 182), or write cogent reports (see **Language Arts [Essays and Reports],** page 141).

SUGGESTED CORRECTIVE STRATEGIES

In School

1. If you feel your child has an atypical learning problem, request an evaluation by the school psychologist. If she does not qualify for testing (see **Parents' Rights,** page 201) or does not qualify for learning assistance, consider having her privately tested.

2. If you conclude that your child is struggling because she lacks effective study skills, request that she be provided with assistance in this area (see page 292).

3. If the teacher can identify specific academic deficit areas, brainstorm how the deficiencies might be resolved. Supplemental materials in spelling, reading, math, vocabulary, or specific subject areas could be provided for use at home. If your child might benefit from a tutor, ask the teacher to refer you to one who is creative, knowledgeable, and motivating.

4. Inquire if it is feasible to create a system of incentives in school that encourages your child to improve her work, such as extra-credit projects or some sort of public acknowedgment for effort and accomplishment. Perhaps the teacher could give a weekly award for the student who has made the most improvement. This system would permit struggling students to be acknowledged and affirmed for their progress.

At Home

1. Encourage your child to establish realistic goals for improving her work in specific subject areas (see **Goals,** page 84). For example, she might aim to improve her performance on the weekly spelling tests or her Spanish grade from a C– to a B–.

2. Consider enrolling your child in a private learning center if she requires specialized help, has study skills deficits, or does not qualify for learning assistance in school.

AUDITORY DISCRIMINATION

Identifying and differentiating the sounds that letters and groups of letters produce is fundamental to learning to read and spell phonetically. The process of distinguishing sounds is called *auditory discrimination*.

Children are first taught basic auditory discrimination skills in kindergarten and first grade. In a phonetically oriented reading program students are expected to break words down into phonetic fragments or phonemes (called *word attack* or *sounding out*) and to blend the sounds together (see **Phonics,** page 217). Auditory discrimination is central to the word attack/blending process. A child must be able to hear the difference between the sounds *a* and *o, fla* and *plo,* and *t* and *p* if he is to read words such as *flap* and *plot.*

Auditory discrimination skills are also vital to spelling (see page 283). Children usually use three overlapping perceptual processing skills when they spell: auditory discrimination, auditory memory (see page 22), and visual memory (see page 326). Although good spellers rely primarily on visual memory and "see" the letters of words in their mind, auditory discrimination can be very important when a child is unfamiliar with the word being spelled and the word follows prescribed pronunciation rules. Students who cannot discriminate between the short *i* in the word *pig* and the short *e* in the word *peg* can be expected to have spelling problems.

Children with severe auditory discrimination deficits will require assistance from a resource specialist or speech pathologist. Highly effective remedial methods have been developed to help students overcome auditory discrimination problems. If the auditory discrimination problem is severe, the student's hearing should be tested by a pediatrician or licensed audiologist. Most children who struggle to discriminate sounds, however, do *not* have a hearing loss. They can hear the sounds with acuity, but for complex neurological reasons they have difficulty decoding the auditory input.

The "sight method" is another system for teaching children to read that deemphasizes phonics and auditory decoding and sequentially introduces entire words to students according to their level of difficulty. Students learn to read through repeated exposure and practice, without having to sound out the words. The sight method is generally effective with children who have good visual memory (see page 326) and no underlying reading or learning disabilities (see page 157). Children with reading problems, however, usually do better in a phonics-oriented program. Although the instructional pendulum periodically swings from the sight method to the phonics method, at the present time most schools are teaching reading phonetically (see **Phonics,** page 217, and **Nonphonetic Words,** page 191).

SUGGESTED CORRECTIVE STRATEGIES

In School

1. If you suspect that your child has an auditory discrimination deficit, request that she be evaluated by the school psychologist, speech therapist, or resource specialist. There are many excellent tests that can quickly pinpoint deficiencies. An especially effective and comprehensive test designed to detect these auditory discrimination deficits is called the LAC Test, published by Developmental Learning Materials.

2. If deficits are identified, request that your child be provided with remedial assistance by the resource specialist, speech therapist, or reading specialist. In some schools teachers and parents have been trained in the Lindamood Auditory Discrimination in Depth Program (also referred to as the ADD Program). This highly specialized program has proven to be very effective.

At Home

1. **(ES)** Go to a teacher supply house and ask about tapes, books, software, and games that teach auditory discrimination skills. An extensive range of materials is available, and publishers are always adding new materials. You might want to look at those listed in the Resource List at the back of this book.

2. **(ES)** Write the consonants on a sheet of paper and practice pronouncing with your child the name of each letter and the sound it makes. (If your child is very young or is having an especially difficult time with discriminating sounds, use only *one* sound each time you work with your child.) Say a word that begins with one of the consonants (e.g., *top*). Have your child underline the beginning consonant she hears. Later use a word with a consonant in the middle (e.g., *sitting*). Ask your child to identify the beginning

and middle consonants. Later, have your child identify beginning, middle, and ending consonants. Make the activity a game, perhaps even giving your child points for each correct answer and encouraging your child to improve her score each time you play. Repeat the activity over several weeks. Be patient and be prepared for plateaus and occasional regression. Know when to quit for the day, stopping if you find yourself or your child losing patience or becoming frustrated. You may have to go over the same sound for several days before your child masters it. Another option is to spend time watching *Sesame Street* with your child. Reinforce the sound or sounds that they introduce for the day, using some of their highly creative ideas. You could also put plastic alphabet letters into a hat, have your child pick a letter, and then have her try to think of as many words as she can that have the letter (or sound) in it. Many of the materials you can purchase in a teacher supply store or bookstore will suggest other games and activities you can play with your child. *If you conclude you cannot work with your child, consider hiring a well-trained tutor or enrolling your child in a specialized learning center.*

3. (ES) Write the five vowels on a sheet of paper and follow the same procedure. Say a single-syllable phonetic word (e.g., *peg, top, pin*) and have your child write down the vowel sound she hears in the middle of the word. Once your child becomes proficient at identifying the five vowel sounds, begin using multisyllable words (e.g., *hanging*) and have her write down both of the vowel sounds she hears. Make this a game, and make it fun by giving her points for correct answers. Keep track of your child's score each time you play and encourage her to improve her score the next time. Be careful not to lose your patience if she struggles or has difficulty identifying a sound you felt she had already mastered. When she has mastered these sounds, progress to vowel sound combinations (e.g., *en, un, in, an*) and follow the same procedure.

AUDITORY MEMORY

Students are constantly being bombarded with verbal information in school. They must remember their teachers' instructions about how to format an English book report, fill out a test answer sheet, and solve an algebraic equation. They must remember which science exercises to complete in class and which pages in their history text to read for homework. For reasons that cannot be easily explained, some children have difficulty with auditory memory tasks. These children are at a significant disadvantage in school. If their memory deficits are chronic, their performance in every subject area could be undermined.

If your child is struggling to remember what he is told in school, he will probably also have difficulty remembering what you tell him at home. He may appear to be listening, but thirty minutes later you discover that he has not set the table, fed the dog, or brought in the newspaper. Your child's explanation is usually quite simple: "I forgot."

Students with auditory recall and auditory sequencing (remembering information in the proper order) deficits usually receive a great deal of negative feedback. (Some of these children may also have concentration problems—see **Attention Deficit Disorder,** page 5.) Because they are not compensating effectively for their auditory dysfunction, they may appear confused and disoriented. Their memory lapses may lead their parents and teachers to conclude erroneously that they are disinterested, inattentive, and/or lacking in intelligence.

The most obvious way for children to compensate for their poor auditory recall is to write down important information (see **Notetaking,** page 193, and **Recording Assignments,** page 258). Smart students recognize this solution and avail themselves of it (see **Smart Thinking,** page 275). Some students, however, overcompensate and try to write down *everything*, which usually interferes with their listening to or understanding what they are told (see **Listening in Class,** page 166).

Even students with good auditory memory skills must record assignments and instructions. Ironically, the children with the greatest need to record information are usually the most resistant to doing so. They are either too lazy to make the effort or they insist on deluding themselves that they will remember. The consequences are inevitable: they omit important details, forget to do assignments, fail to follow instructions, submit incomplete work, and miss deadlines (see **Following Verbal Directions,** page 78).

Youngsters with short- or long-term auditory memory deficits are at a particular disadvantage in classes in which teachers do a great deal of lecturing. These children often feel insecure and anxious whenever they are required to follow and understand instructions and explanations. The net effect is frustration, demoralization, and diminished self-confidence. By the age of eight, many bright and potentially capable children have already concluded they are inept. This conclusion can have tragic academic and vocational consequences.

With systematic training and sufficient practice, most children *can* significantly improve their auditory recall skills. They can learn a range of memory "tricks" that utilize other sensory modalities to compensate for their memory deficits. A child, for example, who is given verbal instructions could compensate for his memory deficits by visualizing the steps as opposed to trying exclusively to *hear* them in his head. (See specific strategies below.) As children develop more skills and more confidence in their ability to remember, they will be amazed at how proficient they can become at recalling what they hear.

SUGGESTED CORRECTIVE STRATEGIES

In School

1. If you believe your child has an auditory memory problem, discuss your concerns with the teacher. If the deficits are manifesting themselves in the classroom, request that your child be tested by the school psychologist or resource specialist. Highly reliable tests can quickly confirm if he has a short- or long-term memory problem.

2. If an auditory memory deficiency is revealed by the tests, request that the resource specialist provide your child with special assistance. If this request is denied because your child's problems are not deemed sufficiently serious, you may need to become assertive in insisting that he be provided with help (see **Parents' Rights,** page 201). For teaching materials that are commonly used in resource programs to develop auditory memory skills, see the Resource List at the back of this book.

3. (ES) Request that the teacher initial your child's assignment sheet each day to confirm that he has properly recorded the information. The teacher might also periodically check to make sure your child has understood and remembered instructions for completing in-class assignments. The teacher might ask your child to repeat instructions from time to time, thus serving notice that he must pay attention. This should be done diplomatically to prevent embarrassment, especially if your child has chronic memory problems. As your child's memory skills improve, the monitoring can be phased out.

4. If your child's memory deficits are compounded by concentration problems, refer to the suggestions and strategies listed under **Attention Deficit Disorder,** page 5. Also see suggestions under **Following Verbal Directions,** page 78.

At Home

1. When giving instructions to your child at home, initially limit the amount of information he is required to remember. You might begin with two or three tasks. Ask your child to repeat the instructions and then to close his eyes and see himself doing the tasks. Encouraging your child to take a visual picture of auditory information will help him compensate for his auditory memory deficits.

2. Play auditory memory games around the dinner table. One person says a number (initially two or three digits), and the person sitting next to him says the number in reverse order. Encourage your child to close his eyes and see the number in his mind, perhaps in his favorite color. Urge him to see the number changing position. Follow the same procedure with the names of objects (e.g., a hat, a needle, a plum, and a hairbrush). Have your child take a mental picture and then repeat the objects in reverse order. If reversing the order is at first too difficult, have your child repeat the original order. Control the difficulty until his skills and confidence improve. Make up variations of the game using sounds or clapping patterns (e.g., two fast beats, four slow beats, three fast beats). This will develop auditory memory skills and auditory sequencing skills. Remember, your objective is to set your child up to win and to help him overcome negative associations with his capacity to recall auditorially.

3. Urge your child to make up acronyms to help him remember verbal information (e.g., SOHCAHTOA: sine = opposite over hypotenuse / cosine = adjacent over hypotenuse / tangent = opposite over adjacent). Making up rhymes and simple songs can also help him retain information (e.g., "Go to the store for bread, eggs, milk, and cheese. Then feed the dog and put out the cat.").

4. Encourage your child to record homework assignments and his teacher's directions on an assignment page (see **Recording Assignments,** page 258, and **Following Verbal Directions,** page 78).

5. (ES) Go to your local teacher supply store or bookstore and ask for books, software, and games designed specifically to develop auditory memory skills.

BEHAVIOR AND PERFORMANCE GUIDELINES

Children whose family's rules for acceptable and unacceptable behavior are unclear are invariably confused and unhappy. The absence of clearly defined *external* structure and control prevents them from developing *internal* structure and control. This capacity to self-regulate is vital to the development of self-confidence, self-sufficiency, and self-esteem.

When children do not have a frame of reference for the permissible and the nonpermissible, they almost invariably have problems conforming to society's value system. Because they have not been taught the limits, they never complete the characteristic testing phase of two- and three-year-olds. Children who are unsure of the boundaries may express their confusion by becoming disrespectful, unruly, manipulative, or delinquent. They may blame others for their deficiencies and transgressions and may cut school, act out in class, or continually challenge the "system" and its authority figures. They may become bullies, liars, sneaks, or con artists, or they may cheat, steal, or take drugs.

Children who have not internalized their family's standards and guidelines usually have great difficulty relating to the principles of cause and effect. They tend to be unconcerned about consequences, take unnecessary risks, and disregard the feelings and wishes of others (see **Disregard of Consequences,** page 50). Despite their affected bravado, these children are frequently unsure of themselves, their prerogatives, others' expectations, and their own expectations.

During the first eight years of a child's life, the family is not intended to be a model of democracy. Children must be told when to go to bed, when to turn off the television, and when to stop making noise. They must be taught socially acceptable manners and trained to be sensitive to the feelings of others. They must be taught to be respectful of their parents and teachers and to live by the family's and society's rules. Fair, reasonable, and consistently applied guidelines provide them with a sense of security and allow them to deal more successfully with less clearly defined issues.

Your child must understand unequivocally that he is expected to do his homework, make his best effort, keep commitments, complete projects, submit his assignments on time, take responsibility for his chores, attend to details, and use his head when he confronts danger. If he doesn't learn these reasonable rules, how can he be expected to reject the drugs that are offered him, resist the temptation to cheat on a test, or refuse to drive with a friend who is intoxicated?

As your child matures and demonstrates that he is responsible and that he knows the difference between right and wrong and between smart and dumb, he can begin to create his own personal rules and guidelines. Permitting a responsible child to design his own study schedule is an important step in preparing him to handle the challenges and responsibilities he will encounter later in life (see **Time Management,** page 308, and **Self-Esteem and Self-Confidence,** page 266). This incremental empowerment is vital in preparing your child to become a self-sufficient, independent, responsible adult.

SUGGESTED CORRECTIVE STRATEGIES

In School

1. If your child's teacher has indicated on report cards that your child is having difficulty conforming to the rules of behavior or academic guidelines, request a conference to get as much specific information as possible. Make note of the issues that concern the teacher. Unless you feel he is being unfair or unreasonable, do not be defensive or attempt to excuse your child's behavior. Brainstorm how the unacceptable behaviors might be modified. If your child is manifesting a great many counterproductive behaviors, prioritize the list, as it will be impossible to correct all of the problems at the same time. Ask for ideas about how you might modify your parenting strategy at home. Also explore changes that might be made in the classroom. If, for example, your child has told you that the teacher is embarrassing him in class or continually reprimanding him, and if you believe your child is reacting by misbehaving, discuss how this situation might be altered. Could the teacher make an effort to find something positive for which he can compliment your child? Ask the teacher if he believes your child would benefit from individual or family therapy. (You need not necessarily follow his recommen-

dation.) By convincing the teacher that you appreciate the problems your child's behavior might create in the classroom and expressing a sincere desire to work with him on solving the problem, you will enlist his active support.

2. Ask the teacher if your child may be misbehaving because he is frustrated by his inability to do the assigned work and therefore feeling inadequate and demoralized. If your child has identified perceptual, academic, or study skills deficits, he will need learning assistance. (Refer to the relevant entries for specific corrective strategies.) If you feel your child should be tested by the school psychologist to determine the source of his behavior and/or learning problems, request a diagnostic evaluation (see **Parents' Rights,** page 201).

3. Ask if the school counselor or principal should be involved in counseling and monitoring your child. If he is disruptive or fighting with other children, he may need someone with counseling experience to help him examine his actions and perhaps also redefine the school rules and guidelines. Ideally, this involvement will not be exclusively in a punitive capacity.

At Home

1. Create a checklist of specific behaviors that your child needs to improve. Start out with two or three behaviors you would like your child to modify. Ask the teacher to evaluate your child each day in these areas (e.g., paying attention, following instructions, handing in assignments on time). The teacher could use a simple code: 0 = poor, 1 = fair, 2 = good, 3 = excellent. The process should take the teacher no more than two minutes and will provide you with daily feedback about your child's behavior. Initial the checklist each evening so that the teacher knows you have seen it. You will also need to explain succinctly to your child why you are setting up this system and why school rules are as important as at-home rules. With your child's active participation, establish a system for rewarding improvement. Reward systems usually work better than punishment systems, although punishment may be an appropriate response under certain circumstances. Rely on your judgment. (The ultimate goal, of course, is for your child to behave for intrinsic rewards such as personal satisfaction and not for extrinsic rewards.) The behavior modification process requires time and patience. Generally the more your child understands about his behavior and how it is perceived by others, the more receptive he will most likely become to making changes. And the more actively you involve your child in the process of making the changes, the more success-ful the process will be.* (For additional ideas, see the **DIBS** method described on page 233.)

2. If your child will not accept reasonable behavior guidelines despite your best efforts, and he continues to break the rules at home and in school, you will need to consult a trained mental health professional. Request a referral from your pediatrician, school principal, or school psychologist.

---

* Behavior modification "purists" would contend that it is not necessary for children to understand the underlying issues that are responsible for their behavior. From their perspective, all that matters is that the counterproductive behavior be modified. This approach is debatable.

BOUNCING BACK FROM SETBACKS AND LEARNING FROM MISTAKES

Mistakes and setbacks are inescapable facts of life, and children must overcome them if they are to survive and prevail in a competitive, demanding world. Those who do not develop the ability to analyze challenges and problems, who cannot make tactical adjustments, and who lack the emotional resilience to bounce back are destined to suffer.

The compelling need to understand, to pit one's talents against obstacles, to make things work, to examine miscues analytically, and to learn from mistakes are traits that distinguish successful students from less successful students. To achieving children a setback is an invitation to a wrestling match. Convinced they deserve to prevail and driven by ego (a positive sense of self and one's own power), they persevere until they succeed or until they become convinced the problem is insoluble.

In contrast nonachieving children who lack problem-solving skills and emotional resilience either give up when they experience a defeat and do not consider an alternative plan, or they plow ahead mindlessly and make the same mistakes. As the repeated collisions take their cumulative psychological toll, these children become increasingly frustrated, insecure, and fragile. At this point the temptation to shut down can be compelling. (See **Smart Thinking,** page 275, and **Psychological Problems and Psychological Overlay,** page 239.)

A child's belief in her ability to handle predicaments directly reflects her life experiences. A child who has proved to herself that she can overcome obstacles and survive occasional failures, disappointments, and rejections develops faith in her own powers. Repeated defeats, on the other hand, undermine her faith in herself and trigger demoralization, diminished self-confidence, and self-protecting and often counterproductive behavior.

Children who have not been successful in school are usually sorely tempted to run away from any situation that might expose their inadequacies. By running they can avoid the stress of having to confront and work through problems (see **Learned Helplessness,** page 152). They may blame, procrastinate, manipulate, act irresponsibly, or feel sorry for themselves. On the surface they may appear lazy, resistant, and unmotivated, but beneath the surface they are driven by insecurity, feelings of inadequacy, and a powerful instinct to protect themselves. From their perspective the outcome is inevitable: If they continue trying, they will fail again.

Every child of normal intelligence can be taught how to analyze problems, link errors in judgment with the outcome, identify the consistencies and inconsistencies, find common denominators, and respond more strategically to setbacks (see **Disregard of Consequences,** page 50, and **Smart Thinking,** page 275). Teaching children these skills is every bit as vital as teaching them how to read, write, and do math.

The child who continues to be crushed by mistakes and setbacks despite her tactical survival skills and your best efforts is waving a red flag. If her behavior suggests that underlying psychological or family problems may be undermining her coping skills, professional counseling is essential.

SUGGESTED CORRECTIVE STRATEGIES

In School

1. If you observe that your child lacks emotional resilience and is crushed by setbacks and reversals, ask her teacher if he has observed the same behaviors. If so, explore strategies for helping your child modify her response patterns. For example, if she does poorly on a math test, you might have her analyze the types of problems on the test and the specific difficulties she experienced. Did her problems involve "silly" mistakes, or did she not know how to do the problems? Was she nervous? Did she forget her number facts, or did she not remember how to solve the algebraic equation? Encourage her to develop a strategy for improving her performance on the next test. For example, she might design a very simple checklist to make sure she has completed her homework and checked it over for careless mistakes. Perhaps she might do some simple relaxation techniques before taking a test. The goal is to show your child how she can avoid making many common mistakes and how she can respond strategically to setbacks. Once she becomes convinced she can handle glitches and learn from setbacks, her self-confidence cannot help improving (see **Smart Thinking,** page 275, for additional methods that encourage more strategic planning and problem solving).

2. Ask your child's teacher if other students are also responding inappropriately to setbacks and mistakes. If so, ask if he would be willing to incorporate into his curriculum procedures designed to improve analytical problem-solving skills and response patterns. The class might be given a copy of a facsimile test that received a poor grade. (This should *not* be a student's actual test but rather a test the teacher has intentionally sabotaged for the purposes of illustration.) The class (or small cooperative learning groups) could analyze why the student did poorly and explore specific ways in which he might improve his study strategy for the next test. The problem-solving template that appears below provides a practical step-by-step format for analyzing mistakes.

3. If you would like more specific input from the teacher, ask him to complete the checklists that appear on pages 33 and 34, substituting *this student* for *my child*.

PROCEDURES FOR LEARNING FROM MISTAKES

1. Define the obvious. (E.g., "I didn't know information that was covered on the test, and I made careless mistakes.")

2. Identify the mistake. (E.g., "I didn't make a checklist of important information I needed to learn.")

3. Investigate. (E.g., "What specific study skills techniques might I use in preparing for the next test?")

4. Explore corrective options. (E.g., "I will need to allow enough time to learn the important information, and I will need to figure out a system for memorizing key facts.")

5. Look for the common denominator. (E.g., "If the teacher usually gives this type of test, and if my previous study strategy has not worked, I will need to make adjustments.")

Students will need to practice analytical/problem-solving procedures many times before they master the method and make it an integral part of their responses to problems, challenges, and reversals.

At Home

1. If you have observed that your child is having difficulty with setbacks and mistakes, the following checklist will help you determine if your child is rebounding effectively to reversals and identify specific counterproductive behavior patterns that could undermine your child's capacity to achieve.

2. Use the **DIBS Problem-Solving Method** described on page 233 to help you analyze the issues identified on the checklist that are causing your child to respond nonproductively to setbacks and mistakes. If her nonadaptive response patterns persist, you should consult a mental health professional. Chronic chal-

LEARNING FROM MISTAKES CHECKLIST

	YES	NO
My child:		
Becomes very discouraged when she makes a mistake		
Is afraid of making mistakes		
Tends to give up if she makes a mistake		
Makes the same mistake repeatedly		
Fails to examine her mistakes		
Does not perceive the common denominators that run through her mistakes		
Resists admitting that she has made a mistake		
Demonstrates deficient judgment		
Is very defensive about mistakes		
Is unwilling to discuss mistakes with me		
Blames others for her mistakes		

BOUNCING BACK FROM SETBACKS CHECKLIST

	YES	NO
My child:		
Gets very discouraged when she encounters a setback	____	____
Is tempted to give up when she fails at something	____	____
Tries to avoid things that are difficult	____	____
Is convinced she is dumb when she has a setback	____	____
Regrets having tried something when she doesn't do well	____	____
Thinks people think less of her if they know she has failed at something	____	____
Doesn't like to admit that she has had a setback	____	____
Wants to run away and hide after a failure	____	____
Quits when she is doing something that becomes too difficult	____	____
Is unwilling to ask for help	____	____
Gets so frustrated when she encounters difficulty that she can no longer work efficiently	____	____
Becomes defensive when she must ask for help	____	____

lenge-avoidance tendencies, phobias, insecurity, demoralization, frustration, and exploding or imploding anger can cause serious psychological damage and can erect major academic and vocational barriers. The underlying problems must be addressed and resolved before self-sabotaging behavior patterns become entrenched.

COMMUNICATING WITH THE SCHOOL

The issue of how involved parents should become in their child's education is controversial. Some teachers and school districts welcome active parental participation; others consider this involvement an intrusion, especially when parents *presume* to find fault. Although parents have traditionally been encouraged to participate in organizations such as the PTA, their participation is usually restricted to sponsoring paper drives, helping out on the playground, or chaperoning field trips. The welcome mat is withdrawn when parents attempt to question educational objectives, academic priorities, or teachers' salaries and qualifications. The notable exception occurs in "open" schools, where parents are expected to assist in the classroom and interact with the professional staff.

Teachers opposed to parental involvement generally justify their resistance with the same arguments that physicians might offer in discouraging laypeople from becoming involved in the day-to-day affairs of the local community hospital: They argue that nonprofessionals are unqualified. This elitism is a common by-product of highly specialized training. Experts—be they physicians or educators—tend to acquire an inflated sense of their skills, autonomy, and prerogatives, and they may convince themselves that those outside of their professional circle cannot possibly understand the complex issues that are central to their work.

Teachers and administrators who construe inquiries as criticism, suggestions as threats, or requests for help as exploitive are insecure, lazy, arrogant, and/or incompetent. Something is wrong when reasonable requests for information, flexibility, or special treatment are greeted with resistance and resentment. Providing information and responding to questions is a basic responsibility of educators. Those who forget this obligation disserve their profession and their students.

The fact that most parents lack the expertise to develop a curriculum or critique educational objectives does not negate the value of their questions, perceptions, and insights. Competent teachers and administrators are usually delighted when parents want to take an active role. They realize that when parents understand the issues, provide support at home, and have realistic expectations, their own jobs become easier.

You do not have to be a professional educator to sense intuitively when a teacher or a school is not meeting your child's needs. You have a right to communicate with the school authorities and to expect that teachers and school administrators will consider and examine the issues you raise, even if your perceptions should ultimately prove to be inaccurate and your concerns unwarranted.

The option to become actively involved in your child's educational process is, of course, predicated on your being reasonable and rational. Your right to be consulted, request information, raise questions, and make suggestions is not an unrestricted license to interfere in the operation of the classroom or the school, nor is it a license to make unfair and excessive demands on the teacher's time.

By becoming involved in your child's education, monitoring his progress, clearly communicating your concerns, asking penetrating questions, requesting penetrating answers, and acknowledging teachers and administrators for their accomplishments and contributions, you serve notice that your child is not the only one being held accountable for his performance. The educational establishment is also accountable. Active and informed parental involvement invariably improves the quality of education at the local level.

The first step in becoming involved is to talk with your child's teacher. If you are dissatisfied with her response to your concerns or request for information, you have several options:

- You can resign yourself to accepting the status quo.

- You can discuss your concerns with the principal.

- You can request that your child be placed in another class.

- You can seek private educational therapy or tutoring.

- You can discuss your concerns with the superintendent.

- You can exercise your right of due process and request a hearing if you feel your child's federally mandated rights are being violated (see **Parents' Rights,** page 201).

- You can enroll your child in a private school.

The need to participate in the educational process is more urgent when you become convinced that the teacher's attitude or methodology is causing your child to suffer educationally or psychologically. If you are concerned about a lack of structure, discipline, or standards, you have an obligation to discuss these matters with your child's teacher. Be forewarned, however, that doing so in a hostile or unreasonable manner will trigger resistance and resentment. Teachers who feel attacked are more likely to defend themselves than to change.

You, your child's teacher, and the school administration have a mutually shared objective: to help your child become skilled, productive, self-sufficient, and self-confident. This goal is attainable only when everyone is willing to work together.

SUGGESTED CORRECTIVE STRATEGIES

In School

1. If you feel that you and your child's teacher are having difficulty discussing or resolving issues relating to your child's education, you must diplomatically express your concerns. You might say: "I sense that we may be having some communication problems. I need to identify problem areas so that I can provide appropriate support for my child. You are a vital source of information. If positive changes are to occur, we have to be able to work together." If the teacher is overly sensitive or defensive, you might say: "I am not here to criticize you or to make your job more difficult. My objective in becoming involved in monitoring my child's progress is to find solutions to problems and to help him remove obstacles that are blocking his academic success."

2. The more specifically you can identify deficits and develop corrective strategies, the better. You might say to the teacher: "You've said that my child procrastinates and is unmotivated. What exactly can you do to help him, and what activities should we be doing to help him overcome these behaviors? (To get specific feedback about your child's possible deficits, refer to the student evaluation forms on pages 160–163.)

At Home

1. The information your child's teacher provides about classroom performance, effort, behavior, and attitude can be a catalyst for discussion and problem solving at home. If she tells you that he is not handing in his assignments on time, you might say: "Your teacher is concerned about your late assignments. She says your last book report, for example, was handed in two days late. Let's take a look at how you could solve this problem. . . ." (See **Planning Ahead,** page 222, **Priorities,** page 228, **Disorganization,** page 46, **Smart Thinking,** page 275, **Inadequate Study Time,** page 116, and **Time Management,** page 308, for additional suggestions.)

2. If you feel your child is not making adequate effort in school, let him know that you will be staying in close communication with his teacher. Realizing that you "mean business" about his being responsible and conscientious can be a powerful deterrent to counterproductive behavior.

CONFERENCING WITH SCHOOL OFFICIALS

When parents cannot resolve their concerns about their child in direct discussions with the teacher or resource specialist, they have two basic options: They can accept the status quo, or they can go up the chain of command and discuss their concerns with the vice principal, counselor, dean of students, school psychologist, principal, and superintendent. Legitimate topics for discussion include disagreements about educational goals, teaching methodology, classroom discipline, grading criteria, and homework assignments. Concerned parents would also want to discuss with the school administration major decisions about whether their child should repeat a grade (see page 262) or be transferred to another class or school.

Parents who are anxious about conferencing with school officials may have negative associations with childhood authority figures. They may remember being sent to the office when they misbehaved as children, and they may still have misgivings about having to deal with a school principal or counselor. The best antidote for such anxiety is for parents to remind themselves that their taxes pay the salaries of school officials and that they have a compelling responsibility to represent their child when problems arise in school.

Apprehension about dealing with school officials may also be linked to the tendency by educators to use technical jargon. Terms such as *attention deficit disorder, dyslexia, auditory discrimination,* and *visual memory* (all defined in this book) can be incomprehensible and intimidating to an uninitiated parent. In fairness, it should be noted that this specialized vocabulary serves the legitimate function of permitting educators to discuss complex issues with precision. At the same time, however, educational jargon can be wittingly or unwittingly used to exclude parents from understanding matters that are vital to their child's welfare. Professionals who intentionally employ technical terms as a smoke screen or to deflect dissent are either insecure or incompetent and deserve to be challenged.

Any competent educator can explain your child's academic issues and educational problems in terms that you can understand. If you are confused about the meaning of a standardized achievement test score or about diagnostic terminology, you should not hesitate to ask for clarification (see **Understanding Diagnostic Test Results,** page 316, and **Performance on Standardized Tests,** page 212). If you are still confused, *ask for further clarification.* You have the legal right to all educational information that pertains to your child, and you have the right to insist that this information be explained in language you can comprehend.

Conferences with school officials are most productive when the participants are reasonable, nonadversarial, nonstrident, and committed to working together. Avoiding conflict is clearly in everyone's best interest. Presenting your position, expressing doubts, and communicating disapproval without triggering defensiveness and resistance can be a monumental test of your diplomatic skills.

Federal law requires that your child's school provide learning assistance if her needs can be clearly documented and if she meets the defined qualification criteria (see **Parents' Rights,** page 201). If your child's school cannot provide the necessary help because of limited resources, you may agree to a less-than-ideal compromise, or you may decide to do battle with the school system. Compromising, however, does not mean passively acquiescing to your child's being damaged by an incompetent teacher, an inadequate program, or an inflexible and insensitive bureaucracy.

If you conclude you cannot procure the help your child requires within the public school system, you may decide to seek help outside the system. Tutoring, educational therapy, counseling, or private schooling may be your only recourse. Unfortunately, these services can be expensive.

SUGGESTED CORRECTIVE STRATEGIES

In School

1. The guiding principle in conferencing with the school administration is to ask focused questions and address specific issues. Problems must be accurately identified before they can be solved. The student evaluation forms for elementary school children (page 160) and junior and senior high school students (page 163) will identify specific deficits and can help you establish priorities in the learning assistance program.

2. Request clarification if you're confused about any of the issues raised during the meeting. Your child's future may be at stake, so continue to ask questions until you're satisfied.

3. If you feel it would be beneficial, request that the teacher and resource specialist participate in any conference with the principal or other school personnel. This request is reasonable even if you've already met with these people at the IEP (Individual Educational Program; see page 126) or PPT (pupil/parent/teacher) meeting.

4. You may want to have your child attend the meeting with the principal, school psychologist, and/or counselor if everyone agrees her participation is appropriate. Students obviously should not participate when sensitive issues regarding their performance or emotional state are being examined. It may be best to discuss these matters with your child at home or have school personnel do so after a clear strategy has been determined.

At Home

1. You should prepare for conferences with school officials by formulating important questions in advance and by making a list of issues you want to discuss. Review recent test scores, report card grades, and written or oral communication with your child's teacher. If the teacher or resource specialist has completed an evaluation form, identify the deficits that concern you and discuss them during the conference.

2. Examine with your child selected issues discussed during the conference. Follow your instincts about what subjects are appropriate for discussion. Gear the discussion to his developmental maturity and use language, examples, and metaphors he can understand. For example, you might say: "I met with the principal today, and we discussed your behavior on the playground. Do you have any ideas about what her concerns are? Well, you seem to be getting into fights with other children. I'm curious if you're angry at these children. . . . Well, this is what we decided to do about the behavior. . . ."

3. Brainstorm with your child about how she might contribute to resolving identified academic, social, or behavior problems. Use the **DIBS** method described on page 233. For more ideas about how to involve your child actively in the problem-solving process, consult *Smarter Kids* (see "Study Skills" in the Resource List at the back of the book).

CRITICAL THINKING

If children are to master advanced academic material, they must develop their capacity to focus their intelligence and get to the *heart* of an issue or a concept. This higher-level critical thinking requires them to:

- analyze information

- identify and understand key ideas

- ask penetrating questions

- use reason and logic

- consider the pluses and minuses of events and decisions

- question the validity of assumptions

- identify contradictions, inconsistencies, and deceptions

- see matters from different perspectives

- relate new information to previously learned information

Although the ability to think critically is linked to intelligence, critical thinking is also an acquired skill that must be systematically developed, improved, and refined with good coaching and practice.

American schools have traditionally been preoccupied with teaching children academic skills and with pouring information into their heads. Students are required to memorize and regurgitate chemical formulas, historical dates, Spanish verb conjugations, and vocabulary definitions. This approach may produce *quantitative* learning, but it does not necessarily guarantee *qualitative* learning. Most students quickly forget, or never bother to learn, information and data they perceive as irrelevant. Even information acknowledged to be relevant and important is often quickly forgotten, as most physicians and attorneys can attest two months after passing their licensing exams.

During the last thirty years critical intelligence has been largely ignored by primary and secondary schools. The effects of this neglect are very evident. Each day thousands of cerebrally anesthetized youngsters make tragically flawed decisions that lead to drug and alcohol addiction, car accidents, unwanted babies, suicides, gang killings, and prison time.

Recently there has been a renaissance in teaching critical thinking in American schools. More and more teachers are training their students to reason and apply logic (see **Logic,** page 169). They are showing children how to use their intelligence like a scalpel and how to expose the important issues that lay beneath the surface. The goal is for students to use this scalpel deftly in school and in their personal lives.

Children face frightening perils today. Those who do not know how to assess temptations and problems analytically, evaluate their choices, and consider carefully the potential effects of their actions are at risk.

Encouraging children to "stretch" and develop their thinking skills is certainly beneficial. Demanding that they comprehend what they are incapable of understanding, however, can create stress and cause psychological damage. Children who are clearly struggling to grasp concepts, relationships, and meanings should be tested to determine their intellectual capacity (see **IQ Test Scores,** page 130). Although expectations should be high, these expectations must also be realistic and congruent with an *accurate* assessment of a child's aptitude.

You cannot expect your child's teacher to assume the entire responsibility for teaching your child how to think critically. The environment you create for your child at home is just as crucial. By encouraging your child to reason and think analytically, you will significantly improve the chances that she will ask astute and incisive questions and make reasonable and appropriate decisions.

SUGGESTED CORRECTIVE STRATEGIES

In School

1. If your child has difficulty thinking critically, ask her teacher to assign in-class supplemental materials designed to improve this skill. The teacher might also be willing to provide some extra help after school or before class. Classroom materials that develop critical thinking are included in the Resource List at the back of the book.

2. If your child is in a learning assistance program, diplomatically suggest that the resource specialist devote time to working on critical thinking materials. The specialist may wish to remediate your child's basic skills deficits first, and this is a sound approach as long as there is a commitment to incorporate critical thinking skills at the appropriate time. The materials cited in the Resource List could be used to teach *both* reading *and* critical thinking skills.

At Home

1. To develop your child's thinking skills, urge her to think about what is happening in the world at large and in her own world. The starting point in the process is to emphasize the basic "thinking questions"—*how, why,* and *what.* At the dinner table you might ask: "How do you think the problem of the homeless might be solved? Why do you think the government has launched this 'Say No to Drugs Program in Schools'?" The child studying American history might be asked: "Why do you think religious freedom was so important to the Founding Fathers? What is the link between religious freedom and the concept of the separation of church and state?" These interactive sessions will produce another valuable payoff: Your child's communication skills will improve. When you discuss topics in the news, encourage your child to recognize that events can be seen from another point of view. A person living in Rio de Janeiro might perceive the issue of ecology differently from a person living in Omaha.

2. If your child is having difficulty with critical thinking, ask her teacher if he can recommend a workbook to be used at home. Perhaps he could provide you with extra critical thinking worksheets that you and your child could do at home. Ask him to suggest how best to monitor your child and how to respond to wrong answers or confusion. Extra assignments should not require more than ten to fifteen minutes of homework per evening. To overload your child would be perceived as a punishment. Work together and make the sessions enjoyable. Be patient and supportive if your child struggles.

3. If you observe that your child is having significant difficulty acquiring critical thinking skills, or if you discover that you lose your patience when working with her, she may need a tutor. Signs that should alert you to a problem include chronically poor logic and reasoning and confusion, frustration, and resistance. Select a tutor with whom your child has rapport, ideally someone who has had experience in teaching critical thinking skills. Ask your child's teacher for a recommendation. If your child continues to struggle despite your best efforts and the tutor's best efforts, request that the school psychologist administer an intelligence test.

4. Read with your child. Use school textbooks, newspaper articles, or library books. Select materials within your child's reading "comfort zone." If you are unsure of your child's reading level, ask her teacher. As you read together, ask questions about related issues. You should not, however, become a question "machine gun." A stream of questions will cause your child to become resistant. Make the process enjoyable and stimulating. For example, if the article is about drugs in schools, you might ask: "Why do you think the police would be concerned about drugs being sold near schools? Why would they want to arrest the sellers? What would happen if kids could buy drugs without any difficulty? What would you do to solve the problem?" After modeling how to ask questions, urge your child to ask *you* questions. Make these sessions short (no more than ten to fifteen minutes). Be patient! Developing problem-solving skills takes time. If you communicate exasperation or disappointment, you will demoralize your child and cause resentment and resistance.

5. Request at your local teacher supply store materials or games expressly designed to develop children's critical thinking skills. Select materials appropriate to your child's age and reading level. Materials you might want to examine are included in the Resource List at the back of the book.

DISORGANIZATION

The chronically disorganized child is on a collision course with his teachers and parents. Energy that should be devoted to studying and learning is dissipated in looking for misplaced materials and struggling to meet deadlines. Because he "spins his wheels" with little or no forward momentum, the disorganized child rarely achieves in school at a level commensurate with his true ability.

Several key traits differentiate organized students from their less organized classmate:

- They establish goals and priorities.

- They plan ahead.

- They budget time effectively and meet deadlines.

- They develop an effective system for recording assignments.

- They have the materials they need to do their work (paper, pens, textbooks, notebooks, pencils, dictionary, etc.).

- They keep their desks and study areas neat.

The poorly organized child must be constantly reminded to straighten his room, put away his toys, make his bed, put his dirty clothes into the hamper, and clear the mess off his desk. To insulate himself, he will probably tune out the predictable sermons and threats.

Realizing that chronic disorganization can cause monumental problems for your child throughout his life, you will probably feel determined to intervene. Unfortunately, the traditional parental methods of intervention—lectures, bribes, and punishment—are rarely successful and usually trigger active or passive resistance. Youngsters with the most urgent need to alter their behavior are often the most unwilling to change and the most oblivious of the effects of the chaos they create in their environment (see **Disregard of Consequences,** page 50, and **Smart Thinking,** page 275).

Because children are as resistant as anyone else to changing their habits, they must become convinced that *organization will make their lives easier* and that the payoffs for the new behaviors are superior to the payoffs for their old behaviors. Experimenting with organizational strategies, systematically teaching the fundamentals of good organization, and involving your child actively in applying the new procedures are vital to eliciting his cooperation. You must show your child how to organize his notebook and desk and how to budget his study time. You must encourage him to practice the methods, and you must diplomatically monitor and affirm his progress until he can demonstrate mastery (see specific suggestions below).

You will know your child has made a breakthrough when he voluntarily begins to organize specific areas of his life. Creating a system for organizing his baseball cards could be the first step. Your child cannot be realistically expected to transform himself overnight. He may make progress and then plateau or even regress. Although these blips in the learning curve are frustrating, you must be patient, supportive, and consistent. Once he becomes convinced that order will create more free time to do what he wants to do and allow him to achieve at a level previously beyond his reach, he will be more receptive to becoming organized.

SUGGESTED CORRECTIVE STRATEGIES

In School

1. (ES) If your child appears to be chronically disorganized in school, ask the teacher to help you identify the specific areas in which he is disorganized, using the following checklist. Make modifications to include your child's particular deficits.

At Home

1. Teaching your disorganized child *how* to organize his life is a far more effective strategy than lecturing or punishing him. Here are guidelines for making the strategy work:

■ *Demonstrate the value of organization with relevant examples.* (E.g., "Let's do a flowchart that outlines the steps required to finish this history project." See **Planning Ahead,** page 222.)

■ *Model how to use study materials more efficiently.* (E.g., "Let's see how we can organize this material and put it on index cards. Then we'll see if we can

DAILY ORGANIZATIONAL CHECKLIST

Code: *1 = Poor   2 = Fair   3 = Good   4 = Excellent*

	MON.	TUES.	WED.	THURS.	FRI.
Desk is neat	___	___	___	___	___
In-class assignments are neat	___	___	___	___	___
Work handed in on time	___	___	___	___	___
Notebook is neat	___	___	___	___	___
Homework assignments recorded	___	___	___	___	___

Brainstorm with the teacher how you might work together in reorienting the counterproductive behavior. Ask the teacher to affirm your child when his performance begins to improve. Keep track of the points your child receives each day and have your child apply them to earning a prize or reward.

develop a filing system for keeping track of what you're doing and your other school materials." See **Notetaking,** page 193.)

■ *Provide clear how-to guidelines.* (E.g., "Let's write down the steps for doing this research report in an order that makes sense." See **Priorities,** page 228.)

■ *Provide repeated opportunities for practice and application.* (Monitor your child to make sure he is using the techniques you have developed together.)

■ *Be patient, affirming of progress, and supportive when there are plateaus or temporary regressions.*

2. Find a disorganized area in your house (the attic, the garage, the workshop, or your own closet or desk). Develop a reorganization strategy with your child and then implement the plan. Encouraging your child to experiment with reorganizing a specific area of the family's life can defuse resistance to change. A family project for designing and building closet shelves, for instance, would demonstrate in very concrete terms the principles of organization. Input from your child during the planning stage and hands-on active participation in the implementation are vital. Once you have modeled how to reorganize, work together on developing a strategy for reorganizing your child's closet or desk. You may need to buy a shoe organizer or build a box for toys or sports equipment. Make the project fun and resist any temptation to give a lecture or a sermon.

3. (ES) Set up a point/reward system at home that acknowledges your child when his desk, room, notebook, backpack, assignment sheet, and homework are neat and organized. To keep track of points, you might use a format similar to that of the daily organizational checklist presented on page 48, and you might even combine the points earned in school with those earned at home.

DISREGARD
OF CONSEQUENCES

Some youngsters—either because they are oblivious to the basic principles of cause and effect or because they consciously or unconsciously choose to disregard them—do not consider the consequences of their actions. Their thinking is so rooted in the present that they do not plan ahead or consider risks. These children pay the price for their subsequent mistakes, indiscretions, and flawed decisions, and their repeated miscues often place them in conflict with their parents and teachers and, in extreme cases, with the judicial system.

Children who think more strategically and who have integrated cause-and-effect principles into their decision-making process analyze problems, learn from mistakes and setbacks, define goals, consider options, develop fallback positions, and formulate strategies for attaining their objectives (see **Smart Thinking,** page 275, and **Bouncing Back from Setbacks and Learning from Mistakes,** page 30). The child who considers consequences would repair a loose wheel on a skateboard *before* having an accident. The child who disregards consequences would have to fall repeatedly and injure himself before he would take the time to fix the wheel.

Mastery of cause-and-effect principles is essential to success in school. Students who apply these principles carefully weigh the implications of a decision to study or not to study, to cheat or not to cheat, or to take drugs or not to take drugs. Their future-oriented thinking reduces the chances of repeated crash landings and contrasts with the present-oriented thinking of children who are impulsive and demand immediate gratification.

Some parents assume that children naturally learn cause-and-effect principles. Unfortunately, countless potentially capable children do not intuitively connect poor performances with lack of preparation. Thinking and acting irresponsibly and mindlessly, they misbehave in class, submit incomplete or sloppy assignments, and spend inadequate time studying. Because they are not attuned to the implications of their decisions and actions, they perform below their potential and are often labeled underachievers. Their poor schoolwork obscures their talents and causes their self-confidence to erode (see **Study Skills,** page 292). As success appears increasingly remote, underachievers often lower their expectations and perform congruently with their diminished expectations.

Reprimands usually elicit resistance and resentment and rarely motivate children to change their behavior. The far more effective alternative is to teach children how to make more astute decisions and to *train* them to ask key questions such as "What's going on here? What are my options? What are the possible consequences of my choices?" This analytical questioning process must be practiced until it becomes a reflex.

Children who do not naturally apply cause-and-effect principles can be systematically taught to do so. Without this training, they will probably continue to make nonjudicious choices throughout their life. Epidemic substance abuse, teenage pregnancy, gang killings, and tens of thousands of high school dropouts each year attest to the catastrophic effects of our society's failure to teach children to think about the potential consequences of their actions. Those children who arrive at life's critical junctures and do not consider the effects of their choices are in grave danger. If a pattern of mindlessness becomes entrenched, they could self-destruct.

SUGGESTED CORRECTIVE STRATEGIES

In School

1. If your child is continually getting into trouble or repeatedly making errors in judgment, it is likely that she has a marginal understanding of cause-and-effect principles. Ask your child's teacher to complete the checklist on page 52 so that specific thinking deficits can be pinpointed.

2. Discuss with the teacher ideas for helping your child better understand cause-and-effect principles. Focus initially on one or two specific deficit areas identified on the checklist.

For example, you might help her develop a plan for organizing her notebook and desk. The teacher might be willing to monitor her to make sure she is using the organization system, if she is in elementary school. You, in turn, will need to monitor her at home. Beware, however, of making your child overly dependent on supervision and help (see **Learned Helplessness,** page 152).

3. (ES) The teacher might be willing to integrate cause-and-effect

CAUSE-AND-EFFECT CHECKLIST

	Yes	No
This child:		
Leaves projects and assignments until the last minute	____	____
Does not allow sufficient time to complete projects	____	____
Is disorganized	____	____
Acts impulsively and without thinking	____	____
Does not plan ahead	____	____
Makes nonjudicious choices	____	____
Is chronically forgetful	____	____
Repeats the same mistakes	____	____
Resists assistance	____	____
Rarely establishes short-term or long-term goals	____	____
Has little sense of purpose	____	____
Gives up easily	____	____
Avoids responsibility	____	____
Tends to blame others for problems	____	____
Does not weigh potential danger or risks	____	____
Does not change behavior even when reprimanded or punished	____	____
Appears satisfied to do a second-rate job	____	____

activities into her curriculum so that the entire class can practice and apply the principles. Below are some examples of scenarios that could be used for class discussions:

■ You forget to bring your homework to school.
*Effect:*_____

■ You do not chain your bicycle to a tree at the park.
*Effect:*_____

■ You receive a poor grade on your science report.
*Cause:*_____

■ You win an award for the most improvement in school.
*Cause:*_____

If students are to develop a heightened awareness of the implications of their decisions and choices, they must practice identifying possible and probable effects and deducing possible and probable causes. The process can be fun for everyone. Encourage students to list as many as possible in the activity above to reinforce their appreciation of the cause-and-effect connection.

4. (J/HS) Diplomatically encourage teachers in the upper grades to spend time discussing choices and consequences. A history teacher cannot assume that all of his students realize how much time and planning are required to do a first-rate report. Nor can he assume that his students realize the implications of not allocating sufficient time for proofreading or properly formatting footnotes. Teachers who value strategic thinking skills must be prepared to devote sufficient instructional time to teaching their students the nuts and bolts of the analytical process.

At Home

1. You too have a primary responsibility to teach your child cause-and-effect principles. Because preaching or delivering sermons is usually ineffective, you must actively involve your child in thinking about what is happening to her and around her. Events described in the newspaper or on TV can be excellent catalysts for discussion. You might explore the reasons why reservoirs become polluted or examine the causes of acid rain. You might discuss factors that could contribute to the "greenhouse effect" or to the destruction of rain forests. You might explore the effects of raising the gasoline tax or of no-fault insurance. You might also examine the consequences of not submitting work on time.

2. (ES) Make up simple cause-and-effect scenarios similar to those described in strategy 3 under "In School." For example:

■ Your friend decides to steal something from the supermarket.
*Effect:*_____

■ A child throws rocks at moving cars.
*Effect:*_____

■ You get a D on your math homework.
*Cause:*_____

■ A teenager gets arrested on the freeway.
*Cause:*_____

3. Examine real-life problems your child is having. You might ask: "What are the behaviors that might have caused your teacher to get upset with you? What could you do to change her attitude about you? If your goal is to do better on the next spelling test, what specific steps could you take?"

DISTRACTIONS WHILE STUDYING

Parents and teachers with traditional attitudes about education generally have strong opinions about how children should study. They believe that noise, distractions, and interruptions undermine effort and performance and usually justify their position by contending that they were able to study more effectively in a quiet environment when they were in school.

These traditional attitudes set the stage for repeated parent-child confrontations. The adults want the TV and stereo off, nonessential phone calls eliminated, and breaks kept to an absolute minimum. Children argue that TV, music, and breaks for phone calls and snacks do not negatively affect their ability to study.

Many parents and teachers will be surprised to learn that some respected educators support the children's position. These educators have analyzed the performance of students who study with the radio or TV playing and have compared their work with that of students who study without environmental distractions. They have found no significant differences. One authority who has coined the term "Walkman Learner" maintains that many children in modern society have become so acclimated to loud rock music, pulsating videos, and blaring TVs that they may actually study and learn *best* under these conditions.

Although this may be true, it is important to keep in mind that students with chronic concentration deficits are an exception. They usually must struggle to stay on task even under the most controlled conditions and often become academically dysfunctional when allowed to create diversions (see **Attention Deficit Disorder,** page 5).

If your child has difficulty concentrating and you believe she is studying inefficiently and performing below her potential because of distractions, you probably will be tempted to try nagging, lectures, and threats first. These measures not only are usually ineffective but also can cause bitterness, hurt feelings, and showdowns. The autocratic response—simply insisting that your child turn off the TV or stereo—typically produces similar reactions. Children who are forced into compliance tend to become resentful, defensive, and resistant and may even retaliate for what they see as unfair treatment by intentionally sabotaging themselves. They are often so enmeshed in resisting their parents' authority that they either do not recognize or choose to deny that their behavior is hurting them as well as their parents (see **Anger and Frustration,** page 1).

The alternative is to assess your child's schoolwork objectively and decide if intervention is required. If your child does her homework while watching TV and receives good grades, she can make a persuasive argument for studying in her own way. If, however, her grades indicate she is not working up to her potential, developing reasonable study guidelines would certainly be justifiable. A cooperative approach ("Let's figure out how you might improve your grades") requires more parenting skill but is usually more effective than the heavy-handed, autocratic imposition of rules (see the **DIBS** method, page 233). If the cooperative approach doesn't work, you may have no choice but to define the study rules autocratically.

SUGGESTED CORRECTIVE STRATEGIES

In School

1. Some teachers run a tighter ship than others. They don't want their students to talk to each other in class or get up from their seats without permission. Other teachers prefer a less structured interactive classroom and cooperative learning. Although many students thrive in this system, others have more difficulty ignoring the distractions. If you feel your child cannot handle too many stimuli, diplomatically discuss your concerns with her teacher. Be aware, however, that although a highly structured classroom may be best for your child, it is not necessarily best for all students. One solution may be to transfer your child to a more structured, traditional classroom. If this is not feasible, ask the teacher to help your child learn how to adjust to the realities of her class. You cannot expect the teacher to change her style to suit your child, but she may agree to make some accommodations. Your child's desk, for instance, might be placed closer to the teacher's desk. The teacher might also develop some simple signals to alert your child when she is becoming diverted by distractions (see **Attention Deficit Disorder,** page 5, and **Working Independently,** page 332, for more specific corrective strategies).

At Home

1. Children with concentration problems who discover they can improve their schoolwork by reducing the distractions in their study environment are generally more receptive to making changes than those who are lectured. Discuss with your child in a nonconfrontational manner how distractions and concentration problems are linked. Brainstorm how she might reduce distractions when she studies. For example, she might eliminate incoming and outgoing telephone calls during study periods (see **Time Management,** page 308, **Monitoring Homework,** page 185, and **Study Breaks,** page 288). Although showing your child how to engineer her environment will not resolve chronic atten-

tion deficit disorder, it can help her figure out some of the logical "dos and don'ts" of efficient studying.

2. Involve your child in an experiment to determine if distractions are undermining school performance. Have her record her most recent grades. Then ask her to make up a list of specific distractions she agrees to eliminate for three weeks. Each day, have her use the checklist below (or create your own) to record that she successfully eliminated the distraction when studying. After three weeks, compare her current grades with those she received before making the changes.

STUDY ENVIRONMENT EXPERIMENT

	MON.	TUES.	WED.	THURS.	FRI.
No TV or music while studying.	——	——	——	——	——
Telephone calls only during breaks.	——	——	——	——	——
Concentrated study sessions of 25 minutes without taking a break.*	——	——	——	——	——
2 breaks of no more than 15 minutes.	——	——	——	——	——

If your child's performance in school improves after doing the experiment, discuss the obvious payoff of intentionally limiting distractions when studying. You might want to create a reward system that acknowledges her for improvement and encourages her to continue using the system. The ultimate goal is for her to control her study environment voluntarily because she likes the rewards and enjoys doing a first-rate job.

* The duration of study sessions for highly distractible younger children might initially be ten minutes and then slowly be increased to fifteen and ultimately twenty minutes.

DYSLEXIA

Dyslexia means different things to different people. Some educators use the term to describe any type of serious reading problem. Others use the term to describe a very specific type of reading dysfunction characterized by letter reversals (*b*/*d*, *q*/*g*, etc.), number reversals ("flipped" numbers), upside-down letters and numbers (*b*/*q*, *6*/*9*), word reversals (*saw*/*was*), letter and word transpositions (out of sequence), and word omissions. (Although letter and number reversals are quite common in kindergarten, parents should become concerned when the reversals persist beyond the fourth month of first grade.)

The process of reading is a grueling, emotionally draining nightmare for students who see letters, words, and numbers backward. Asking a seriously dyslexic youngster to read is the equivalent of asking a child to play baseball with his hands tied behind his back. The continual battle to make sense out of words that dance, wiggle, and tumble across the page will inexorably corrode the child's self-esteem and self-confidence and leave in its wake profound feelings of inadequacy, hopelessness, and embarrassment.

To protect themselves psychologically, many demoralized dyslexic children become phobic about reading and develop elaborate ego-protecting behaviors. Their defense mechanisms may range from laziness, irresponsibility, procrastination, acting out, and manipulation to truancy and drugs. Although these behaviors call attention to the very deficits the children are attempting to camouflage, the children are too enmeshed in their own drama to recognize this irony.

The reasons that children reverse letters and numbers are complex and not fully understood. The most common theories include right-left confusion ("directionality" deficits), poor ocular muscle control, disequilibrium, neurological dysfunction (sensory processing deficits) and cranial misalignment (a controversial theory promulgated by some chiropractors).

Although there is no consensus about the causes of dyslexia, specialists in the field generally agree that the condition is genetically based. Dyslexia may affect several members of the same family as well as family members from previous generations. Experts also generally agree that although dyslexia is mysteriously linked to the neurological processing of sensory data, the condition rarely involves measurable organic brain damage.

Methods for treating dyslexia include perceptual training (teaching children how to focus and process sensory data more efficiently), tracking exercises (workbooks, handouts, and other materials), eye muscle therapy (practiced by specialists in developmental optometry), kinesthetic/neurological imprinting, (incorporated in the Slingerland and Orton-Gillingham methods), colored lenses (used to treat a condition called *scotopic dyslexia* in which the letters run together or "fall" off the page), visualization methods, auditory discrimination therapy (see page 19), drug therapy (Ritalin, Dexedrine, etc.), motion sickness medication (see *A Solution to the Riddle of Dyslexia* by Harold Levinson, M.D., included in the Resource List at the back of the book), and cranial adjustments (a controversial chiropractic technique).

Dyslexic children may respond positively to a wide range of different remediation techniques. Most resource and reading specialists focus on developing children's visual discrimination skills (the ability to see the difference between letters such as *b* and *d*) and improving visual tracking skills (the effectiveness with which the eyes move from left to right across the printed line). That dyslexic children can respond positively to so many radically different remedial methods strongly suggests that rapport with the teacher and the "halo effect" must be factored into any attempt to assess the efficacy of a particular remediation technique. The halo effect (also referred to as the Hawthorne effect) acknowledges that some improvement may be attributed to extra attention and may not reflect the efficacy of a particular intervention method. A child's skills may improve because he likes his tutor and wants to please her and/or because he is receiving affirmation, encouragement, and individualized help. Certain remediation methods may also prove more successful with some children than with others, and well-trained educational therapists often combine different methods until they discover the most effective prescription for a particular child.

Significant breakthroughs in treating dyslexic children have occurred in the last twenty years. Thanks to more effective learning assistance programs and better-trained teachers, children who might never have learned to read are now overcoming or compensating for serious reading deficits. Unfortunately, many school districts provide only marginal learning assistance for dyslexic students. These districts insist that children be at least two years below grade level to qualify for remedial help despite compelling evidence that early diagnosis and intervention can prevent the devastating psychological damage that occurs when stymied, frustrated, and demoralized children become convinced that their problems are insoluble and that they are hopelessly defective. Parents cannot permit this tragedy to happen. They *must* find help for their dyslexic child, either within the system or outside it.

SUGGESTED CORRECTIVE STRATEGIES

In School

1. The primary symptoms of dyslexia usually become apparent in first grade. Chronic decoding (sensory processing) problems are red flags, and children manifesting these deficits should be diagnostically tested. If your child is enrolled in a district that insists that students be two years below grade level to qualify for help, you must be persistent and, if necessary, aggressive in requesting an evaluation. Federal law 94-142 stipulates that children with learning problems be tested (see **Parents' Rights,** page 201). Your child should be provided with help *before* she becomes demoralized and phobic about reading.

2. If your child is identified as dyslexic, inquire if the school has a resource specialist trained in the Orton-Gillingham or Slingerland method. The Lindamood Auditory Discrimination in Depth Program is also effective in helping some children with visual discrimination problems. Materials specifically designed to improve visual discrimination (seeing the difference between letters) and decoding that are available to resource specialists are included in the Resource List at the back of the book.

At Home

1. If your child is dyslexic, you should anticipate resistance when you propose to provide assistance in reading. Youngsters who struggle to decode written words are emotionally vulnerable and highly sensitive, and because of profoundly painful associations with reading they will often make every effort to avoid reading. They are especially reluctant to expose their deficiencies to their parents. Patience is vital. Be sensitive to your child's feelings and be creative in making reading a positive experience. Select high-interest stories and have your child sit next to you and encourage her to try to follow along as you read. Your goal is to help her realize that reading can be an enjoyable experience.

2. **(J/HS)** Most older students with a long and painful reading track

IMPROVING YOUR CHILD'S READING SKILLS

1. Ask the teacher what your child's reading level is and choose materials that are slightly below her comfort reading level. (The teacher or resource specialist should be able to recommend appropriate books. Also consult with the librarian at your local library.)

2. Read a line to your child slowly and then ask her to read the same line. Be patient when she struggles. (You may need to read the line several times before she feels comfortable reading the line aloud.)

3. As your child's reading improves, you can experiment with reading two lines aloud before asking her to read. The goal is to progress to reading an entire paragraph or page before she reads the same section. At some point she will ideally be able to read to you *without* your having to preread the material.

4. Gently point out when she reads a *b* as a *d*.

5. Ask your child if her teacher or resource specialist has taught her methods for recognizing the difference. (For example, she could make two fists. The knuckles of the right hand should touch the knuckles of the left. She should then point the right and left thumbs up. The left hand is always the *b*, and the right is always the *d*. This kinesthetic [body] association can help children recognize the difference between the two letters.)

6. Make the process of reading fun and note when your child is becoming tired. Be prepared to quit for the day even if you have not covered as much ground as you would have liked.

Your goal is to improve your child's skills through practice and to convince her that reading can be a pleasurable experience. Be prepared for temporary plateaus and regressions. These setbacks are common with dyslexic children. Stress is counterproductive. Be affirmative. Children thrive on affirmation!

record are highly resistant to reading aloud with their parents. You may be able to defuse this resistance by explaining the rationale for reading together. If your child is unwilling to read aloud with you, propose that she work with a tutor. This person should ideally be a specialist who can show her methods for tracking words more proficiently. With practice she will become more proficient, and her sensitivity should diminish.

EFFORT AND MOTIVATION

A child's motivation is directly linked to his desire to attain objectives he believes will provide immediate or long-term gratification. The short-term goal might be a hit in the next baseball game or an A on the next spelling test. The long-term goal might be an A in English on a report card, a part in the school play, a varsity football letter, a car, or a college scholarship.

The value a child attaches to a specific objective is affected by a complex mix of family, personality, societal, peer, and mass media factors. The wish list may include a specific toy, spending money, popularity, a car, security, competence, prestige, power, or free time to play basketball.

A young child is continually absorbing data from his environment as he observes and responds to his parents, siblings, peers, and teachers. His value system, attitude, goals, and work ethic cannot help being profoundly influenced by this ongoing process of storing life experiences.

Although environmental factors will influence a child's effort and motivation, inherited personality traits can also profoundly affect his attitudes, choices, and actions. Research has demonstrated that certain behaviors once believed to be exclusively determined by environmental forces are linked, at least in part, to genetically transmitted and hormonally based factors. Chronically shy children, for example, have been found to have a high level of the hormone cortisol in their saliva. Although cortisol and adrenaline are secreted in response to fear, some chronically timid and inhibited children may have a continually elevated cortisol level. Research done by Jerome Kagan, a developmental psychologist at Harvard University, has shown that this anomaly can be measured even in newborn infants.

Inherited intelligence, academic skills, study skills, and strategic thinking skills must also be factored into the motivation equation (see **IQ Test Scores,** page 130, **Smart Thinking,** page 275, and **Study Skills,** page 292). Children are usually motivated and conscientious when they believe they have the ability to achieve their objectives. Those who possess good skills and self-confidence are more willing to accept challenges, establish short- and long-term objectives, risk setbacks, and work diligently (see **Learning Disabilities,** page 157, **Atypical Learning Problems,** page 16, **Underachievement,** page 312, **Goals,** page 84, **Bouncing Back from Setbacks and Learning from Mistakes,** page 30, and **Fear of Failure/Success/Competition,** page 74). Children who have struggled and repeatedly failed often shut down and become irresponsible, lazy, and unwilling to accept challenges or risk potential ego-bruising defeat (see **Self-Esteem and Self-Confidence,** page 266).

If you conclude that your child is lazy and unmotivated, you will undoubtedly want to intervene. The most effective way to do so is to develop a system for communicating family values, expressing concerns, defining problem areas, teaching practical achievement-oriented skills, modeling productive behaviors, affirming progress, and conveying positive expectations. Certain guidelines can facilitate this process:

- Communicate clearly and unequivocally your position on effort and motivation (see **Behavior and Performance Guidelines,** page 26).

- Resist preaching.

- Encourage and model honest communication and feedback.

- Be consistent.

- Be patient.

- Be reasonable.

- Urge your child to establish short-term and long-term goals.

- Acknowledge and affirm progress and success.

- Be sensitive.

- Express love and positive expectations.

Children who continually sabotage themselves by refusing to work and who resist their parents' best efforts to get them on track will require professional counseling. Ignoring the problem increases the risk of academic and emotional shutdown. The problem won't, in all likelihood, disappear of its own accord. Responsible parents admit when they cannot deal with a problem and recognize that procuring professional help can be the wisest investment they can make in their child's future.

SUGGESTED CORRECTIVE STRATEGIES

In School

1. Discuss any concerns you might have about your child's unacceptable work ethic with his teacher and/or school counselor. Ask for suggestions about how you might work together in improving his motivation and effort. Also ask the teacher if she feels your child has the requisite skills to do the work. If his skills are deficient, it is imperative that learning assistance be provided, either in school or privately.

2. It is vital that you and the teacher pinpoint the specific factors that might be impeding your child academically and undermining his willingness to establish goals and work diligently. Refer to the specific deficit areas described in this book and to the many checklists that are designed to help you identify underlying problems. If, for example, your child has problems with reading comprehension, phonics, spelling, vocabulary, or auditory memory, these learning deficits must be addressed before you and the teacher can reasonably expect a great deal of effort and motivation. Your child must feel he has a chance to succeed academically before he will be willing to sustain his effort and take the risks inherent in defining goals and working toward attaining these goals.

At Home

1. Discuss your concerns about effort and motivation with your child. Ask him if he has any theories about why he is unwilling to establish goals and work diligently (refer to the **DIBS** method on page 233). Don't be surprised if your child resists acknowledging the problem and denies he is "coasting." Help him define the specific factors that could be undermining his effort and motivation. The factors may include learning problems, study skills deficits, and family issues. Once you identify the sources of your child's poor motivation, you must develop a strategy for resolving the deficits (educational therapy, tutoring, or counseling). Explore ways in which the agreed-on plan can be monitored without triggering resentment. Be careful not to preach or lecture.

2. If specific learning or study skills deficits are causing your child to resist working diligently, refer to the appropriate entries in this book for suggestions about how to correct these problems. (See student evaluation, pages 160–163.) It may be advisable to work with your child on goal setting (see page 84), planning (see page 222), disorganization (see page 46), problem solving (see page 231), or time management (see page 308).

3. If your child is chronically angry at you or his teacher, and you cannot defuse this anger, he will require professional counseling. Resisting work and acting lazy can be weapons that your child uses consciously or unconsciously to express his unhappiness, anger, or depression. If you do not provide the resources for him to examine and resolve his unhappiness, he may become so habituated to doing the minimum possible that the counterproductive behaviors could persist throughout his life.

ESSAY TESTS

Students who are required to take essay tests must be able to demonstrate that they have retained key information, have understood important underlying concepts and issues, and can tie the relevant information together. They must organize their thoughts, present facts that support their position, and express their ideas cogently and persuasively.

A typical high school essay test might instruct students to discuss the historical issues that led to the civil rights movement in the 1960s. The students may have twenty minutes to pull together all the relevant information they know. Although facts are important, facts alone do not guarantee a good grade. The students must select information that clearly demonstrates their understanding of the subject, and they must cull, distill, and shape the data into a well-crafted three-page essay. If they are strategic (see **Smart Thinking,** page 275), they will probably take a few moments to make a mental or written thumbnail outline of what they want to include. They will begin with a powerful topic sentence, write neatly, spell accurately, tie the information together, express their ideas succinctly and sequentially, and make their points convincingly.

There are two basic formats for writing an essay. For the most common, the *deductive method*, the student makes a general overview statement in her opening or topic sentence, such as "Two hundred years of oppression, prejudice, and discrimination made the civil rights movement of the 1960s inevitable." She then describes historical events and sociological conditions that contributed to the movement and includes data to substantiate her analysis and document her knowledge. In her concluding paragraph she ties the information together and concisely reiterates her position.

The deductive method can be visualized as a triangle or pyramid with the introductory topic sentence at the point of the triangle and the substantiating data in expanding layers below the tip. The concluding sentence, which encapsulates the information presented in the essay, is the base of the triangle.

For the alternative *inductive method* the student presents information and supporting data and carefully leads the reader to the main point that she states in the concluding sentence or paragraph. The first sentence of her essay might be "Blacks were brought to this country as slaves during the early colonial period." After presenting relevant information that describes the sociological conditions and historical issues, she might conclude her essay by stating "It was inevitable, given centuries of oppression, prejudice, discrimination, and widespread denial of basic rights and freedoms, that American blacks would ultimately demand equality in school, on the job, in housing, and at the ballot box. They would no longer tolerate second-class citizenship. Their demand for basic civil rights, which were constitutionally guaranteed, finally exploded in the 1960s and dramatically changed the course of American history and the values of American society."

The inductive method can be visualized as an inverted triangle. Information is stacked in descending layers that lead to a logical conclusion. This conclusion, which is expressed in the final sentence or paragraph, is the inverted point of the triangle. Although inductive essays can be very persuasive, they require advanced planning, organization, and expressive language skills (see **Language Arts [Essays and Reports],** page 141). For this reason most students choose the deductive model when taking an essay exam.

There is another method for writing essays that incorporates a dialectic format. This method involves stating and documenting a well-reasoned position on a subject (the thesis), stating and documenting a contrasting position (the antithesis), and blending the best components of both positions into a balanced conclusion (the synthesis). The Hegelian dialectic format (named for the philosopher Hegel) is used extensively in European countries. The method can be highly persuasive but students clearly require extensive practice before they can use it effectively.

Practice, feedback, constructive criticism, encouragement, and patience are vital components in the equation that ultimately produces good essay-writing skills. Because expository writing and analytical thinking skills improve slowly and incrementally, children must receive systematic instruction, incisive feedback, and constructive criticism (see **Language Arts [Essays and Reports],** page 141). Students must write hundreds of essays and reports before they can reasonably be expected to express themselves effectively in a timed essay exam. Even children with natural writing talent must make a concentrated, sustained effort to develop and refine their expressive language skills.

Students in elementary and junior high school who have taken only multiple-choice, short answer, and true/false tests usually become overwhelmed and demoralized in high school when they encounter teachers who give essay exams. Memorizing facts, circling the correct answer, writing *True* or *False*, or responding to a test question with one or two words does not prepare these children for the rigors of having to organize, distill, and communicate what they know about a subject in a two- or three-page essay.

Some educators contend that multiple-choice tests can adequately measure information retention and comprehension and that the tests are easier to grade and are less subjective than essay exams. But exclusive use of multiple-choice tests deprives students of an opportunity to master expressive language skills that are fundamental to a complete education. The widespread practice of denying children this opportunity to develop their thinking and language arts abilities has had a catastrophic impact on American education. The effects are eloquently and incisively described in Allan Bloom's book *The Closing of the American Mind*.

SUGGESTED CORRECTIVE STRATEGIES

In School

1. (ES) Many elementary school teachers erroneously believe that their students cannot reasonably be expected to take essay exams. Most fourth-graders can learn to write cogent essays, assuming they have been systematically taught how to condense information and express their ideas sequentially. Many innovative programs (see the Resource List at the back of the book) have produced documented and dramatic improvement in written expressive language skills.

2. (J/HS) If you feel your child's teachers are not giving enough essay exams, diplomatically express your concerns and be prepared for resistance from teachers who have developed their own teaching style and testing system and may construe your suggestions as interference. These teachers may reject your suggestion on the basis of some of the arguments described above, without considering the logic of your position. If you feel strongly that your child should have more opportunities to develop and refine her essay-writing skills and the classroom teacher does not concur, discuss your concerns with the department chairman and/or the principal. Even if they agree, they may not be able to require a tenured teacher to change his testing philosophy. Effecting major changes in educational philosophy at the local school level usually requires a concerted effort by a significant number of concerned parents.

At Home

1. For specific suggestions about how to help your child develop her essay-writing skills, refer to **Language Arts (Essays and Reports)**, page 141.

EVALUATING SPECIAL EDUCATION PROGRAMS

Most parents of children who are struggling in school are delighted if their child qualifies for learning assistance. They realize that individualized help from a resource specialist is an ideal means to make certain their child gets the remedial help she requires.

There are two types of learning assistance programs: a *self-contained program* ("special day class") where children spend most or all of the school day and a *resource program* ("RSP class") where children spend only a portion of the day. Children in special day classes generally have more severe learning handicaps and lack the requisite skills to keep up with a regular class. Children in RSP programs generally have less debilitating learning problems and can usually keep up with their class if provided with forty-five to sixty minutes of learning assistance each day.

Not all parents are receptive to learning assistance programs. Some fear that if their child is officially classified as "learning disabled" or "learning different," she will be permanently stigmatized. Other parents worry that having to leave the classroom each day to work with the resource specialist will embarrass their child. They may also fear that their child will miss important classwork while participating in a pullout program. These misgivings may be justified. Children in RSP programs often do miss important work, and they are frequently held responsible for this work. Students in learning assistance programs in fact often find themselves in a "Catch 22" situation: they require remedial assistance, but while they are out of the classroom receiving help, they fall further and further behind.

Classroom teachers who are flexible and understanding about missed classwork can significantly reduce the stress on students. The work, however, must somehow be made up, and this can pose a monumental challenge to even compassionate teachers. To alleviate the problem, some schools now send their RSP teachers and teacher aides into the regular classroom to provide on-site remedial assistance. There is a potential disadvantage to this strategy: focusing on helping children complete their daily classwork takes valuable time away from remediating their underlying learning deficits.

Many parents of children assigned to special day classes have other concerns. They may fear that their children will never learn the skills needed for successful reintegration into the mainstream. These parents may also be apprehensive about negative behaviors and attitudes that may be prevalent in classes comprised of children with a long history of serious learning problems. Teasing, taunting, and social rejection by other mainstream students on the school campus are another consideration. Social ostracism can be traumatic for special education students. Although these children may have perfectly normal IQs, they may be rejected by mainstream students because they are considered "strange" or retarded. This stigma may cause students to resist placement in special programs.*

Before you can intelligently decide whether or not to accept the recommendations of the school authorities, you must understand the issues and take the time to observe and evaluate the proposed remedial program (see **Individual Educational Program [IEP],** page 126). If you agree to have your child participate, you should monitor her progress and periodically reassess the program. Conferences with the resource specialist or special day class teacher are vital (see **Parent-Teacher Conferences,** page 198). These meetings do not necessarily have to be face to face. Telephone contacts and progress checklists are often sufficient. You need updates, but you must be reasonable. Checking in with the teacher every two months is usually sufficient.

Remediation programs rarely follow a precise and predictable timetable. Although some children improve quickly and dramatically, most make slower progress. Students may also respond differently to the same remedial program. You must be realistic when assessing the efficacy of your child's program. Serious problems usually take longer to resolve, even if your child is enrolled in a first-rate program. You must also be prepared for occasional temporary setbacks; your child may show improvement for several months and then plateau or even regress. You should, however, expect improvement after a reasonable period of time. Reexamine the program if you conclude your child is not achieving the agreed-on goals established during the IEP, or if you conclude that the goals are

---

* Prevalent teasing reflects an incompetent school administration. In well-run schools, principals and teachers make certain that their students treat children with special academic and physical needs with sensitivity and respect. Teasing and taunting are simply not tolerated.

insufficient to permit successful reintegration into the mainstream. Be prepared to discuss your concerns diplomatically with the resource specialist.

You have a right to understand why an RSP program or special day class is not achieving the educational goals defined during the IEP conference, and if you find the explanation unacceptable, you must insist that the remedial program be revised (see **Parents' Rights,** page 201).

SUGGESTED CORRECTIVE STRATEGIES

In School

1. Periodically request that the teacher and resource specialist re-evaluate your child. The student evaluation forms (page 160 for elementary students and 163 for junior and senior high students) will provide substantive information to give focus to the parent-teacher conferences (see page 198). Strategies for correcting your child's deficits should be assessed and, if necessary, reexamined. Ask for recommendations about how you might help your child at home. If you cannot work successfully with your child, discuss with the teacher whether hiring a tutor would be advisable. Ask for guidelines about how much help you should provide and how much homework your child should be expected to do. This discussion is vital if you feel your child is doing too much or too little homework. (See appropriate suggested corrective strategies under relevant entries in this book.)

2. Make a list of the concerns you want to explore during your next conference, IEP meeting, or PPT (pupil/ parent/teacher) meeting. This conference should examine substantive issues. Your role is to ask penetrating, nonantagonistic questions. Do not allow yourself to be overwhelmed or intimidated by the professionals in attendance. If you don't understand their jargon, ask for clarification. Your comprehension is vital to the quality of your child's remedial program.

At Home

1. It is vital that you communicate with your child about his progress and any problem areas. Decide which issues discussed during parent/teacher conferences to examine with your child. You may need to simplify the issues, and you may decide to withhold certain information. Trust your intuition. A simple explanation about the rationale and goals for the learning assistance program or about changes in your procedures for providing help or supervision at home may be sufficient for younger children. Older children may want a more comprehensive explanation. Use examples your child can relate to and understand. (E.g. "Do you remember how your Little League coach had you practice your swing for hours? Well, you're going to have to do some more practice learning the parts of speech.") As a general rule, informing your child about the issues and actively involving him in the remediation program produces the best results.

2. Periodically review the objectives of the learning assistance program with your child. Explore strategies for achieving the goals and examine problem areas. Actively involve your child in the process of brainstorming solutions and attaining short-term and long-term goals (see **Smart Thinking,** page 275). Discuss homework, study habits, and schedules. If your child has become overly dependent on you, discuss the problem and explore solutions with her (see **Learned Helplessness,** page 152).

FEAR OF FAILURE/ SUCCESS/COMPETITION

When faced with danger, a child's brain triggers an involuntary neurological, hormonal, psychological, and behavioral chain reaction. The child may respond to the perceived threat by escaping, fighting, or neutralizing the danger. However he responds, he will instinctively attempt to protect himself from harm.

When fear functions as intended by nature, it warns children not to climb on dangerous rocks, jump from a bridge into water of unknown depth, get into a stranger's car, or ride with a friend who is drunk. Fear, however, is not always an ally. When it is excessive, inappropriate, or irrational, it can distort a child's perceptions and judgment and be emotionally and academically debilitating.

The demoralized child who has repeatedly experienced pain in school and who lacks self-confidence and emotional resilience is especially vulnerable to fear. If he believes his academic situation is hopeless, he may become school phobic and run away from any challenging situation that might cause additional pain or frustration. He may retreat into a "circle the wagons" stance and refuse to venture outside the perimeter of his defenses, or he may charge ahead mindlessly and continue to make the same mistakes.

Once children become convinced that effort is futile and failure is preordained, they usually acquire a pattern of counterproductive compensatory behaviors that may include procrastination, resistance to help, irresponsibility, denial, blaming, manipulation, laziness, cheating, and lying. Some children will act out aggressively. Others will become timid and withdrawn and may shut down. The list of nonadaptive behaviors attributable to poor self-esteem, insecurity, and fear is extensive, and the behaviors invariably impede problem resolution (see **Anger and Frustration,** page 1, **Effort and Motivation,** page 63, **Bouncing Back from Setbacks and Learning from Mistakes,** page 30, **Disregard of Consequences,** page 50, **Behavior and Performance Guidelines,** page 26, **Negative Attitude Toward School,** page 188).

Children with healthy self-esteem, good academic skills, and a successful track record respond with confidence to challenges. They have faith in themselves and their abilities because their achievements have confirmed their talents. They enjoy competition and believe they deserve to win. They are willing to take reasonable risks and to devote the requisite time and effort to attaining their goals, and they revel in their accomplishments. When they do experience a setback, they possess the emotional resilience to bounce back. After analyzing the situation they will either try again or move on to another challenge (see **Goals,** page 84, **Self-Esteem and Self-Confidence,** page 266, and **Smart Thinking,** page 275).

Academically deficient children, in contrast, are often preoccupied with protecting themselves from failure. Youngsters traumatized by the fear of failing perceive each new challenge as potential defeat and respond to each glitch as a confirmation of their inferiority. To cope with their fear, they often capitulate, rationalizing that they haven't really failed because they haven't really tried.

A struggling child who is accustomed to marginal achievement may become so habituated to doing poorly in school that he may actually fear success. Marginal performance may provide a sense of identity and security, and he may perceive success as a scary, uncharted territory. Once he becomes accustomed to limited achievement, he may convince himself he doesn't want to succeed.

Ensconced in a comfort zone where relatively little is expected by him and from him, an insecure and fearful child may passively or aggressively resist leaving the safety of his refuge. Achievement would require him to revise his assessment of his abilities and potential. This drastic revision could be threatening and unsettling. His relationship with his parents and teachers would change. Instead of accepting Ds or Cs, they would probably begin to expect Bs or even As, and they would be less willing to offer help and accept excuses (see **Learned Helplessness,** page 152). Meeting the new standards would also require additional effort and work. He might also face the prospect of being rejected by his nonachieving friends, and he would have no guarantee that achieving students would accept him.

With assistance and guidance most children can conquer their fears of failure, success, or competition. Your role is to orchestrate repeated opportunities for success, affirm your child's accomplishments, build his self-confidence, and provide the academic and study skills he needs to prevail in school. If his fears are chronic and are linked to deep-seated psychological issues, he will require help from a mental health professional. Hoping that his fears will disappear of their own accord could be a tragic miscalculation with catastrophic emotional, social, academic, and career consequences.

SUGGESTED CORRECTIVE STRATEGIES

In School

1. (ES) If you believe your child's ability to function in school is being undermined by excessive fear, discuss your concerns with his teacher. Do not automatically assume that he is afraid of failing. He may actually be afraid of succeeding. Consider whether he has become so habituated to his comfort zone that he is unwilling to change his attitudes and behavior. Consider also whether he is afraid of succeeding because he perceives himself as being unworthy of success. Take a close look at your child's behavior. Identify his specific strengths and deficiencies. Observe how he responds to setbacks. Identify his desired payoffs. Does he act like a clown to elicit attention? Does he act helpless to elicit assistance (see **Learned Helplessness,** page 152)? Does he intentionally try to elicit sympathy and concern? What triggers his anxiety and stress? Once you and the teacher have assessed the possible underlying sources of your child's fears, brainstorm how you might orchestrate successful experiences for him. For example, you might use new strategies for helping him study for his spelling test. The teacher might agree to reduce the number of words for which he is

responsible. Suggest that she intentionally acknowledge and affirm him for even relatively minor successes. This acknowledgment may initially trigger discomfort, especially if your child has become habituated to negative feedback and comments. Fear is not easily overcome. The process requires patience and insight. Children with chronic fears will require professional counseling.

At Home

1. Encourage your child to examine the situations that frighten him. If he has difficulty identifying or discussing the specific factors, you might say: "Let me tell you some of the situations that frighten me. For example, when I was in school I was afraid to try out for plays because I was sure I would forget my lines. I've noticed that you sometimes give up at the last minute. You do this even when you've been doing a good job. Let's list the reasons why someone might give up on something and then let's list the possible consequences. I'll start with the first reason. The person is afraid that his work will not please his teacher. The consequences he fears are that she might get upset or his parents might get upset when they see his grade. Now you give a reason and a consequence." Using the third person (*he or she*) may provide some emotional distance and be less threatening to your child. Be patient as you attempt to draw out your child. This may be a very difficult exercise. Most children do not think consciously about their fears and being asked to identify underlying issues may be difficult and emotionally unsettling. Do not make negative judgments about your child's responses. If he says that the teacher would get mad at him, you might respond: "How could someone deal with this?" Your objective is to encourage your child to begin looking at his fears so that he can "process" them and overcome them.

Resist the temptation to try to solve your child's problems. Give him something to think about. For example, you might say: "If the teacher did get upset with the child's work, what could the child do? Could he talk to her about it? What might he say? Could his parents help in any way?" Be prepared for "I don't know." Your objective is to plant seeds, encourage thinking, and elicit the expression of feeling.

At this point you might make a transition to one of your child's fears, and say: "You have told me you are afraid when you have to read aloud in front of the class. Let's list the reasons why you are frightened. . . ." Follow the same procedure described above. Don't expect immediate resolution. Processing fear usually takes time. Assistance from a trained mental health professional will be necessary if your child is unresponsive and unable to examine and resolve his fears.

2. Be patient. Altering your child's attitude and imprinted behavioral responses to fear of failure, success, or competition is a slow process. Once you and the teacher identify the underlying issues, you will want to make changes incrementally. You do not want to overwhelm your child or produce unnecessary anxiety. You might begin to provide a bit less help with his homework (see **Learned Helplessness,** page 152). You might encourage him to take karate, swimming, or tennis lessons. This could be especially valuable if he has poor coordination or chronically lacks confidence. Do not let him quit when the class begins to get difficult. To do so would be tantamount to "setting him up" for failure. Before he begins, insist on at least a six-month trial before a reassessment and a decision about whether or not to continue the program.

FOLLOWING
VERBAL DIRECTIONS

During a typical school day children are expected to respond to a constant barrage of instructions. Some children can assimilate these instructions effortlessly. Others struggle to make sense of even the most basic verbal directions (see **Auditory Memory,** page 22).

Children who have difficulty following verbal instructions are in a constant state of confusion. Because their class work and homework rarely conform to the teacher's guidelines, their grades inevitably suffer. To keep up, either they must constantly ask the teacher for clarification or they must somehow figure out through observation what their classmates are doing. In desperation they may ask other students for help, possibly getting into trouble for talking in class. As the possibility of academic success appears increasingly remote, their behavior, self-confidence, and attitude will deteriorate. Those who are repeatedly reprimanded for not paying attention will probably feel hopelessly inept and shut down whenever verbal directions are given. From their vantage point there can be only one explanation for their ineptitude: They are "dumb." And to cope with the resulting feelings of incompetence, they adopt an attitude of indifference.

Difficulty in processing verbal directions can usually be attributed to deficits in one or more of the following areas:

- **Auditory memory** (see page 22)

- **Auditory sequencing** (remembering information in the proper order)

- **Concentration** (see **Attention Deficit Disorder,** page 5)

- **Impulsivity** (see **Attention Deficit Disorder,** page 5)

Before your child can realistically be expected to improve his ability to follow instructions, he must be taught specific techniques that will help him process, remember, and respond to verbal input more effectively. Systematic instruction, practice, and carefully orchestrated successes are requisites to breaking the cycle of poor performance, frustration, demoralization, negative expectations, and deteriorating self-confidence.

SUGGESTED CORRECTIVE STRATEGIES

In School

1. If you observe that your child is having difficulty following verbal directions and the teacher concurs, request that he be evaluated by the school psychologist or the resource specialist. Tests should indicate if he has short-term or long-term auditory memory or auditory sequencing deficits. If deficits are revealed, specific remediation methods and materials can be used to develop your child's skills in these critical areas. (See the suggested corrective strategies under **Auditory Memory,** page 22.)

2. (ES) Ask the teacher if she would be willing to give your child instructions in smaller "chunks" and monitor him more closely to make sure he has understood the directions. This should be done diplomatically to prevent embarrassment. As your child's listening skills improve, the teacher can begin to phase out this simplification/monitoring procedure.

3. (J/HS) It is difficult for junior and senior high school teachers to supervise students as closely as do elementary school teachers. If your child

tells you he is having difficulty following verbal instructions, discuss the issue with his teachers. (Many teachers *assume* that students should be able to follow verbal instructions by the time they reach seventh grade, and they may consider those who don't listen in class to be irresponsible.) Ask if they would be willing to monitor your child more closely (without embarrassing him) to make sure he has understood the directions.

4. If your child is having difficulty following verbal directions because of attention deficit disorder, refer to the suggested corrective strategies under that listing (page 5).

At Home

1. (ES) Practice is essential if your child is to improve his ability to follow verbal instructions. If your child resists your help, make the process of improving listening skills fun. For example, create a game in which something is hidden (an inexpensive little toy or a cookie) and give your child explicit instructions on how to find the prize. Start out with two or three directions. Increase the complexity as your child's skills improve. Have your child close his eyes and picture going into the living room and picking up the left-hand cushion on the couch. This visualizing process reinforces the auditory process and is especially effective when children have intrinsically weak auditory skills. To further reinforce auditory memory, ask your child to repeat the instructions before following them.

2. When giving your child a series of instructions (e.g., "Please set the table, feed the dog, and bring in the garbage pail"), encourage your child to follow the visualization procedure described above. Have him form a visual picture in his mind of what you have asked him to do and then have him repeat the instructions.

3. (ES) Play Simon Says around the dinner table. ("Simon says cut your chicken into twelve pieces, put your fork down for five seconds, eat a forkful of peas, put your fork down, and then eat a piece of chicken.") Have your child take a visual picture, repeat the instructions, and then follow them. Then have your child give you a series of instructions.

FOLLOWING
WRITTEN DIRECTIONS

A child spends a significant portion of the typical school day responding to instructions written on the chalkboard, in textbooks, on dittoed handouts, and in workbooks. The youngster who has difficulty understanding and following written directions faces an uphill struggle, which will be reflected in his grades.

Relatively few children intentionally or capriciously disregard instructions. Most are confused because they cannot decipher, understand, remember, and/or apply what they read. They may do the wrong assignment, format a report improperly, or misinterpret the directions on a test. The consequences for these mistakes become increasingly grave as students progress into the upper grades.

Difficulty following written instructions can usually be attributed to deficits in one or more of these areas:

- Decoding words (see **Dyslexia,** page 58)

- Reading comprehension (see page 250)

- Working independently (see page 332)

- Concentration (see **Attention Deficit Disorder,** page 5)

- Visual memory (see page 326)

- Visual sequencing (remembering written information in the proper order—see **Visual Memory,** page 326)

- Impulsivity (see **Attention Deficit Disorder,** page 5)

When children see their classmates effortlessly following written instructions and working efficiently while they are continually confused, they will eventually conclude that they are hopelessly inept and will probably try to protect themselves psychologically with an elaborate system of nonadaptive behaviors such as procrastination, irresponsibility, and resistance.

SUGGESTED CORRECTIVE STRATEGIES

In School

1. If your child is struggling with written instructions, discuss the issue with his teacher. Request that he be evaluated by the school psychologist or resource specialist (see **Parents' Rights,** page 201). Once the underlying deficits have been identified, the resource specialist can develop a focused assistance program. See the Resource List at the back of the book for a list of remedial materials.

2. Ask your child's teacher to monitor him to make certain he has understood the directions. Because elementary school teachers have fewer students than do junior and senior high school teachers, they are generally more willing to provide this individualized supervision. If your child is in junior or senior high school, you might elicit his teachers' cooperation by explaining the problem and your concerns. His school counselor should also be involved in the monitoring process. The ultimate goal, of course, is to remove this safety net. Until his skills improve, however, supervision is vital.

At Home

1. Refer to suggested corrective strategies listed under the specific deficits that the school psychologist or resource specialist identify as causing your child's difficulty following written directions (e.g., dyslexia, attention deficit disorder, visual memory, etc.). Your own observations should also guide you in targeting specific areas to work on at home.

2. Monitor your child closely to make certain he has understood the directions for doing his homework or preparing for tests. Ask him to read the instructions and then explain to you what he is being asked to do. Suggest that he close his eyes and see himself doing what the instructions say. These visual pictures should be very detailed and precise. If his problem is caused by a visual decoding problem (see **Dyslexia,** page 58), he may be expending so much energy to decipher the words that he has little left to devote to understanding what the words mean. Once he has read the words with your assistance, discuss what the instructions mean. Be gentle and patient if he is confused and always be affirming and positive. If your child concludes that you are continually judging him negatively or are disappointed in him, he will be reluctant to accept your help. As his skills improve, begin to withdraw this monitoring/

support system incrementally (see **Learned Helplessness,** page 152).

3. If your child does not qualify for help in school and/or is not responding as quickly as you would like, consider hiring a trained tutor or enrolling your child in a private learning center. The resource specialist or your pediatrician may be able to make a recommendation.

GOALS

Successful students grasp the cause-and-effect relationship that links the procedure of establishing goals and achieving them. They may not consciously think about this connection at all times, but their focused effort, astute choices, and strategic behaviors and attitudes attest to the fact that goal setting is an integral part of their modus operandi.

A goal-directed child might decide she wants an A on her math test, a part in the next school play, a hit in the next inning, or a music scholarship to Yale. Like a guided missile, she plots her trajectory and relentlessly closes in on her target. She may not be the most brilliant student in the class, but she typically ranks among the highest achievers.

Several key traits distinguish goal-oriented students:

■ *They select their objective.* ("I want an A on the book report.")

■ *They identify the barriers that stand in the way.* ("To get an A, I have to reduce my spelling errors.")

■ *They consider their options and develop a strategy.* ("I'll allow extra time to proofread my report carefully.")

■ *They learn from mistakes.* ("Even when I proofread carefully, I still miss some spelling errors. I have to figure out a plan for dealing with this.")

■ *They anticipate potential problems, make adjustments, and establish contingency plans.* ("I'll ask John to proofread my paper, and I'll offer to proofread his.")

Goal-directed children thrive on challenges. They enjoy pushing themselves beyond their own limits. They want to run a faster fifty-yard dash, to speak French fluently, and to win the school science award. They are motivated and conscientious because they have faith in their ability to prevail over the challenges they create for themselves. Their accomplishments generate pride, self-confidence, and the desire for more success. This achievement loop naturally recycles itself. Once these children attain their objective, they quickly establish a new goal.

The obvious advantages of encouraging your child to become goal-directed are offset by certain dangers. You are placing your child at emotional risk when you:

■ wittingly or unwittingly impose your own achievement agenda on your child

■ overtly or covertly pressure your child to actualize your own thwarted ambitions (e.g., to become a physician or a concert pianist)

■ encourage your child to aspire to goals incongruent with his interests, needs, personality, and talents

Goals are a double-edged sword. They can provide inspiration and motivation if they mesh with your child's abilities. They also can trigger emotionally destructive stress, guilt, anger, and depression if they do not mesh.

Intensely goal-directed children face other dangers. Children who are unrealistic about their abilities or who seek specific goals to appease their parents will probably not achieve their objectives. Their repeated failures can trigger frustration, demoralization, despair, and damaged self-confidence. Other children may unconsciously orchestrate failure because they feel unworthy of success or because they have a need to punish themselves. Their defeats will further undermine their already tenuous self-esteem and self-confidence and could cause depression, hostility, and socially nonadaptive behavior (see **Anger and Frustration,** page 1). Children manifesting chronic self-sabotaging behavior desperately require psychological counseling.

Our society's materialism creates additional hazards. Goal-oriented children may fall into the trap of equating achievement with happiness. Although success may enhance self-confidence, it does not guarantee self-esteem. This irony is apparent when one examines the personal lives of many ostensibly successful actors, rock stars, and business tycoons. The achievement-equals-happiness illusion underscores a perplexing paradox: Achievement may not guarantee happiness, but chronic nonachievement almost invariably guarantees unhappiness.

As a parent, you face a monumental challenge. You must help your child realize that goals and achievements are important but that her value as a person is not exclusively contingent on what she achieves. This insight can prevent subsequent disillusionment and, perhaps, an emotionally devastating mid-life crisis forty years down the road.

If your child is to attain her goals, she must acquire an essential skill: She must learn how to plan. Some children intuitively figure out how to create a practical strategy for achieving their objectives and require little formal instruction in strategic thinking. Most children, however, must be shown how to get from point A to point C. You cannot assume that if your child declares she wants an A in science, she knows how to make this happen. If she has not had a successful academic track record, she will need to be taught systematically how to establish short-term goals (e.g., A's on quizzes and weekly tests). She will also need to be taught how to prioritize, how to manage study time, how to take notes, how to remember information, how to check over her daily homework assignments, how to anticipate what is likely to be asked on tests, and how to write a term paper (see **Smart Thinking,** page 275, **Priorities,** page 228, **Note-taking,** page 193, **Preparing for Tests,** page 225, **Essay Tests,** page 67, and **Language Arts [Essays and Reports]**, page 141).

Your child does not need to know at the age of ten, or even at the age of eighteen, what she wants to do with the rest of her life. Relatively few ten-year-olds who profess that they want to become professional basketball players, ballerinas, or airline pilots will actually attain these objectives. These transitory goals, however, serve a vital purpose. They provide your child with a sense of direction and produce an appreciation for the cause-and-effect principles that link focused effort and self-actualization.

SUGGESTED CORRECTIVE STRATEGIES

In School

1. (ES) During your next parent-teacher conference, discuss the value of encouraging students to establish goals in each subject. You might diplomatically suggest that at the beginning of the semester students write their specific grade goals for the semester on pieces of paper that are then sealed in envelopes. These envelopes could be placed in a "time capsule." (The content, of course, would be private.) The teacher might also discuss her specific grading criteria for getting an A, B, or C. She might brainstorm with the class methods for meeting these standards, and the class could create facsimile strategies for achieving a specific grade. Students would then know precisely what they need to do to attain their goal. The students also could include in their time-capsule envelope their personal strategy for achieving their objectives. After report cards have been issued, the teacher could open the time capsule and return each student's unopened letter. A class discussion about strategies and goals would then be appropriate. Students, however, should *not* be pressured to reveal their goals or their grades.

2. (J/HS) Students in junior and senior high school should also be encouraged by their teachers to record their personal grade goals for each se-mester. Ideally the teacher will devote time to explaining her grading criteria and will show students strategies for attaining their target grades. (Practical techniques for helping junior and senior high school students establish academic and career goals are described in the school edition of *Getting Smarter*. See the Resource List under "Study Skills.")

At Home

1. At the beginning of the school year, make it a family tradition to establish specific goals. You could use the following format to record these goals.

Long-Term Goals
(Career, College, etc.)

1. _____

2. _____

Short-Term Goals

1. _____

2. _____

Medium-Range Goals

1. _____

2. _____

2. At the beginning of each semester, have your child establish specific grade goals for each subject. Then examine her strategy for achieving her objective. If appropriate, you might help her integrate a study schedule and a task completion checklist into the strategy. Place the target grades in an envelope and, at the end of semester, see how close your child came to achieving her goals. You might want to establish a reward system if it is obvious that your child will have to "stretch" to achieve her goals. Suggest that she tape a copy of her target grades near her desk. If your child does not achieve her goals, discuss in a nonemotionally-charged and nonjudgmental way what might have gone wrong and what obstacles were encountered that weren't anticipated. Brainstorm possible adjustments in her study strategy. For more specific ideas, see the suggested corrective strategies under **Priorities,** page 228, **Planning Ahead,** page 222, **Recording Assignments,** page 258, **Smart Thinking,** page 275, and **Time Management,** page 308.

GRADES

Establishing quality standards and evaluating students' work are two of a teacher's most important responsibilities. The teacher's clearly defined requirements, standards, expectations, deadlines, verbal and written criticism, and grades are an initiation into the real world where people are rewarded and advanced on the basis of their effort and performance. Grades are a rite of passage that prepares children for the harsh realities of life in a competitive society. Youngsters who learn how to adapt to their teacher's criteria for judging their work generally have less difficulty adapting to the demands and pressures of adulthood. They realize that to succeed in school they must study conscientiously, complete their work on time, write legibly, attend to important details, remember important information, demonstrate that they have understood key concepts, and behave (see **Smart Thinking,** page 275, **Attention to Details,** page 12, and **Disregard of Consequences,** page 50).

Although the grading process serves an important function, it is fraught with potential danger. A child who does poorly because he lacks the ability to meet his teacher's standards and fulfill her expectations can be psychologically damaged. A prolonged pattern of poor grades and negative comments cannot help undermining his self-confidence. If he concludes he cannot win in school, he will become demoralized and overwhelmed by feelings of frustration and futility. At this juncture he has three options: He can persist, lower his expectations, or give up. Most struggling children select option two or three.

Grades reflect a teacher's objective and subjective assessment of a child's skill mastery and the quality of his work. The criteria may be narrow or broad, fair or unfair. One teacher may give a student good grades because he is well behaved and personable or because he diligently completes reams of Dittos. The teacher may give another student with equivalent skills lower grades because he does not acquiesce to her behavior, attitude, or performance standards. The child may hand in sloppy, incomplete, or late work, or he may spend hours working on a creative writing assignment but neglect to proofread his history report or finish his math problems. Under the circumstances the teacher can clearly justify giving the child poor grades (see **Effort and Motivation,** page 63, and **Behavior and Performance Guidelines,** page 26).

Factors that can negatively affect your child's grades include learning disabilities, study skills deficits, family problems, emotional problems, uninspiring teaching, drugs, and negative peer pressure. The child with learning problems and the child who is depressed, angry, or in conflict with his family and who consciously or unconsciously sabotages his schoolwork will require learning assistance or counseling before his grades can realistically be expected to improve.

Teacher-designed tests are the foundation of the grading process. These tests are typically "criterion-referenced" (that is, the questions are linked to material contained in textbooks or presented in class). In grading these tests teachers generally use both objective and subjective criteria. Some educators consider the standardized (nationally normed) achievement tests administered to students throughout the country to be a more objective measure of students' skills (see **Understanding Diagnostic Test Results,** page 316). The lack of statistical objectivity in teacher-designed tests, however, does not diminish their validity in measuring skill mastery.

Although teachers are required by their districts to cover certain designated material in the curriculum, they are generally given some latitude in choosing their priorities and teaching methodology. When developing lesson plans and performance standards, one teacher may emphasize writing skills and another may emphasize reading comprehension, handwriting, and spelling. The selection of course content, teaching methods, and grading criteria reflects the teacher's training, educational philosophy, and classroom experience. If her tests are properly designed and fair, they should provide valid and important information about her students' skill proficiency.

Unless you have evidence to the contrary, you should assume that the grading criteria used by your child's teacher are fair. Poor grades are red flags. Additional warning bells should go off when poor grades are accompanied by low scores on standardized tests. If your child does poorly in class, on standardized tests, and on teacher-designed tests, it is critical that he be diagnostically tested for a learning disability.

In an ideal educational system all teachers would be highly skilled, open-minded, unbiased, organized, affirming, reasonable, dedicated, motivating, and sensitive. It is unlikely, however, that an ideal educational system will ever exist. The realities of the classroom are not always congruent with the theories taught in graduate school. Many teachers are indeed outstanding, dedicated, and inspirational. Others are, at best, marginally competent. They may be insensitive and biased, or they may not have had a creative thought or taught a dynamic lesson in twenty-five years.

Your child must be able to produce in school despite any shortcomings his teachers might have, just as someday he must be able to produce at work for a less-than-perfect boss. The grading process may not always be fair, and the teaching may not always be superb, but these are facts of life your child must learn to handle. There are also other "hard" facts he must handle:

1. His work will be continually evaluated.

2. His grades will reflect how well he is able to adjust to each teacher's guidelines and standards.

3. His grades in upper-level courses will profoundly affect his academic and vocational choices and opportunities.

4. The system is designed to judge his skills and not those of the teacher. *

Every child can be taught practical strategies for improving his grades. The subsequent rewards—achievements, personal satisfaction, pride, and acknowledgment—are addictive. Children with good academic skills and a winning game plan will be motivated and will strive to excel with little or no parental prompting.

SUGGESTED CORRECTIVE STRATEGIES

In School

1. The first step in helping your child improve his grades is to identify specific problems. Communicating with his teacher is vital. The objective of the conference is to examine deficits, understand the grading criteria, and develop, with your child's active participation, a plan for improving perfor-

---

* Although teachers are initially evaluated by administrators and supervisors before they are given tenure, once they receive tenure they are rarely held accountable for their performance. The system usually provides for dismissal, censure, and peer criticism only in cases of egregious incompetence or malfeasance.

mance. The teacher may make specific suggestions ranging from spending additional time studying to checking assignments more carefully for mistakes. The teacher may be willing to provide extra help before or after class. If his poor grades are the result of negative attitude and behavior, help him identify the causal factors (e.g., either not handing in assignments or writing illegibly). If his study skills are deficient, explore with the teacher a plan for helping him improve his skills. Consult the relevant entries and implement the appropriate corrective strategy.

2. If you feel your child's teacher is using unfair or biased criteria to evaluate your child, diplomatically express your concerns. The teacher may help you understand her criteria. You will elicit far more cooperation if you are nonadversarial, reasonable, and sensitive to the challenges the teacher faces (see **Parent-Teacher Conferences,** page 198). Your objective is to resolve problems. Being confrontational or making the teacher "wrong" is nonstrategic and counterproductive. People who feel attacked stop listening and spend most of their energy defending themselves. If you remain convinced that the teacher's criteria are flawed and cannot resolve the issue, request a conference with the principal.

3. If you or the teacher suspect your child has a learning disability, request that he be diagnostically tested. He may require tutoring in specific academic subjects. You may need to be persistent, especially if the school does not consider the problems grave (see **Parents' Rights,** page 201).

At Home

1. Help your child establish specific short-term goals. Ask him to indicate what grades he is aiming for on spelling tests, math tests, book reports, etc. Start with an immediate goal: the grade he wants on his next homework assignment.

2. Have your child indicate long-term goals: what grades he wants in each subject on his next report card. The following form can be used to record goals. These should be reviewed periodically with your child to determine if his strategy is working and if scheduling adjustments need to be made. Be careful *not* to dictate what grades you want your child to target. Encourage him to stretch, but do not suggest unrealistic objectives. A child getting a D in math is probably setting himself up for a defeat if he aims for an A on the next report card. If he insists, have him complete a second form. Explain that these grades should be an acceptable fallback position in the event he doesn't achieve his first choice. Although you want to encourage him to strive for the A, you also want to help him understand that raising a D to an A usually requires more than one semester. (See **Goals,** page 84, for a more comprehensive de-

DESIRED GRADES

Elementary School

SUBJECT	MOST RECENT REPORT CARD GRADES	GRADES DESIRED ON NEXT REPORT CARD
Reading	——————	——————
Spelling	——————	——————
Math	——————	——————
Social Studies	——————	——————
Science	——————	——————
——————	——————	——————
——————	——————	——————

scription of how to help your child establish long-term and short-term goal-setting strategies.)

3. Help your child develop a study strategy that will allow him to achieve his objectives. Specific (and realistic) amounts of time should be allocated for each subject, and a daily schedule should be developed. (See **Time Management,** page 308, for methods for creating a study plan.) Check to see that the teacher's instructions are being followed.

4. Set up regular meetings with your child to evaluate his progress and problems. The tone should be upbeat and cooperative. If you assume the role of drill sergeant or grand inquisitor, you are certain to trigger resentment, resistance, and defensiveness. Your goal is to gather information about what is happening in school and to engage your child actively in the problem-solving process. You might say: "We need to meet on a regular basis to examine how things are going in school. We can see if you are on target in achieving your goals. If there are problems, you may need to reexamine your goals and adjust your study schedule. We can work together on this. Once things are going well,

DESIRED GRADES

Junior and Senior High School

SUBJECT	MOST RECENT REPORT CARD GRADES	GRADES DESIRED ON NEXT REPORT CARD
English	_____	_____
Math	_____	_____
Science	_____	_____
Social Studies	_____	_____
_____	_____	_____
_____	_____	_____
_____	_____	_____

the conferences will no longer be necessary. Let's look at a checklist that will help you pinpoint issues that can affect your schoolwork." (See the self-evaluation checklist opposite.)

5. Ask your child's teacher(s) to complete the teacher evaluation checklist on page 96. Compare the teacher's perceptions with your child's perceptions in a nonaccusatory way. If there are discrepancies, you might say: "It seems that your teacher doesn't think you're submitting your assignments on

time or coming to her for extra help. How could you convince her that you are being responsible about your homework?"

6. If your child continues to receive poor grades despite his best efforts to establish and attain his goals, manage time, and study efficiently, he may require special assistance. If he does not qualify for help in school, consider hiring a tutor or enrolling him in a private learning assistance or study skills program.

SELF-EVALUATION CHECKLIST

	YES	NO
I aim for a specific grade in each subject.	——	——
I aim for a specific grade on each test, report, or project.	——	——
If I am having difficulty in a subject, I have spoken to the teacher and asked for help.	——	——
I have identified and understand the specific reasons why I am having difficulty.	——	——
If I need extra help, I have informed you about the problem.	——	——
I spend sufficient time studying and doing homework.	——	——
I hand in my assignments on time.	——	——
I pay attention in class.	——	——
I hand in neat and legible assignments.	——	——
I take the time to proofread my work carefully to correct spelling and grammar mistakes.	——	——
I use a study schedule.	——	——
I have the materials that I need to do my work.	——	——
I feel I am doing the best job I can.	——	——

TEACHER EVALUATION CHECKLIST

	YES	NO
This student:		
Asks for help when having difficulty	———	———
Appears to be spending enough time studying and doing homework	———	———
Pays attention in class	———	———
Hands in assignments on time	———	———
Hands in neat, legible assignments	———	———
Proofreads work carefully to correct spelling and grammar mistakes	———	———
Brings to class the materials needed to do work	———	———

GRAMMAR

All languages are bound by rules that regulate the mechanics of spoken and written speech. These rules are called *grammar.*

Children begin to assimilate the conventions of English grammar during infancy. As they listen to their parents speak, they begin, at a genetically predetermined developmental stage, to mimic the sounds, words, intonations, and grammatical constructions they hear. During the early stage of language development the process of mastering the rules of language is relatively painless. Children are motivated because they want to make themselves understood.

By the time children enter kindergarten, they have already learned a great deal about grammar. Although they may not be able to cite the rule for subject-verb agreement, most children know that "the boy *goes,* and the girls *go.*" They know how to use adjectives and adverbs properly in most circumstances. They can speak in the past, present perfect, and future tenses. They may not know how to identify or define a participle, but they can use it in everyday speech.

For many children assimilating grammar becomes less natural and more painful when the learning arena shifts from the informal context of home to the more formal context of the classroom. Here children are often required to memorize grammar rules and practice these rules ad nauseam. Most children perceive these rote procedures as another boring, irrelevant academic chore intentionally created by adults to make their lives miserable.

The "memorize the rules" approach has endured despite ample evidence that it turns kids off and often fails to achieve its stated objective. Teachers committed to the memorization method usually direct their students to fill in the blanks in textbook exercises, workbooks, or duplicated forms. For most youngsters the rules are at best only remotely related to the language they speak at home and with friends. That many of these students find grammar complex, mysterious, and impenetrable and that they actively or passively resist the mind-numbing exercises should surprise no one.

Grammar deficiencies manifest themselves in four areas:

1. **Difficulty using grammar correctly in reports and essays (run-on sentences, nonparallel construction, mixed tenses, etc.)**

2. **Difficulty speaking with grammatically correct language**

3. **Difficulty identifying parts of speech**

4. **Difficulty citing the rules**

To help your child overcome her grammar difficulties, you must identify her specific deficits (see the following checklist). The next step is to teach her specific techniques for checking over what she says and writes so that she can begin to eliminate her mistakes. When you hear or see a specific grammatical mistake, examine the appropriate rule for correct usage and practice together applying the rule to other examples. *Use this technique selectively.* If you continually correct each grammar mistake, your child will probably become resentful and begin to tune out what you say. Also take time to show your child how much grammar she *already* knows. Without consciously thinking about it, for example, she can correctly use parallel tense usage. She *knows* that it is grammatically correct to say "While I was watching the movie, I *ate* popcorn" and that it is incorrect to say "While I was watching the movie, I *eats* popcorn."

Helping your child master the rules of grammar can actually be *fun* if you make the process creative and relevant. (If you need to brush up your own grammar, consult *The Goof-Proofer.* See the Resource List under "Grammar.") Hire a tutor who is imaginative and dynamic if you conclude that you lack the skills, inclination, or patience to help your child.

SUGGESTED CORRECTIVE STRATEGIES

In School

1. To identify your child's specific grammar deficits, ask the teacher to complete the following checklist (see the grammar checklist opposite).

2. If specific deficits are noted, request supplemental materials from the teacher that reinforce the grammar concepts your child does not understand. Ideally these materials should be interesting and relevant. To have your child repetitively go over dittoed copies that have already proved ineffective, boring, or irrelevant will do

GRAMMAR CHECKLIST

	Yes	No
This student:		
Uses parallel constructions when writing[1]	___	___
Recognizes subject-verb agreement	___	___
Avoids run-on sentences	___	___
Uses tenses properly when writing	___	___
Writes complete sentences	___	___
Knows the parts of speech	___	___
Uses punctuation correctly	___	___
Uses adverbs and adjectives correctly[2]	___	___
Uses pronouns correctly[3]	___	___
Avoids dangling or misplaced modifiers[4]	___	___
Uses transitive and intransitive verbs correctly[5]	___	___

[1] *Incorrect*: She is singing, dancing, and *likes* to have a good time.
  Correct: She is singing, dancing, and *having* a good time. (parallel construction)
[2] *Incorrect*: She feels *good*.
  Correct: She is *good*. (predicate adjective modifies subject.)
      She feels *well*, or she is *well*. (adverb modifies verb)
[3] *Incorrect*: It is between *she* and *I*.
  Correct: It is between *her* and *me*. (object of preposition)
[4] *Incorrect*: We learned that Pearl Buck wrote the book *in English class*.
  Correct: We learned *in English class* that Pearl Buck wrote the book. (properly placed modifier)
[5] *Incorrect*: I want to *lay* down.
  Correct: I want to *lie* down. (intransitive verb)
      I want to *lay* it down. (transitive verb)

little good, especially if she already has negative associations with learning grammar. Materials you might request from the teacher or resource specialist are included in the Resource List at the back of the book.

At Home

1. Compose a short essay with glaring grammatical mistakes (e.g., "How he go to the store is him business. What I wants were candy quick . . ."). *Play* at finding the mistakes together. Gear your expectations to your child's grade level. The skills of elementary school students will obviously be less developed than those of high school students. Later, have her try to find the mistakes on her own in longer paragraphs that contain grammatical mistakes. Give her a point for each mistake. Explain why "they wants" is incorrect (subject-verb agreement) and give other examples. For fun, have her write paragraphs with mistakes and correct them. Consult *The Goof-Proofer* (see Resource List) for verification.

2. After completing the process described above, have your child check over her own reports and essays to see if she can correct the mistakes her teacher has identified. Urge her to experiment with different grammatical constructions to communicate her ideas more effectively. If your child is willing, rewrite the essay together. The tone you establish during these interactive sessions is vital. Be creative and make the sessions enjoyable. Stop when your child becomes fatigued, distracted, or resistant. The duration of the sessions should depend on the age and maturity of your child. Be patient if she makes a mistake even if you have covered a particular grammatical concept several times. Do not express disappointment. Children usually require several exposures before they achieve mastery.

GUILT

When children do poorly in school, they are vulnerable to a range of painful emotions that include frustration, embarrassment, shame, discouragement, feelings of inadequacy, demoralization, defensiveness, and insecurity. These feelings are often compounded by anger at being placed in a seemingly no-win situation and guilt about being unable to fulfill their teachers' and parents' expectations. The never-ending battle to survive academically must inevitably take a toll on children's attitudes, behavior, and self-perceptions (see **Anger and Frustration**, page 1, and **Fear of Failure/Success/Competition**, page 74).

Ironically the anger a child may consciously or unconsciously feel toward his parents and teachers for making "unfair" demands often triggers additional guilt. Most children are conditioned from early childhood to believe that it is wrong and disrespectful to express anger openly to parents and teachers. The angry child is thus in a double bind. If his anger explodes and he throws tantrums, talks back, fights, bullies, etc., he will get into trouble, be punished, and perhaps feel guilty. If his anger implodes, he will either become depressed or express his hostility through passive aggression (self-sabotaging behavior, manipulation, resistance, sarcasm, teasing, whining, deviousness, belittling others, etc.). The child, however, does not *consciously* choose to explode or implode. His unconscious decides how to cope with the unpleasant feelings.

When children openly express anger to authority figures, the anger manifests itself as defiance. This generally elicits reprimands and punishment that trigger additional anger and guilt. If not treated through counseling or psychotherapy, the chronic, volatile, and consuming hostility will most likely lead to delinquent behavior.

Children with academic problems can become so enmeshed in the struggle to survive in school that they have difficulty identifying and understanding the underlying feelings and issues responsible for their guilt. These children often attempt to flee from their pain, fear, shame, anger, and guilt by disowning, denying, or hiding the "unacceptable" feelings.

When children repress or disown an unpleasant emotion, other emotions are usually also repressed, with profound psychological implications. Children who are compelled to disown distasteful feelings cannot possibly like or respect themselves. To cope with their "badness," they may resort to misbehavior, delinquency, alcoholism, drug abuse, and, in extreme cases, suicide.

Repressed children tend to be noncommunicative, withdrawn, and non-responsive. Some may retreat into a fantasy world. Others may become obsessed with one or two interests. Beneath the appearance of calm, however, is a powder keg of combustible emotions and the ever-present danger that the keg will suddenly explode and spew shrapnel.

The guilt experienced by a child who is having difficulty in school is distinct from the remorse felt by a child who steals, lies, or cheats. Remorse has socially redeeming value. A remorseful child is signaling that he realizes he has violated a code of conduct and that he has a conscience. If he decides not to repeat the act, his remorse has served a positive social function. The child who commits antisocial acts and feels no remorse is manifesting sociopathic behavior that could lead to prison.

Guilt associated with learning problems has *no* redeeming value. The emotion distorts children's perceptions, undermines reasoning powers, erects barriers to identifying and resolving problems, impedes communication, and causes emotional damage.

Parents who intentionally use guilt to modify their child's behavior or improve his performance are creating a ticking time bomb. Denigrating a child, continually expressing disappointment, or comparing a child with other, more successful children or siblings to make the child feel guilty must inevitably undermine self-esteem, trigger defensiveness and nonadaptive behaviors, and produce guilt, anger, and resentment. This strategy will produce a dysfunctional child and a dysfunctional family (see **Psychological Problems and Psychological Overlay,** page 239).

Smart parents do everything in their power to reduce guilt. Their objective is to build their child's self-confidence, and they are committed to helping their child acquire the academic skills he needs to succeed in school. They have realistic expectations and establish reasonable and consistent performance guidelines. They intentionally orchestrate opportunities for success, and they provide emotional support by repeatedly acknowledging and affirming improvement (see **Behavior and Performance Guidelines,** page 26, **Self-Esteem and Self-Confidence,** page 266, **Learning Disabilities,** page 157, **Underachievement,** page 312, **Atypical Learning Problems,** page 16, and **Effort and Motivation,** page 63).

The parents of nonachieving children are also vulnerable to feeling guilty. Admitting that one's child has a problem can be especially threatening to parents who have difficulty accepting "imperfections." Some parents may fear that they are genetically responsible for their child's learning problems or that they did something to damage their child's learning capacity. To protect themselves, they may deny an obvious problem despite irrefutable evidence, or they may blame the teacher or the school system for the problem.

Just as guilt can distort a child's perspective, it can also distort a parent's perspective. Parents may attempt to assuage their guilt by expecting very little from their child or by serving as an on-call tutor, surrogate teacher, or constant monitor. Those who conclude their child can do the work on his own and refuse to help may also feel guilty (see **Learned Helplessness,** page 152, **Monitoring Homework,** page 185, and **Behavior and Performance Guidelines,** page 26).

Denial-oriented parents often give marginal support to those providing help for their child. They may go through the motions of being supportive, but then they may impulsively decide to withdraw their child from a valuable learning assistance or counseling program, or they may look for a scapegoat if there is not immediate and dramatic improvement. They may blame the child's lack of progress on an incompetent resource specialist, classroom teacher, or educational system. Sensing his parents' lack of commitment, the child will also lack commitment. The parents have in effect set their child up to fail.

Some parents respond to guilt with excessive concern that undermines their judgment and impedes the remediation process. A mother may, for instance, volunteer to help in the classroom. On the surface there is nothing wrong with this. If, however, the parent's real agenda is to monitor her child's performance more closely, the strategy may backfire, and her child may become anxious, resentful, or dependent on her constant supervision. Although the parent may recognize intellectually that her intense anxiety is contributing to her child's stress, guilt may prevent her from allowing her child to "own" his problems and trust those providing help.

When guilt causes parents to think and act irrationally, friction often develops between the parents and school personnel. The school psychologist, for example, may recommend that a child be enrolled in a learning assistance program, but the child's parents may reject this recommendation and justify their position by arguing that enrolling their child in the program would cause her to be permanently labeled as handicapped (see **Individual Educational Program [IEP],** page 126). This guilt-driven reasoning clearly disserves the child and prevents vital remediation. Any parental concerns about the short-term disadvantages of labeling a child are clearly offset by the advantages of having the child's learning problems identified, treated, and remediated.

At any given time as many as eight million students in the United States are struggling in school. This represents the potential for eight million frustrated, demoralized, angry, guilt-ridden children and sixteen million frustrated, demoralized, angry, guilt-ridden parents. Parents can choose to feel guilty, or they can choose to respond constructively. Smart parents select the constructive option.

SUGGESTED CORRECTIVE STRATEGIES

In School

1. If you feel your child is embarrassed by his learning deficits and that this is causing frustration, demoralization, shame, anger, and guilt, discuss your concerns with his teacher or resource specialist. If he is not already receiving learning assistance, request that he be evaluated by the school psychologist (see **Parents' Rights,** page 201). Examine with the teacher not only how your child's learning deficits might be resolved but also how he might be protected from embarrassment. If you believe the teacher may be causing your child to feel guilty about his deficits (e.g., "You'd do a lot better in school, young man, if you would just remember what I tell you!"), communicate your concern that this approach is counterproductive and could be emotionally damaging. Although you do not want to defend your child's misbehavior, you have a compelling responsibility to protect him from a teacher who is insensitive to his underlying problems. As you wrestle with how best to respond to your child's problems and needs, you must consider what is in his best interests. Are you continually rescuing him? Are you rationalizing his deficits and defending him when he doesn't need to be defended? Are you encouraging learned helplessness (see page 152)? Are you providing legitimate and necessary help that will insulate him from unnecessary frustration, pain, and demoralization? There is no absolute formula for determining the appropriate strategy. Your responsibility is to acquire information from school personnel so that you can make an informed decision. If appropriate, consult with your pediatrician or an independent counselor. You must then make an intuitive judgment call based on the data. If you and the teacher cannot agree on an acceptable strategy, ask the principal or assistant principal to participate in the discussions.

2. If you believe your child is compensating for his learning deficits by misbehaving in school, explore appropriate in-class and at-home behavior modification strategies with the teacher (see **Behavior and Performance Guidelines,** page 26).

At Home

1. If you feel guilty because you believe you are in some way responsible for your child's learning difficulties or because you are constantly angry at your child, you must do some introspection. If you cannot resolve the issues on your own, seek a qualified counselor or therapist. It is easy to lose perspective when deeply enmeshed in a problem. Admitting that you need help testifies to your concern, integrity, and responsibility.

2. If you believe your child feels guilty because he feels he is disappointing you or because he is frustrated and angry at you or his teacher, encourage him to express his feelings, identify problem areas, and develop a practical plan for resolving the issues (see the **DIBS** method, page 233, and **Anger and Frustration,** page 1). If you cannot make inroads into the problem, request a referral to an educational therapist or a family therapist, social worker, psychologist, or psychiatrist. Guilt can be an insidious emotion. It is vital that you provide help before serious emotional damage occurs. If damage has already occurred and your child is manifesting red-flag symptoms, getting help is all the more urgent.

HANDWRITING

Teachers are obligated to read their students' work, and they are usually very unhappy when assignments are illegible and sloppy. Poor handwriting can be caused by deficits in fine motor control, spatial awareness, copying, or concentration. The child who chronically submits hard-to-read assignments may be struggling with one or more of these problems at the same time.

Fine motor control deficits interfere with children's ability to regulate their fingers as they grasp and move a pencil, pen, or chalk. When a child's fingers are "uncooperative," letters and numbers are invariably misshapen and uneven.

Spatial awareness deficits signal that children are having problems recognizing proportions. Individual letters and the space between letters and words are not uniform. These spatial deficits can also create major problems for children when they attempt to line up number columns while adding, subtracting, dividing, and multiplying.

Near-point deficits can cause children to make mistakes when they copy words and numbers written in textbooks or on assignment sheets. Children with *far-point deficits* make mistakes when copying words and numbers written on the chalkboard.

Children with chronic concentration problems also tend to have poor handwriting. They are characteristically oblivious to details (see page 12). They forget to indent, cross their *t*s, and dot their *i*s and frequently "slap down" their work on the paper without caring if anyone can actually read it (see **Attention Deficit Disorder,** page 5).

Attitude must also be factored into the poor handwriting equation. Children who have received continual criticism about their poor handwriting often conclude they are incapable of writing legibly and become resigned to doing sloppy work. Having accepted their "fate," these children are rarely willing to invest the extra effort required to improve the legibility of their work.

Many children who have the ability to write neatly and legibly nevertheless submit substandard work. Most of these youngsters have failed to assimilate the principles of cause and effect. Their cavalier attitude about effort, diligence, and attention to details and their disregard of the consequences of laziness could become an entrenched habit that will plague them throughout life (see **Disregard of Consequences,** page 50, and **Attention to Details,** page 12).

The first step in helping your child correct her poor handwriting is to identify the causal factors. If your child has poor fine motor control, specific remedial techniques can improve this skill. If she has a near-point or far-point copying deficit, she should be evaluated by an ophthalmologist or optometrist. (Developmental optometrists specialize in identifying and treating copying, reading, and word tracking deficits [seeing letters and words in proper sequence]—see **Inaccurate Copying,** page 113). Although concentration problems are difficult to treat, there are specific methods for helping your child focus and take responsibility for her distractibility (see **Attention Deficit Disorder,** page 5).

Positive expectations, acknowledgment for effort, and patience are as vital as identifying the source of your child's handwriting problems and implementing a corrective strategy. You must guide your child to the realization that she *can* improve her handwriting if she is willing to make the necessary effort.

SUGGESTED CORRECTIVE STRATEGIES

In School

1. (ES) Ask the teacher if your child's handwriting problems or sloppy work might be caused by poor fine motor control, poor spatial awareness, attention deficit disorder, or copying deficits. If so, request that the teacher assign materials that your child could use in class or at home to remediate the deficits. Specific materials that focus on correcting handwriting deficits are included in the Resource List at the back of the book.

2. If you suspect underlying deficits in fine motor control, spatial awareness, near- and far-point copying, and concentration, request an evaluation by the school psychologist or resource specialist.

3. If your request for testing is denied, you may want to assert your right to have your child evaluated. Ask to see the district's parents' rights manual (see page 201). Having your child privately tested is another option.

At Home

1. (ES) Explain to your child that you would like to do some experiments together. As a pretest, have her carefully copy every letter of the alphabet in capitals and small letters. Younger children should print, and older children should use cursive. This exercise will reveal which letters are difficult for your child to form.

2. (ES) Now give your child a timed test. Ask her to copy a paragraph in her very best handwriting. Remind her to space her letters carefully and to use capitals and periods. *Do not tell her now why you are asking her to do this.* Allow her to take as much time as she needs. When she has finished, acknowledge her for her effort. Because of the deficits described above, her work will probably be far from perfect. The sample represents a baseline of your child's careful work and a starting point for improvement.

3. (ES) Have your child copy another paragraph as quickly as she can. *Stop her after two minutes.* This sample provides a baseline of your child's "fast" work. Fast work is rarely as neat as slow, careful work. Nevertheless, your child must be able to write legibly even when writing an essay on a timed test in school.

4. (ES) Place the *carefully* copied paragraph in a plastic sleeve (this can be bought at an office supply store). Explain that this sample will serve as a new standard for homework assign-

ments. Whenever written work is below this standard, take out the paragraph and simply say, "You've shown me that you're capable of doing work as good as this. I'd like the assignment you just did to be as neat and legible. So I'm going to ask you to redo the assignment using this paragraph as your standard." Be careful not to sound harsh, punitive, or disappointed. Be matter-of-fact and express your conviction that she can equal or excel the standard. Enthusiastically acknowledge and affirm her when she does. By actively engaging her in the process, by encouraging effort, and by demonstrating that the standard is attainable, you can help her take pride in her work and stretch toward a higher standard.

5. (ES) Copy a sentence in neat, legible handwriting. Have your child trace over your sentence several times. Then have her copy the sentence in her best handwriting. If your child is in elementary school, have her use graph paper (1/2-inch boxes) to help with spacing and letter proportions. This paper is available in teacher supply stores. If your child is having difficulty lining up columns of numbers when doing math, follow the same procedure. Create a model for properly aligned, legible addition, subtraction, and/or multiplication problems. Have your child trace over your numbers and then copy the problems on graph paper. As she shows improvement, she can begin to use graph paper with 1/4-inch boxes. Make the sessions short and nonstressful and communicate positive expectations. Children respond far better to praise than they do to negative comments. Be patient. Do not expect miracles overnight.

6. **(ES)** Every few months, have your child recopy the original paragraph. Acknowledge her for the progress she is making, perhaps establishing an actual reward such as a toy or an excursion to an amusement park. Insert the new sample in the plastic sleeve. This will now be the new standard. In time this procedure should become unnecessary.

7. **(J/HS)** Copy a short paragraph very carefully. Then copy the same paragraph quickly, intentionally making it illegible. Show your child the illegible sample and ask her to read it. Tell her to pretend she is the teacher.

Ask her what grade she would give a report or an essay answer on a test that was written with this handwriting. Now show her the legible sample. Identify the specific handwriting components that make something legible (the slant and size of the letters, spacing, margins, cross-outs, care, etc.). Examine some of your child's previously submitted assignments with her. Ask her to pinpoint illegible words or sentences. Brainstorm how she might develop a plan for improving her handwriting and legibility. Encourage her to establish specific performance goals. You might want her to complete the following simple checklist before handing in each assignment.

8. **(ES)** Consider buying some handwriting development materials at your local teacher supply store and using them with your child at home.

HANDWRITING CHECKLIST

	Yes	No
I have carefully recopied my rough draft.	____	____
I have done the best I can to make my work neat and legible.	____	____
I have paid attention to the size and slant of my letters.	____	____
I have followed my teacher's directions (indented paragraphs, skipping a line after the title, etc.).	____	____

IDENTIFYING IMPORTANT INFORMATION

Each day in school, children are assaulted with prodigious amounts of information. Because they cannot realistically be expected to recall everything they are taught, they must develop the ability to sort through the plethora of facts, rules, formulas, procedures, concepts, and definitions and identify what is truly important. This targeting ability is especially vital in high school and college. Children who have difficulty identifying what is important and prioritizing what they must learn and remember can easily become overwhelmed by the barrage of information in upper-level classes.

To get good grades, your child must be able to identify not only what *she* considers important but also what *her teacher* is likely to consider important. This discrimination skill is integral with effective studying (see **Study Skills,** page 292).

Successful students are pragmatic. They are alert to the types of information their teacher emphasizes in class and on tests. Does he want students to remember the date when Fort Sumter was attacked, or does he want them to be able to discuss the social, political, and economic conditions responsible for the American Revolution? This ability to distinguish *concepts and ideas* from *details and facts* and to recognize their teacher's value system is standard operating procedure for successful students. Good students may not always be aware they are "psyching out" their teachers, but their test performance and grades testify to their strategic study skills—they figure out what they need to do to win in school.

Some educators may argue that children should not be encouraged to devote their intellectual energy to "psyching out" their teachers. This argument is naive; pragmatic, goal-oriented, cause-and-effect thinking is fundamental to achievement in school and in life. Thinking strategically does not preclude having an inquisitive mind or a genuine enthusiasm for learning (see **Smart Thinking,** page 275).

Smart students recognize that there is an infinite amount of data to assimilate and a finite amount of time and energy available to do this. Therefore they use their time efficiently, distinguish what is important, anticipate what is likely to be asked on tests, and develop individualized methods for retaining information (see **Preparing for Tests,** page 225, **Visual Memory,** page 326, and **Auditory Memory,** page 22). They relate what they are currently learning to what they have already learned. These skills are fundamental to academic achievement.

SUGGESTED CORRECTIVE STRATEGIES

In School

1. If your child is having difficulty identifying important information in her textbooks, ask her teacher if there is a reading comprehension problem. Review her performance on standardized reading tests. If her scores are below grade level, request supplemental remedial materials she can use at home to improve her skills (see **Reading Comprehension,** page 250, for specific materials and learning assistance strategies). If her comprehension is more than one year below grade level, request that she be evaluated by the Child Study Team,* the school psychologist, or the resource specialist to identify the underlying learning deficits. An "item analysis" of her answers on a standardized reading test can also be used to identify her specific comprehension problems (see **Reading Comprehension,** page 250, for an explanation of this procedure).

2. If your child is having difficulty identifying important spoken information, ask that she be diagnostically evaluated to determine if she has auditory memory, auditory sequencing, or concentration deficits (see **Auditory Memory,** page 22, **Following Verbal Directions,** page 78, and **Attention Deficit Disorder,** page 5). If deficits are revealed, request specialized help from the resource specialist. An auditory acuity test from the school nurse, your pediatrician, or an audiologist may also be advisable to rule out the possibility of a hearing impairment.

3. If you suspect other students in your child's class are also having difficulty identifying important information for reasons other than poor reading comprehension, diplomatically suggest that a study skills component be integrated into the cur-

---

* Many school districts require that a team of educators review a child's performance and test scores and make an in-class observation to determine if a comprehensive diagnostic evaluation by the school psychologist is advisable.

riculum. Most children need to be taught systematically how to identify key information and take notes (see **Notetaking,** page 193).

At Home

1. Select an article from a magazine or newspaper that you believe will interest your child. Read it to her and discuss it in general terms. Ask her if it contains anything of importance that should be remembered. Then reread the article paragraph by paragraph. Work together at picking out the key ideas or facts. Use a highlight pen to mark this information. As you go through each paragraph and select important facts, ask your child if the information is a detail or a main idea. Discuss the difference between the two. When you have finished, summarize aloud what you remember from the article and then ask your child to summarize what she remembers. You might leave out some information intentionally from your summary and then affirm your child for including this information when she does her summary.

2. After using the procedure described above several times, change roles with your child and have her read the article to you. (This assumes, of course, that she has the necessary reading skills to read the article. If not, ask the teacher to recommend high-interest material written at your child's skill level.) Encourage your child to play teacher and lead the discussion. Have her again summarize the article. Each of you should then *independently* highlight the important information in separate copies of the article. Discuss the criteria you used for making your choices. Create a quiz from the material. This will help your child begin to "think like a teacher." Urge her to use the preceding identification techniques when studying. Refer to strategies under **Reading Comprehension,** page 250, and **Notetaking,** page 193, for additional methods for improving your child's ability to recognize key information.

INACCURATE COPYING

The inability to copy accurately can undermine academic performance in every subject area. A child may know how to do a multiplication problem but may write down the wrong answer because he copies a 6 instead of a 9 or because he misaligns the columns and adds incorrectly (see **Dyslexia,** page 58). He may know how to spell the word *perform* but may transpose the letters and write *preform* when doing the final draft of his book report. He may fail to study for his history test because he wrote down that the test would be on Thursday when his teacher actually wrote Tuesday on the chalkboard.

Children copy inaccurately from textbooks (near-point copying) and from the chalkboard (far-point copying) for diverse reasons. The first step in identifying the cause of the problem is to have the child's eyes examined by an optometrist or ophthalmologist. Nearsightedness, farsightedness, and astigmatism can be major sources of copying problems. If no visual impairment is detected, further testing by a school psychologist, resource specialist, or developmental optometrist (see below) is the next step in the diagnostic process.

Some children copy inaccurately because they cannot perceive spatial relationships accurately or distinguish the nearground from the background. These children characteristically struggle to decode printed letters and symbols and often do not perceive the difference between an *n* and an *m* or between *bed* and *bet*. These deficits are primary symptoms of a perceptual dysfunction.

Visual tracking difficulties (inefficient, jerky eye movements) can also cause inaccurate copying. The ocular motor muscles that control the horizontal movement of the eyes as they move across the printed line must function efficiently if a child is to see letters and words accurately. Children with tracking deficits usually have problems differentiating letters such as *b/d* and *p/q* or numbers such as *6/9*. When copying, they may omit or transpose letters and words and "flip" words (*saw* is seen as *was*—see **Dyslexia,** page 58). Convergence deficits (the eyes do not work together) may also cause reading and copying inaccuracies.

Developmental optometrists are now using specific training exercises to treat chronic tracking problems. Although some ophthalmologists dispute the value of these methods and argue that eye muscles cannot be "trained," clinical and classroom observations generally substantiate the claims that children with tracking problems read better after having received this training.

Concentration problems, impulsivity, and inattention to detail may also cause inaccurate copying (see **Attention Deficit Disorder,** page 5). Children who lack impulse control and who cannot focus on important details when they write usually make careless mistakes.

Your child *can* be trained to copy more accurately. If he chronically makes careless mistakes, he must be conditioned to assess his work objectively and to take responsibility for finding and correcting his inaccuracies. He must be taught how to self-edit, how to become more vigilant, and how to tenaciously ferret out his errors. This extra effort will determine whether the quality of your child's work is first-rate or, at best, marginal.

SUGGESTED CORRECTIVE STRATEGIES

In School

1. If your child is making careless copying mistakes, ask the teacher if she can help you identify the possible causes. If the problem appears to be attributable to inattentiveness, see the suggested corrective strategies under **Attention Deficit Disorder,** page 5.

2. (ES) If you or the teacher suspects your child has perceptual processing problems (i.e., spatial, figure ground, and/or visual tracking deficits), request that he be evaluated by the school psychologist or resource specialist. See the suggested corrective strategies under **Dyslexia,** page 58, for specialized remedial materials. If your child appears to read and copy inaccurately because of visual tracking deficits, consider having him evaluated by a developmental optometrist who specializes in treating visual dysfunction. (The school should be able to make a referral.) Children with suspected visual impairment should be tested by an ophthalmologist or optometrist.

At Home

1. (ES) Purchase wide-ruled paper at your local teacher supply store. Have your child carefully copy a sentence from one of his favorite books. If there are mistakes, brainstorm with him how he might develop his own system for finding and correcting his mistakes.

2. (ES) Make a game out of find-ing mistakes. Intentionally make er-rors when you copy sentences and/or math problems and award him a point for each error he can find. Show him how to align columns when adding, dividing, and multiplying and have him practice. Award additional points for neatness. The points can be used for earning a prize or a special treat.

3. (J/HS) Brainstorm with your child a procedure for writing and copying more accurately. He should as-sume his work contains errors and should be prepared to make an extra effort to find these errors. He will have to reread his assignments carefully and search for the errors that he tends to make. You might design a pro-cedure that lists four or five steps for finding common errors. The pro-cedure might include the following steps:

a. Read over each assignment aloud two times and listen to the words to make sure they "sound" right.

b. Check over every *d, b, p,* and *q* to see if it has been written correctly.

c. Look for any words that might be left out.

d. Look for transposed numbers.

e. Look up any word that doesn't "look" right.

f. Make sure punctuation has been inserted.

g. Check math columns to make sure numbers have been properly aligned.

Encourage your child to use this procedure before submitting all as-signments. Individualize the pro-cedural steps so that they address the particular errors he is prone to make. As an experiment, encourage him to use the procedure conscientiously for three weeks to determine if his assign-ments are more accurate. He could use an acronym to help him remember the steps: SPORT-A (*S*pelling, *P*unctua-tion, *O*missions, *R*eversals, *T*ransposi-tions, *A*lign).

INADEQUATE
STUDY TIME

Students who are unwilling to spend adequate time studying face predictable consequences: substandard work, poor grades, parental lectures, and the denial of privileges. Despite these consequences, many capable children continue to study as little as possible.

No matter how bright your child may be, she must still review, practice, and assimilate at home the rules, concepts, formulas, and procedures taught in class if she is to master the material she is being taught. If she circumvents this procedure, her learning and performance will suffer.

If the homework battle has become an unpleasant nightly ritual in your home, you must be willing to take an objective, analytical look at the situation. Chronic resistance can usually be linked to one or more of the following factors:

■ academic skills deficits

■ specific learning disabilities

■ a cavalier attitude about cause and effect (no thought or concern about probable consequences)

■ poor study skills

■ failure to establish short-term and long-term goals

■ frustration

■ demoralization

■ laziness

■ procrastination

■ psychological problems

- family problems
- negative associations with learning
- negative expectations ("Why try? I'll fail anyway")
- negative peer influences

Lectures, punishments, threats, and sermons are seldom effective antidotes for poor study habits. Determining if your child has the requisite academic skills to do the assigned work is a far more effective starting point. A conference with your child's teacher, school counselor, and/or resource specialist and a review of her scores on standardized achievement tests and diagnostic tests will provide this information (see **Parent-Teacher Conferences,** page 198, **Performance on Standardized Tests,** page 212, and suggestions below for specific strategies for gathering and interpreting these data).

Children with learning disabilities are often the most resistant to studying. For frustrated academically defeated students, school is a painful ordeal. When the bell rings at three o'clock, they've had enough unpleasantness for one day. Spending additional time studying is the last thing they want to do. (See **Learning Disabilities,** page 157, and other relevant entries for suggestions about how to help your child overcome her learning problems and phobias about school.)

Some children resist studying for another reason: They don't know *how* to study. Students who do not record their assignments properly, establish goals or priorities, manage time efficiently, or create a study plan will derive little benefit from the time they spend studying. Once they conclude that studying will produce no positive payoffs for them, they will shut down. (See **Study Skills,** page 292, and other relevant entries for specific strategies to improve study skills.)

In some cases children resist studying for no readily apparent reason. They have no identifiable learning or study skills deficits, and yet they show little desire to be in school. Their passivity and lack of motivation is usually indicative of underlying psychological or environmental issues. If they have low self-esteem and poor self-confidence, they may intentionally orchestrate their own failures to express their unhappiness and to confirm their negative feelings about themselves. Angry or demoralized children who sabotage themselves by cutting class, chronically misbehaving, refusing to do their schoolwork, taking drugs, or becoming delinquent may consciously or unconsciously be using poor grades as a weapon against their parents. These children urgently require counseling (see **Psychological Problems and Psychological Overlay,** page 239, **Anger and Frustration,** page 1, **Fear of Failure/Success/ Competition,** page 74).

Some children are unwilling to study adequately because of negative peer group pressures. Underachieving children with poor self-esteem often seek friends who share their values, attitudes, and behaviors, and the collective negative energy of the peer group reinforces their alienation, defense mechanism, and nonadaptive behavior. Children who perceive themselves as nonachievers and strongly identify with other nonachieving children realize that they would have to seek new friends if they decided to achieve in school.

Changing one's peer group can be a frightening prospect, and many children are unwilling to take this step. Professional counseling can help these youngsters develop a healthier self-image. As they begin to perceive themselves more positively, they will naturally gravitate toward children who share these positive feelings.

Parenting styles may also contribute to a child's attitude about studying. Parents who have been lax in asserting the family's position on such issues as effort, responsibility, and commitment must do some introspection. Although they may feel they have clearly defined their position on the subject of studying conscientiously, they may need to reassert unequivocally their commitment to this position. The starting point is to formulate fair, reasonable, and consistent guidelines. Children are invariably confused by double messages. Knowing the rules and standards provides them with a sense of security. (Parents of children who are in counseling or psychotherapy should discuss appropriate parenting and behavior modification strategies with their child's therapist.)

Academic and study skills assistance, supervision, emotional support, consistency, clearly defined structure, reasonable standards, positive expectations, carefully orchestrated victories, and effusive praise for improvement are vital components in the equation that can transform negative attitudes about school and studying into positive attitudes and improved performance.

Success is addictive. Once your child begins to achieve in school, she will be more willing to relinquish her "victim" role and the attitude that homework and studying are cruel punishments intentionally designed by her parents and teachers to make her life miserable. This change of attitude is an important signal that she is ready to participate more actively and enthusiastically in the learning process.

SUGGESTED CORRECTIVE STRATEGIES

In School

1. (ES) If you believe your child is not spending adequate time studying because she is unsure about how much work is required or expected, arrange a conference with her teacher. Your child should attend this conference. Ask the teacher to explain her homework requirements and her grading criteria. (If she hasn't already done so, this clarification would be beneficial for the entire class.) You cannot assume that your child can figure out on her own how much homework she should do. You might write down the guidelines in language your child can understand and have her sign the document. In this way she formally acknowledges that she understands the standards and agrees to conform to them.

2. If you believe your child's teacher is not showing students how to get organized, schedule and budget time, record assignments, and plan ahead, diplomatically discuss your concerns. These activities could be integrated into the curriculum and require as little as five hours of instruction.

At Home

1. Help your child determine how much homework is required on the average each evening in each subject. To make this determination, you will need input from her teachers. (Refer to the suggested corrective strategies under **Time Management,** page 308, **Planning Ahead,** page 222, and **Smart Thinking,** page 275, for specific ways to schedule and utilize study time more effectively.)

2. If the teacher concurs that your child is not spending sufficient time studying, be prepared to monitor her more closely. Explain the reason for this supervision and advise her that the monitoring will cease when she demonstrates that she is spending adequate time studying and doing homework. This will be determined by your observations, her performance in school, and the teacher's feedback. Your expectations, however, should be realistic and congruent with your child's skills. Communicate positive expectations and provide acknowledgment and affirmation for improvement. (See **Time Management,** page 308, **Planning Ahead,** page 222, **Goals,** page 84, **Procrastination,** page 235, **Priorities,** page 228, **Monitoring Homework,** page 185, and **Preparing for Tests,** page 225.)

3. If your child is failing to study adequately because of learning problems, academic deficiencies, or study skills deficits, learning assistance in the form of tutoring or help from the school resource specialist is vital (see relevant entries for suggestions about how to handle specific learning problems).

4. If you suspect your child is sabotaging herself because of unresolved family or psychological issues, seek professional counseling. Such behavior invariably becomes worse if it is not treated. Your pediatrician, the school psychologist, or your local mental health organization can refer you to a qualified mental health professional. (Sliding fee schedules are usually available to families with limited budgets.)

INCOMPLETE ASSIGNMENTS

You have legitimate cause for concern if your child chronically submits incomplete work. Teachers associate this practice with irresponsibility and usually express their disapproval with poor grades. This behavior also has serious long-term implications. Your child must one day compete in a society that rewards substandard effort and performance with substandard pay, limited career options, and limited advancement.

The following factors could cause your child to submit incomplete work:

- Academic deficits
- Poor assignment recording skills
- Lack of awareness or concern about consequences
- Difficulty following or remembering instructions
- Poor planning skills
- Poor organizational skills
- Inadequate motivation
- Poor time management skills
- Laziness and irresponsibility
- Procrastination
- Frustration and demoralization
- Psychological problems
- Family problems

Poor academic skills and learning problems are the two most plausible explanations for incomplete assignments. Children who cannot do their assigned work and who are convinced in advance that they will get poor grades no matter how hard they try frequently develop poor work habits (see **Learning Disabilities,** page 157, and **Underachievement,** page 312). They may refuse to do their homework, or they may complete only the easy sections. Although this response is clearly escapist, the struggling child may conclude that escape is the only solution to an intolerable and seemingly insoluble situation.

Children who protect themselves from frustration by not completing their work either do not recognize or choose to deny an obvious irony: Not completing their assignments calls attention to the very inadequacies they are trying to hide. Unless they receive help and develop alternative strategies for dealing with their frustration, their self-defeating behaviors will probably persist into adulthood (see **Disregard of Consequences,** page 50, and **Bouncing Back from Setbacks and Learning from Mistakes,** page 30).

The natural instinct when parents recognize that their child has acquired a pattern of chronic counterproductive behaviors is to intervene and protect the child from the mistakes, defeats, and pain he is certain to experience if his behavior does not change. Threats, lectures, punishment, and showdowns, however, are usually ineffective and typically trigger denial, defensiveness, resentment, anger, and active or passive resistance. The following six-step procedure is far more effective:

1. Determine if your child has academic deficiencies (see the student evaluation forms on pages 160 and 163).

2. If you identify deficits, get help. If he has severe learning problems, your child should be enrolled in the school resource program. He may also require supplemental tutoring or educational therapy after school to overcome his deficits and catch up with his class (see **Parents' Rights,** page 201, **Underachievement,** page 312, and **Learning Disabilities,** page 157).

3. Gear your expectations to a realistic assessment of your child's skills. If he is being asked to do work that demands abilities he does not yet possess, ask his teacher to adjust his assignments to his current skill level. As his skills improve, the academic demands can be increased incrementally.

4. Provide a carefully controlled amount of help and supervision (see **Learned Helplessness,** page 152).

5. If your child does not know how to study, you, the teacher, or a tutor will need to teach him practical study skills (see **Study Skills,** page 292, **Time Management,** page 308, **Monitoring Homework,** page 185, and other relevant entries).

6. Develop reasonable and consistent homework and performance guidelines and clearly assert the family's position on effort, commitment, and follow-through (see **Behavior and Performance Guidelines,** page 26).

Your child's work ethic is directly linked to his academic self-confidence (see **Self-Esteem and Self-Confidence,** page 266). If he receives academic help, begins to receive better grades, and starts to enjoy his success in school, he will be far less likely to submit incomplete work than if he is floundering hopelessly. If your child refuses to relinquish his self-defeating behaviors after his learning deficits have been corrected, he will require counseling. Depressed and angry children often resort to self-defeating behavior to express their unhappiness, get attention, and punish their concerned parents.

SUGGESTED CORRECTIVE STRATEGIES

In School

1. If your child habitually submits incomplete work, ask his teacher if he possesses the necessary academic skills to do his assignments. If she indicates that his skills are weak, request that he be evaluated by the Child Study Team (see page 126), the school psychologist, or the resource specialist. If diagnostic tests confirm that he has learning deficits, request remedial help (see **Parents' Rights,** page 201). The resource specialist may decide to focus on helping your child with his daily class work and assignments or to work on improving his basic skills (see **Mainstreaming and Special Day Classes,** page 173, and **Evaluating Special Education Programs,** page 70). If the work demanded of your child in his regular classes is not reasonable, request modifications until he can catch up.

2. If your child's incomplete work is attributable to poor planning, poor organization, or inadequate recording of assignments, discuss with the teacher the possibility of integrating into the curriculum a study skills segment that teaches these skills. (See **Study Skills,** page 292, and other relevant entries for suggestions.)

At Home

1. If you conclude you have not clearly communicated your position on diligence and responsibility, you may be tempted to assert aggressively a new set of rules. Assaulting your child with a radically different standard without first explaining calmly and in understandable terms the rationale for the new rules could overwhelm him and trigger confusion, active or passive resistance, and resentment. It would be far more strategic to explain why you are establishing new rules and to implement the guidelines in increments your child can assimilate. Spell out the rewards for compliance and the consequences for noncompliance. Consistency is essential. Equivocating about the rules sends a confusing double message: "You better do this, but you really don't have to if you don't want to." The child on the receiving end of double messages rarely respects the rules and rarely respects his parents.

Once the rules are in place, you must clearly communicate that you expect conformity to the rules. Insisting that your child complete his work on time and in neat, legible handwriting is legitimate and reasonable, assuming he has the necessary academic, spatial, and fine motor control skills to complete the work and write legibly (see **Handwriting,** page 106). His acceptance of a work ethic at home is a vital requisite to his ultimate acceptance of a work ethic in the more demanding and often harsher world that awaits him after he completes school.

2. Examine your child's homework assignment sheet (see page 259) to make certain that he is including essential instructions and information. Have him check off each assignment after he has *completed* it (see alternative below). Also make sure he is bringing home the books and materials he needs to do his work. If he is not recording his assignments properly, patiently show him how to do so. Encourage him to use abbreviations (e.g., p. = page and ex. = exercise), but make sure that your child can read his abbreviations and is not taking so many shortcuts that he is becoming confused (see **Recording Assignments,** page 258).

3. Encourage your child to use the following project completion checklist. Feel free to modify the checklist.

4. If your child has academic deficits and does not qualify for assistance in school, consider hiring a tutor or enrolling him in a private learning assistance program. Make certain his specific deficits have been accurately identified. Your child may require intensive educational therapy, tutoring in a specific subject, a study skills pro-

PROJECT COMPLETION CHECKLIST

I have made certain I have followed the instructions for
the assignment.   _____

I have checked to make sure I have completed everything recorded
on my homework assignment sheet.   _____

I have carefully checked over my work.   _____

I have put my completed homework where I will be able to find it
in class.   _____

gram, or simply some short-term help with homework. The efficacy of the assistance program hinges on the accuracy of the diagnosis and the skills of the person providing the learning assistance.

INDIVIDUAL EDUCATIONAL PROGRAM (IEP)

Once a student has been referred by a Child Study Team (a panel of school personnel that examines the child's level of academic functioning—see page 111) to the school psychologist for diagnostic testing and has been identified as learning disabled, his parents are asked to attend an IEP (individualized educational program) conference to identify the child's specific learning deficits, discuss test results, propose a learning assistance strategy, and define specific remediation goals.

Although the composition of the IEP conference may vary from state to state and from district to district, usually the school psychologist, classroom teacher, resource or LH (learning handicap) specialist, principal, and school nurse attend the meeting. A speech therapist may also participate if the child has language or speech problems (see page 280). Parents may invite a private educational or clinical psychologist, psychiatrist, educational therapist, or tutor to present additional relevant information and, if necessary, to represent the interests of the child and family. In the event of disagreement, this independent consultant may also function as an advocate who critically evaluates the proposed learning assistance plan and debates legal issues involving local, state, and federal educational codes. Most IEP meetings, however, are nonadversarial, and relatively few parents feel the need to be represented by a consultant or an advocate (see **Parents' Rights,** page 201).

If parents concur with the recommendations presented at the meeting, they are asked to sign the IEP document and formally authorize the proposed learning assistance plan. An abbreviated IEP review is scheduled annually. At this meeting recent academic scores are examined (the test frequently administered is called the Woodcock Johnson) and the remediation goals are reassessed and perhaps redefined. A more comprehensive reassessment is scheduled every three years, and the results are discussed at another formal IEP conference. At the end of this meeting parents are again asked to sign the IEP document.

The IEP meeting provides an invaluable opportunity for parents to ask questions, express concerns, and examine remedial strategies with the assembled professionals. A primary objective is to coordinate everyone's efforts and facilitate progress. Issues that are typically examined include homework guidelines, the amount of assistance to be provided at home, techniques for monitoring homework, criteria for evaluating progress, responses to counterproductive behavior, and procedures for maintaining communication between parents and the school personnel. If the learning assistance program appears to be failing, you do not need to wait for the next regularly scheduled conference. You can request an IEP review at any time.

Parents who feel intimidated by school authority figures or disconcerted by complex educational jargon may feel anxious about participating in their child's IEP meeting (see **Conferencing with School Officials,** page 39, and **Communicating with the School,** page 35). They may think that questioning this team of highly trained professionals would be presumptuous and that they have nothing to worry about with these experts overseeing their child's needs. Unfortunately these parents may be placing too much trust in a fallible system. Even competent, well-intentioned professionals can make mistakes, and these mistakes can have serious academic and psychological consequences.

Parents who are dissatisfied with their child's IEP conference have every right to ask questions until they feel that the issues have been explained to their satisfaction. Professionals who are not adequately prepared, who use excessive jargon, who gloss over issues, or who are patronizing deserve to be challenged.

Your role at the IEP conference is to serve as your child's representative and make certain that he receives the best help available. You must serve notice—diplomatically, calmly, and unequivocally—that you expect the school personnel to do everything in their power to help your child achieve the defined educational goals and that you expect alternative plans to be implemented if he does not respond as anticipated. Active and informed parental involvement can profoundly affect the ultimate success or failure of the learning assistance program.

Participating actively in monitoring your child's learning assistance program and progress, however, does not translate into being obtrusive, hostile, or unreasonable. You have the right to expect improvement, but you must also be realistic. Serious learning deficits usually resist quick fixes. Imposing an arbitrary and unrealistic remediation deadline, for example, is unfair to your child and his instructors. Your objective and, ideally, those of the school should be the following:

▪ To improve your child's academic skills to the point where he is functioning at or above grade level or at a level commensurate with his intelligence

▪ To improve your child's academic self-confidence (see **Self-Esteem and Self-Confidence,** page 266)

▪ To determine if your child is applying his skills in his regular classes

▪ To determine when your child is able to work independently and no longer needs the support of a learning assistance program

The speed at which your child will attain these objectives will vary depending on the severity of his learning problems, the quality of the learning assistance program, and the nature of his coping mechanisms (see **Psychological Problems and Psychological Overlay,** page 239). Some children make quick and dramatic progress, and other children require more extensive and extended learning assistance.

At some point you will need to trust your intuition about when it is appropriate to question the efficacy of the learning assistance program. If your child is not making *reasonable* progress after a *reasonable* period of time, you have a responsibility to request that alternative strategies be explored. You may also have to consider seeking supplemental learning assistance in the private sector.

SUGGESTED CORRECTIVE STRATEGIES

In School

1. If you question the validity of the test results, and/or if your child does not qualify for learning assistance despite obvious learning difficulties, request a conference with the school psychologist or principal. If appropriate, request that your child retake specific subsections of the test. If this request is denied, you may want to have your child tested independently. Although you should not be afraid to make waves, communicate your concerns in a reasonable, nonhostile way. Your goal is to elicit cooperation if possible. You do have clearly defined rights, however, in the learning assistance equation! (See **Parents' Rights,** page 201.)

2. If you are perplexed by the test results or by the proposed remediation strategy and feel your questions and concerns have not been adequately addressed at the IEP conference, consider consulting an independent educational psychologist or educational therapist. You may want to have this consultant represent you at the IEP conference. Discuss the fees for this service in advance.

3. You may request a conference with any or all of the professionals involved in your child's case before the next regularly scheduled IEP meeting. Realize, however, that teachers and school personnel have many demands on their time and that there should be a valid reason for requesting this meeting. Requesting periodic updates from the teacher or resource specialist is both reasonable and legitimate. A quick, informal in-person or telephone conference is usually sufficient.

4. Make sure you and the school personnel agree about the amount of homework required from your child and the procedures for progress updates. You do not want to discover in April that your child hasn't been making any effort or submitting any work for six months.

At Home

1. There may be aspects of the IEP that can be reinforced effectively at home. Drilling spelling words or reviewing math facts may facilitate your child's progress, assuming you are able to work with your child without triggering resentment or resistance. Hire a tutor if you feel you cannot implement the suggested corrective strategies.

2. Once there is agreement about how much homework is reasonable each evening, you will need to help your child design a study schedule (see **Time Management,** page 308, **Monitoring Homework,** page 185, and **Learned Helplessness,** page 152). You will also need to monitor her to make sure she is doing what is expected (see appropriate entries for specific study skills strategies).

3. Periodically review the IEP document. Make notes about issues that might need to be discussed with the school personnel at the next regularly scheduled meeting or at an "emergency" meeting. Inquire periodically if the plan is still on target. Compare previous IEP documents with the current one. If you feel that the goals are too optimistic or too pessimistic, express your concerns. By asking informed, penetrating questions, you place the professionals on notice that you have expectations and are a force to be reckoned with. This can be done diplomatically. Your goal is *not* to put the school staff on the defensive but, rather, to work together with them in resolving your child's learning problems.

IQ TEST SCORES

Measuring intelligence is considered by some educators and psychologists to be a controversial procedure. This relatively new critical attitude can be traced to the inherent difficulty in (1) defining intelligence to everyone's satisfaction, (2) developing a testing instrument that is culturally and linguistically unbiased, and (3) creating a test that can accurately predict a child's potential to achieve in school and in life.

In theory children with high IQs *should* get the best grades, attend the best colleges, enter the most glamorous, prestigious, or remunerative professions, and make the most significant contributions to society. Sometimes IQ scores do reliably predict subsequent achievement. In other cases the tests fail miserably. Some children with high IQs do poorly in school and in their subsequent careers while other children with lower IQs become highly successful students and major contributors to society. This phenomenon raises serious questions about the predictive value of IQ tests.

Children with high IQs who are not successful in school are generally described as underachievers. These youngsters, who invariably perplex their parents, their teachers, and, ultimately, their employers, are often accused of being lazy and unmotivated.

The success formula is clearly more complex than the simplistic equation High IQ = High Achievement. Environmental, psychological, temperamental, and educational factors must be factored into the formula before IQ tests can be considered to be a reliable means for assessing a child's potential. Despite the relatively widespread use of IQ tests as diagnostic and prognostic tools, some professionals have charged that the tests are intrinsically flawed and consider IQ tests to be highly biased against students from disadvantaged backgrounds. They argue that the scores can be skewed by cultural factors, language deficits, emotional problems, perceptual problems, hyperactivity, anxiety, poor rapport, and inattentiveness. They also contend that the tests do not measure motivation, creativity, and artistic talent and do not make provision for environmental stimulation and the quality of educational instruction. Because disproportion-ately large numbers of minority students have been placed in classes for the retarded, IQ tests are now rarely used by school districts as a primary criterion for the special education placement of minority students.

Despite the limitations and flaws, IQ tests can provide a relatively objective measure of a child's level of intellectual functioning. Parents and educators, for instance, might want to consider the scores in determining fair and reasonable expectations, performance standards, and guidelines for a child (see **Behavior and Performance Guidelines,** page 26). If the test scores indicate that a child possesses average to superior intelligence, encouraging him to reach for chal-lenging goals and establishing fair but demanding standards at home and in school can be important catalysts for intellectual and academic growth. Al-though *all* children should be encouraged to stretch intellectually and to develop their talents to the fullest, below-average IQ scores should be factored into parents' expectations. Making unreasonable or excessive demands on a child with demonstrated intellectual limitations can cause stress, undermine self-esteem, and be emotionally damaging.

A significant discrepancy between your child's IQ test scores and achieve-ment test scores suggests that learning, concentration, emotional, family, or environmental factors could be undermining her school performance. In this case further diagnostic testing by the school psychologist or a private clinical or educational psychologist is essential. Bright children who consistently work below their potential may require learning assistance or counseling.

IQ tests, in conjunction with other personality, aptitude, and vocational interest tests, can also play an important role in career selection. Certain profes-sions require higher-level abstract reasoning or analytical aptitude, while other careers require language or artistic aptitude. The child who wants to become a physician obviously must possess good scientific aptitude, and the child seek-ing a career in graphic arts needs good artistic aptitude. Well-designed test batteries will suggest vocations for which a child demonstrates natural ability and interest.

Although IQ testing can provide clues about why a child is struggling in school or about what a child may succeed at as an adult, the procedure also poses risks. The test may not accurately measure the child's potential or may measure certain abilities while disregarding others. If the measurement is flawed because of test design defects, anxiety, poor rapport with the examiner, or inattentiveness, the child may be assessed inaccurately. As a consequence the child may never be adequately challenged by his teachers or parents to develop his talents, and a tragic waste of potential may occur.

Two popular tests are generally used by psychologists to assess intelligence: the Wechsler (the children's test is referred to as the Wechsler Intelligence Scale for Children, revised—WISC-R) and the Stanford-Binet. Today most school psychologists use the WISC-R. (Other tests have recently been introduced but are not yet as widely used.) Although the format, tasks, and questions vary, both tests evaluate the ability to analyze, perceive, associate, and recall. The number of "correct" answers is compared with scores attained by other students of similar background and age who have taken the same test. Statistical norms are established by administering the test to a broad population of people. The results are tabulated, the child's total number of correct answers on subsections of the test is compared to the norms, and a statistically based score is derived. In determining a child's IQ the examiner can use national or local norms. Local norms permit the examiner to compare children of similar socioeconomic backgrounds, which theoretically reduces cultural bias.

Some school districts place more emphasis on IQ tests than others and many schools use scores as the primary criterion for admitting children into enrichment and gifted programs. Schools may also use the scores in conjunction with achievement test scores as a rationale for skipping students into a more advanced grade.

IQ test scores are usually factored heavily into the eligibility requirements for learning assistance programs. Psychologists consider a significant discrepancy between the highest subsection score on the WISC-R and significant discrepancies between achievement test scores, IQ scores, and classroom performance (e.g., IQ 125, reading comprehension 1.5 years below grade level, and Ds in reading) to be primary symptoms of a learning disability.

Some educators and psychologists claim that parents can raise their child's IQ with systematic instruction, training, and stimulation. More traditional educators and psychologists argue that intelligence is inherited, genetically determined, and unalterable. Other psychologists believe that intelligence is 70 percent genetically determined and 30 percent environmentally determined. Although it is probably true that a child's IQ cannot be significantly altered through instruction, parents and teachers can certainly train children how to use their inherited intelligence more efficiently, effectively, and pragmatically.

By providing intellectual stimulation, systematic guidance, and encouragement, you *can* help your child develop and improve his applied thinking skills.

Your efforts may not necessarily make your child more intelligent, but they certainly will make your child *smarter.* Children who possess developed and enhanced strategic thinking skills and critical intelligence invariably do better in school and in life than those who coast along in cerebral neutral.

SUGGESTED CORRECTIVE STRATEGIES

See **Smart Thinking,** page 275, for specific strategies designed to develop your child's applied thinking skills. Your child's IQ may not increase, but with systematic instruction his *smartness* quotient can be increased dramatically.

KEEPING UP ·
WITH THE CLASS

The most plausible explanation for why children have difficulty keeping up with their class is the most basic: deficient academic skills. Students with reading, math, or language arts deficits obviously face major academic obstacles. These obstacles will appear all the more formidable if the child's classmates have above-average skills. Teachers raise the level of their expectations and their demands when the general ability level of their class is superior. This extra pressure can cause the student with poor skills to fall further and further behind and to become increasingly demoralized. If he concludes the situation is hopeless and effort is futile, academic and emotional shutdown is inevitable.

Unfortunately, many perplexed teachers automatically describe students who cannot keep up with their class as immature. Most of these children are neither immature nor developmentally delayed but, in fact, have learning deficiencies that have never been properly identified (see **Atypical Learning Problems,** page 16, and **Underachievement,** page 312). Recommending that they repeat the year is rarely an effective solution. Unless their underlying learning problems are identified and remedied, these children will remain at risk. (See **Learning Disabilities,** page 157.)

Other factors also can cause children to lag behind: poor study skills (see page 292), poor time management skills (see page 308), inattentiveness (see **Attention Deficit Disorder,** page 5), family or emotional problems (see **Psychological Problems and Psychological Overlay,** page 239), an inability to establish goals and priorities (see pages 84 and 228), a poorly developed appreciation for the principles of cause and effect (see page 51), and a general pattern of self-defeating behavior (see **Procrastination,** page 235). To pinpoint the deficits that are impeding your child's progress, it is vital that you get precise information from the teacher about the nature of your child's problem.

Enlisting help from teachers can be more problematic when students are in the upper grades. Whereas elementary school teachers teach approximately thirty students each day, high school and junior high school teachers teach as many as 150, making them less able to monitor and nurture students who are not keeping up with the class. Elementary school teachers are usually required to take at least one course in identifying and dealing with learning problems to become credentialed or certified, but in many states teachers in the upper grades are not required to take this course.

Most high school teachers are concerned primarily with teaching the subject matter and have little time to identify underlying reasons for a child's academic problems. They generally write off students who do not work conscientiously, act responsibly, and keep commitments, and they penalize those who do not do the assigned work by giving them low grades. In defense of this practice, many high school teachers would argue: "It's not my job to hold a student's hand. If he wants my help, I will give it. Let him come and ask. And then let me see some real effort."

School counselors who should be monitoring and advising struggling students and their parents are frequently overworked, and many children who need help slip through the safety net. In some financially hard-hit school districts, budgetary constraints have forced schools to eliminate their counselors.

Another ironic situation compounds the plight of struggling students. Children whose skills are significantly below those of their classmates and who go to the resource specialist for help often each day miss a great deal of work while out of the room. Although the resource teacher might prefer to use remedial materials to correct the underlying learning deficits, she may be forced to spend her time simply helping the student with homework. The net effect is little or no remediation of the issues responsible for the academic difficulties. Some classroom teachers resent the time academically deficient students spend away from class and actually "punish" these children by holding them strictly accountable for everything covered in class while they were with the resource specialist.

The longer children who cannot keep up with their classes remain in a no-win situation, the greater the risk of demoralization and shutdown. If your child is falling behind, it is essential that you intervene. To avoid academic and psychological damage, everyone—you, your child, the teacher, and the resource specialist—must work together to develop and implement a well-conceived and effective catch-up plan.

SUGGESTED CORRECTIVE STRATEGIES

In School

1. To help identify problem areas, ask your child's teacher to complete the following teacher evaluation, which describes common "problem areas" that can cause children to fall behind. Completing the checklist should require only a few minutes, and it can guide you and your child in developing an effective catch-up plan as well as help the teacher pinpoint deficiencies that might be addressed in class or after school.

TEACHER EVALUATION

Code: *0 = Never*   *1 = Rarely*   *2 = Sometimes*   *3 = Often*   *4 = Always*

THIS STUDENT:

Has difficulty keeping up with the class _____

Has difficulty reading accurately _____

Has difficulty with reading comprehension _____

Has difficulty understanding math concepts _____

Has difficulty with math computations _____

Has difficulty with handwriting _____

Has difficulty with written language arts _____

Has difficulty concentrating _____

Submits sloppy and/or illegible schoolwork _____

Submits incomplete assignments _____

Submits late assignments _____

Procrastinates _____

Is disorganized _____

2. Consult with the teacher about how you can work together to help your child overcome the difficulties. If the teacher is not cooperative or supportive, consider hiring a tutor. If your child is having chronic problems and her skills are below grade level, request an evaluation by the school psychologist (see **Parents' Rights,** page 201). Also request supplemental materials your child might use in school or at home to correct specific problems.

3. (ES) Ask your child's teacher to complete the daily performance checklist (pages 138–139) at the end of each school day. It should require about two minutes to fill out and will provide *daily* feedback about your child's work. Modify the checklist if

TEACHER EVALUATION, CONTINUED

Code: *0 = Never   1 = Rarely   2 = Sometimes   3 = Often   4 = Always*

THIS STUDENT:

Is irresponsible   _____

Is forgetful   _____

Lacks pride in work   _____

Shows little motivation   _____

Avoids hard work   _____

Makes excuses for poor performance   _____

Avoids challenges   _____

Lacks self-confidence   _____

Becomes easily discouraged   _____

Abandons difficult projects   _____

Is easily frustrated   _____

Appears to be functioning below potential   _____

Misbehaves in class   _____ you want other specific information about your child's performance. Initial the checklist each evening to indicate to the teacher that you've seen it. If your child is having difficulty completing assignments on time or writing neatly, set up a meeting with your child and the teacher to explore possible solutions. Involve your child in the process and listen to his ideas and suggestions. He may know how to solve the problem!

Use these checklists to identify problems that need to be addressed and consider setting up a point system to reward your child for attaining specific improvement goals. Make adding up his total points a daily ritual and set specific rewards for achieving a target score in a specific area (e.g., handwriting) for the day, week, month, or semester.

DAILY PERFORMANCE CHECKLIST

First and Second Grade

Code: *1 = Poor   2 = Fair   3 = Good   4 = Excellent*

	MON.	TUES.	WED.	THURS.	FRI.
Reading					
Math					
Handwriting					
Listening in class					
Keeping up with class					
Effort					
Behavior					
Comments					
Parents' initials					

4. Verify that your child has the requisite academic skills to do the work being assigned. The standardized tests (Stanford Achievement Test, California Achievement Test, etc.) given annually in school can provide this information. If you do not understand what the scores mean, ask the teacher to explain them. (See **Understanding Diagnostic Test Results,** page 316.) If your child's skills are deficient, the difficulty or quantity of assigned work should be modified. The demands can be increased slowly as skills improve. If appropriate, request that the teacher or resource specialist provide extra assistance.

At Home

1. Any areas marked 3 or 4 on the teacher evaluation checklist (pages 136–137) should be considered red flags and should be examined with your child. The tone of these sessions should be *nonaccusatory* and *cooperative.* Your child may deny he has problems in the areas the teacher has identified—a common defense mechanism when children feel inadequate

DAILY PERFORMANCE CHECKLIST

Third Grade and Above

Code: *1 = Poor   2 = Fair   3 = Good   4 = Excellent*

	MON.	TUES.	WED.	THURS.	FRI.
Completes assignments					
On time					
Neatly					
Handwriting					
Listening in class					
Keeping up with class					
Effort					
Behavior					
Comments					
Parents' initials					

and threatened. Your job is to communicate your conviction that the problems can and will be resolved and to assure your child that you are there to provide or procure the necessary assistance.

2. Help your child establish specific realistic academic goals such as "complete and submit on time all handouts for science chapters" or "get a minimum of 70 percent on all spelling tests." Discuss strategies for attaining these goals (see **Goals,** page 84, and **Smart Thinking,** page 275). Consider creating incentives or rewards for attaining specific, agreed-on objectives. Perhaps your child could earn points toward something she wants. These extrinsic or external rewards will ultimately be unnecessary once your child begins to succeed and can then be phased out.

3. If your child has specific academic deficits but doesn't qualify for special assistance, consider hiring a private tutor or educational therapist or enrolling your child at a private learning center.

4. Communicate daily with your child about what is happening in school. *Be careful, however, not to nag.* Use the performance checklist as a springboard for discussion. Lectures and recriminations typically fall on deaf ears.

5. Establish reasonable guidelines for the amount of homework expected each evening and help your child set up a study schedule (see **Procrastination,** page 235, and **Time Management,** page 308). If appropriate, suggest an experiment that slightly increases the amount of homework done each evening in each subject. Don't propose this experiment if your child is already doing a great deal of homework.

LANGUAGE ARTS (ESSAYS AND REPORTS)

To write effectively, children must be able to select words that express their perceptions, thoughts, and feelings about events, symbols, objects, and experiences perceived through their five senses. The process of responding to sensory stimuli (e.g., a word, a puppy, or an emotion) is called *decoding*. The process of choosing words to express responses to stimuli is called *encoding*. When children communicate verbally, the decoding/encoding process is generally spontaneous. The process requires more intense and conscious effort when children respond to more complex symbols (e.g., the word *intransigent*) or express more complex ideas (e.g., the definition of *osmosis* or their insights about *Moby Dick*).

Some children inherit natural language aptitude. They easily master the mechanics of writing, learn good self-editing skills, acquire a rich vocabulary, and develop a style and syntax (sentence structure) that are precise and aesthetically pleasing. Researchers have actually pinpointed specific areas of the brain responsible for language; this suggests that the neurological composition of these areas directly influences expressive language ability.

The percentage of the student population that *cannot* master basic writing skills because of intellectual or neurological limitations is relatively small, and these limitations cannot be used to explain the epidemic of poor writing skills in American schools. With systematic and effective instruction most children can learn how to write powerful sentences and produce cogent, well-crafted essays and reports.

To improve written language skills, students must practice continually, and receive continual feedback and criticism. Each writing assignment is an invaluable opportunity for them to develop and refine their skills. Unless their spelling, syntax, organization, and grammatical mistakes are corrected, children will continue to make the same mistakes.

Practice, however, involves more than simply inserting the proper adverb, adjective, or verb tense in reams of mindless language arts quizzes. It involves daily writing assignments, weekly essays, and monthly book reports—a practice that has become an anachronism in schools throughout the United States. Unfortunately, many teachers do not want to spend the time grading these assignments, and even if they tried, they might be *incapable* of finding their students' mistakes. Studies indicate that the writing skills of many new teachers are poor—which should come as no surprise, as these teachers are themselves the products of the same flawed educational system!

Children who believe they cannot write well often become phobic about writing. They make no improvement because they are convinced that the situation is hopeless and that effort is futile.

The recipe for teaching children how to write effectively is quite basic. There are five requirements:

1. Quality instruction and a well-conceived language arts program

2. An emphasis on writing skills in the curriculum

3. Adequate practice (regularly assigned essays, journals, diaries, book reports, and term papers)

4. Meaningful criticism with an emphasis on training children to develop self-editing skills

5. Parental support (parents may need to verify that their child's writing assignments have been completed according to specifications, proofread, submitted on time, and corrected)

Writing deficiencies result when one or more of these requirements have not been provided. The first clear indications of language arts deficits usually appear in the third, fourth, and fifth grades. Chronically poor grammar and punctuation, sentence fragments, run-on sentences, and unintelligible stories are key danger signals (see the following checklist). If not resolved, these deficits can create serious problems in junior high school, high school, and college.

Many effective and innovative methods for teaching language arts have been developed in the last decade, and there is no excuse for having a poor writing skills program (specific programs follow). Learning to write should be one of your child's most enjoyable school experiences. If you observe that she is struggling and conclude that her language arts program is inadequate, express your concerns to her teacher or the principal. You are your child's advocate. Communities that demand a first-rate language arts program in their schools invariably get a first-rate program!

SUGGESTED CORRECTIVE STRATEGIES

In School

1. To identify your child's specific language arts deficits, ask the teacher to complete the language arts checklist on page 144. Students in the lower grades will not have yet learned some of the skills described. You should be concerned only about skills relevant to your child's grade level. The teacher can tell you which skills have been taught and practiced.

2. If the teacher pinpoints specific deficiencies, ask if there are remedial materials that could help your child. Perhaps the teacher would be willing to work with your child before or after class. Remedial materials that could improve language arts skills are included in the Resource List at the back of the book.

3. (ES) Diplomatically ask which language arts program is being used in your child's class. If you believe the program is deficient, check teacher supply stores and bookstores for alternatives you might recommend for review. High school English departments are not usually receptive to parents suggesting writing programs. This should not necessarily inhibit you, however, from expressing your feelings or making suggestions.

4. Check with other parents. They too may have concerns about the language arts program at your child's school. If these parents agree that there may be a problem, discuss the issues with the teacher or principal, who might be willing to consider using a different program.

At Home

1. (ES) For fun you and your child could co-author letters to the editor of the local newspaper. You could also write letters to people featured in the news, expressing your support or disapproval of what they are doing or saying.

2. Write an intentionally complex descriptive sentence (e.g., "The man sat at the table and calmly sipped his coffee, and he seemed oblivious to the commotion that was exploding around him in the elegant restaurant on the Champs Elysée on a hot August day"). If you cannot create a complex sentence, find one in a book. Make a game of rewriting the sentence with your child. Produce as many alternatives as possible (e.g., "Seemingly oblivious to the commotion exploding around him and the heat of the hot August day in the elegant restaurant on the Champs Elysée, the man calmly sipped his coffee"). Experiment with breaking the sentence into two sentences. Discuss the merits of each alternative you create. Repeat this activity many times.

LANGUAGE ARTS CHECKLIST

	YES	NO
This student:		
Uses capital letters when appropriate	——	——
Uses correct punctuation	——	——
Avoids sentence fragments (sentences without verbs)	——	——
Avoids run-on sentences (too many ideas included)	——	——
Uses proper subject-verb agreement ("the boy goes")	——	——
Spells accurately	——	——
Writes neatly and legibly	——	——
Uses topic sentences correctly	——	——
Presents ideas sequentially	——	——
Knows when to start a new paragraph	——	——
Can summarize in writing what has been read	——	——
Writes well-organized stories, essays, and reports	——	——
Can express ideas within a reasonable time frame	——	——
Can edit own work and find most grammatical and syntactical errors	——	——
Writes interesting creative stories	——	——
Can identify parts of speech	——	——

Involve your child in creating the complex sentences and the alternatives. Make the process a game. Your child is learning how to "massage" language!

3. (ES) Co-author creative stories with your child. Suggest a title such as "The Dragon Who Barked Like a Dog" or "Our Trip to Mars." You might want to write the first sentence (e.g., "The little dragon knew there was something terribly wrong the first time he tried to roar like his father"). Have your child write the next sentence, then you write sentence number three, and so on. Later, as she becomes more confident, she may want to write most or all of the story. Make the process fun. *Use your discretion about correcting your child's grammar and spelling.* Being highly judgmental will trigger anxiety, defensiveness, and resistance. The stories don't have to be perfect. From time to time you might diplomatically make suggestions such as "I think this word is spelled . . ." or "Do you think we could play with this sentence and make it even more scary?" Encourage and affirm your child. Your goal is to create positive associations with writing. With sufficient practice the quality of her stories will improve.

4. Read over your child's school assignments. Make a mental note about the spelling or grammatical errors. You might say: "I found five spelling errors. Let's see if you can find them." With younger children you might want to give your child tokens (such as pennies) for every mistake found. The pennies might be placed in a jar and traded in for a special prize each month. As an extra incentive you might say: "If you can find the two run-on sentences, you get five pennies." (You must first, of course, show your child what a run-on sentence is!) Your child might be given a ten-penny bonus for an especially neat and legible assignment.

LANGUAGE DISORDERS

A child is constantly being bombarded with sensory stimuli in the form of spoken or written words, mathematical symbols, chemical formulas, pictures, events on the playground, and feelings of pain, joy, or hunger. Her brain must decode (decipher) these sensory data, retrieve relevant information from her memory, and find the words to encode (communicate) accurately her ideas, feelings, information, and perceptions. Expressive language is the end product of this complex neurological process.

In most instances the decoding/retrieval/encoding procedure is instantaneous and efficient. Your child's teacher might ask her to read a math word problem aloud and explain to the class how to solve the problem. If she can properly decode the words and symbols she reads in the problem, can understand the concepts, and can do the calculations, but cannot intelligibly describe her problem-solving procedure to the other students, she may have an expressive language disorder. If, however, she can describe the procedure but cannot articulate the words properly, she probably has a speech disorder (see page 280).

Children with serious and chronic expressive language problems are generally described as *dysphasic* or *aphasic*. Although these two terms are often used synonymously, they should be differentiated. Children with aphasia have little or no communication skills. Children with dysphasia are able to communicate but do so haltingly. Both conditions require intensive speech therapy, and children manifesting symptoms are usually placed in special school programs.

Autism is another condition that can cause profound communication problems. This little-understood, perplexing disorder prevents children from establishing emotional bonds with the external world. The condition, however, is not related to aphasia and dysphasia.

Language disorders could erect formidable educational and emotional barriers for your child. If she cannot find the words to express her feelings, needs, and ideas, she could easily become frustrated, demoralized, and isolated. Early intervention and specialized language therapy can significantly reduce this risk.

A wide spectrum of specific symptoms should alert you to a possible language disorder. The most obvious symptom is delayed language acquisition. If the normal developmental progression from cooing to babbling to speaking isolated words does not occur, or if the progression is interrupted, you should consult your child's pediatrician. A kindergartner with a possible language disorder may not be able to say the names of the colors, the days of the week, or the months of the year. She may also be unable to count out loud or sing the words to the songs taught in class. (See the inventory below for additional symptoms.)

SUGGESTED CORRECTIVE STRATEGIES

In School

1. The following inventory identifies the primary symptoms of a language disorder. To complete the checklist, consult with your child's teacher and/or resource specialist. (If your child is a teenager and has language problems, the deficits have probably already been identified.)

LANGUAGE DISORDERS INVENTORY

If the inventory indicates that your child has an expressive language disorder, request a speech and language evaluation by the school speech pathologist or the school psychologist (see **Parents' Rights,** page 201).

	YES	NO
Auditory Processing Deficits		
Difficulty paying attention to auditory stimuli	____	____
Difficulty discriminating sound versus no sound	____	____
Difficulty locating where sound is coming from	____	____
Difficulty discriminating different sounds	____	____
Difficulty distinguishing primary sounds from background sounds	____	____

(continued)

	YES	NO
Difficulty associating sounds with source of sounds	___	___
Difficulty filtering out extraneous sounds	___	___
Difficulty sequencing ideas	___	___
Oral reversals (e.g., *emeny* instead of *enemy*)	___	___
Circumlocutions (imprecise, roundabout communication: e.g., "that place down there where they sell the thingamajig")	___	___

Linguistic Processing Deficits

	YES	NO
Poor grammar	___	___
Wrong verb tenses	___	___
Use of only broad meaning of words	___	___
Lack of understanding of subtle meaning or differences between words	___	___
Difficulty understanding spatial prepositions (e.g., *beside* or *beneath*)	___	___
Difficulty understanding comparatives, opposites, and superlatives (e.g., *bigger/biggest, far/near, rough/smooth, fast/slow*)	___	___

Cognitive (Thinking) Processing Deficits

	YES	NO
Difficulty following verbal directions	___	___
Difficulty expressing thoughts and information	___	___
Difficulty classifying	___	___

	YES	NO
Difficulty putting events in sequence or order	____	____
Difficulty making comparisons	____	____
Difficulty understanding or expressing the moral of a story	____	____
Difficulty predicting the outcome of a story or an event	____	____
Difficulty differentiating between fact and fiction	____	____
Difficulty remembering and expressing facts	____	____

Evaluation Deficits

Difficulty drawing conclusions ("Why did she need her gloves?")	____	____
Difficulty relating to cause and effect ("What would happen if he forgot to put gas in the car?")	____	____

Aphasia/Dysphasia

Difficulty making facial motor movements to produce sound (*dyspraxia*)	____	____
Difficulty imitating sounds	____	____
Difficulty remembering words (but being able to repeat them)	____	____
Difficulty formulating sentences (but can use single words)	____	____
Difficulty naming common objects	____	____
Difficulty recalling a specific word	____	____
Difficulty recognizing common objects by touch	____	____

2. If the school's evaluation indicates specific language deficits, carefully examine your options. Nonsevere problems can often be treated successfully at the local school. Most districts, however, place children with severe language disorders in special programs at magnet schools. These programs are usually under the aegis of the county and serve children from districts throughout the county.

3. Make sure you understand the nature of your child's problem. Consult appropriate reference books to learn more about the issues, symptoms, and remediation techniques. (Ask your local librarian or the school speech pathologist for the names of books.) Periodically meet with your child's therapists and teachers to discuss the goals of the program, progress, and criteria for monitoring improvement.

At Home

1. Talk with your child! Provide *nonstressful* opportunities for her to practice her communication skills. Your expectations should be geared to her skill level. Your child is struggling with a handicap, and you must demonstrate that you are sensitive to her struggle and committed to helping her prevail. Your patience, affirmation of her efforts, and emotional support are vital components in the equation that will ultimately allow her to develop more effective communication skills. If your child is struggling to express her ideas in the proper sequence, help her draw a picture, "map," or flowchart that visually represents how the ideas are related. Encourage her to use the map as she orally describes the ideas in the sequence that she represented visually. Urging her to form visual pictures of what she wants to say can be a highly effective tool. You might also suggest that she experiment with closing her eyes and hearing what she wants to say before she actually says it. This "prevocalization" method may be very effective for children who learn best auditorially.

2. Have your child dictate her ideas about topics of interest or relevance to her. Urge her to speak slowly. Draw a map or diagram that visually expresses what she is saying (see mind maps under **Reading Comprehension,** page 250, and **Notetaking,** page 193) as she speaks. Encourage her to make corrections in the map. Discuss the visual representation of her ideas and feelings and brainstorm how the content might be organized differently and how certain vocabulary words might enhance the communication.

3. To reduce your child's anxiety and phobias about verbal communication, have her close her eyes and see herself calmly, effectively, and confidently communicating her ideas. Also suggest that she take one or two deep breaths before beginning to talk. These visualization and relaxation techniques can significantly reduce her stress and fears.

4. If your child does not appear to be responding to her language therapy program, you may want to consider supplemental private language therapy. Ask your pediatrician for a referral.

LEARNED HELPLESSNESS

A powerful instinct impels parents to protect their children when they are in danger and to come to their aid when they are struggling. This mechanism serves a vital function during early childhood, when youngsters are dependent, vulnerable, and incapable of assessing and responding appropriately to risks and dangers. When maturing children remain overly reliant on their parents to support and protect them, there is justification for concern. Excessive dependence signals that the protective instinct may be preventing the child from developing self-reliance (see **Self-Esteem and Self-Confidence,** page 266). This phenomenon is called *learned helplessness.*

A child with poor academic skills and little self-confidence who knows her call for help will bring a concerned parent, teacher, or resource specialist to rescue her will be very tempted to use the "hot line" whenever she experiences a setback or glitch. Although her need for help may be legitimate, the attention and strokes may become a more important payoff than succeeding in school.

Children are rarely consciously aware that they are perpetuating their own helplessness. They telegraph their dependency through their behavior. Red-flag symptoms include chronic forgetfulness, confusion, sloppiness, procrastination, and irresponsibility. Some children actually feign being dense and, in extreme cases, affect mild retardation.

Continual "I can't do this" statements or expressions are another indication that a child has become helpless. Once she accepts her powerlessness, she will become increasingly addicted to the support system. Her responses and demeanor send a clear message: "Don't expect very much from me!" She may manifest her dependency by requiring her parents to sit at her side whenever she does her homework, to remind her to study for tests, to organize her notebook, to verify her assignments, to help her write her book report, to manage her time, to organize her materials, and to check her math problems.

To preserve their on-call rescue service, some children consciously or unconsciously resist overcoming their problems or magnify their needs. These youngsters usually become very skillful at manipulating their parents and teachers. Their continued need for help guarantees that their security blanket will not be withdrawn and that they will not be forced from their comfort zone. Any changes in the status quo can trigger profound anxiety and insecurity.

Even normally astute parents may allow themselves to become enmeshed in their child's helplessness. The most common verbal clue that there is a problem is the pronoun *we*. When parents say *"We* have our math problems to do" or *"We* had difficulty on *our* last spelling test," they are sending a clear message to their child that her dependency is acceptable, when they should be signaling that the responsibility for doing math problems and learning spelling words belongs to the child. This assumes, of course, that the child possesses the basic skills to do the work on her own (see **Monitoring Homework,** page 185, **Spelling Problems,** page 283, and **Math,** page 178).

Parents may rationalize their entanglement in a dependency script by arguing that their struggling child cannot possibly survive without their help. Some parents are reluctantly coerced into the nightly homework ritual. Others *eagerly* participate for complex psychological reasons that may include guilt, inadequately defined ego boundaries, fear of separation, and a host of other dysfunctional-family issues.

Unfortunately, the most common excuse offered by excessively involved parents is usually accurate: Children with learning problems often cannot complete the assigned work on their own and do, in fact, require help. Without assistance these children will fall further and further behind and become increasingly frustrated and demoralized (see **Anger and Frustration,** page 1). With assistance they are at risk for becoming overly dependent. This paradox can cause parents great anguish. As there are no absolute criteria for determining when to assist, when to resist, and how much help to offer, parents must base their degree-of-involvement decision on their child's current skills level, teacher feedback, test results, and their own intuition.

If you conclude you have become enmeshed in a dependent relationship with your child and want to extricate yourself, you must be prepared to make some difficult choices. No parent wants to see his or her child suffer, even if the suffering is exaggerated or self-induced. The process of incrementally withdrawing the security blanket and resisting your child's manipulative behavior will undoubtedly cause stress and unhappiness not only for your child but also for everyone in the family. You must draw your resolve and strength from the realization that it is in your child's best interests to become independent and self-sufficient. These qualities are requisites to developing self-esteem (see page 266).

Children who are allowed to establish dependencies during the formative years often require someone to prop them up throughout their lives. Their sense of helplessness and powerlessness can become so indelibly imprinted on their psyche that they may be continually compelled to seek emotionally destructive co-dependencies.

Helplessness is a mental state that is profoundly influenced by verbalized and nonverbalized parental behavior and expectations. If your child is to reformulate her perceptions about herself and her abilities, you must:

■ Encourage her to reach for goals she can realistically attain

■ Control the difficulty of the problems she is expected to solve on her own and increase the difficulty level in small increments

■ Create repeated opportunities for her to succeed at specific tasks that do not require continual support or supervision

■ Slowly but firmly nudge her from her comfort zone

■ Affirm and profusely acknowledge her successes

■ Express faith in her ability to prevail

■ Encourage her to reach for goals slightly beyond her reach as her skills and confidence improve

Intentionally orchestrating repeated opportunities for success is vital. Allowing your child to experience occasional setbacks is also vital. Children who do not learn to bounce back from setbacks and deal with frustration will be severely handicapped in a highly competitive world (see **Bouncing Back from Setbacks and Learning from Mistakes,** page 30, **Fear of Failure/Success/ Competition,** page 74, and **Anger and Frustration,** page 1).

The transformation from helplessness to independence requires astute planning. You must challenge your child without allowing her to become discouraged, and you must establish expectations and performance standards congruent with her skills (see **Behavior and Performance Guidelines,** page 26, **Keeping Up with the Class,** page 134, **Working Independently,** page 332, and **Effort and Motivation,** page 63). Although you cannot reasonably expect a dyslexic child to read without mistakes, you can insist that she do segments of her homework independently (even if there are errors!) and that she submit her work on time. If she does not have the skills to do the work, you may need to provide a carefully controlled amount of help. You may also need to request that the teacher adjust the difficulty level of her assignments until your child is able to catch up.

The conversion of a helpless child into a self-reliant child can be a long and arduous process. You must be willing to persevere. If the withdrawal of the security blanket causes profound anxiety and resistance, educational therapy coupled with family counseling or individual psychotherapy will be necessary.

SUGGESTED CORRECTIVE STRATEGIES

In School

1. (ES) If you suspect that your child is capable of doing more than she believes she is capable of doing or you conclude that you have taken ownership of your child's problems, ask the teacher for an update about your child's same behaviors and attitudes in class. Also request that she give you an update on your child's skills. Determine what your child can realistically be expected to do on her own in class and at home. Perhaps assignments could be "downloaded" so that she can complete them with little or no help. If she is in third grade and is reading two years below grade level, she clearly will require help from her teacher, resource specialist, and you. The amount of help and the expectations for independent work must be geared to her skill level. Even if her skills are deficient, the amount of independent work expected should be slowly increased, especially if you and the teacher believe your child is capable of doing a particular assignment and the correct pro-

cedure has been adequately explained and modeled. Each decision about how much help to provide will require an intuitive judgment call.

2. (ES) Suggest to the teacher that she involve your child in establishing specific academic and independent work goals for herself (see **Goals,** page 84). The procedure of checking off each goal as it is achieved will make the goals more tangible and should increase her motivation. The teacher's acknowledgment of progress and success is an important component in the behavior modification equation.

At Home

1. Discuss the issue of self-reliance with your child. Explain that you want her to become more independent and self-sufficient. Be specific about how these objectives might be achieved. For example, you might tell her that if you believe she knows how to do her math homework, you will not provide help. If she is truly confused, you will review how to do one or two problems at most, but you will insist that she do the rest on her own even if she does some problems incorrectly or becomes frustrated (see **Working Independently,** page 332). Although she may not be happy with the new "rules of the game," it is important that she understand the rationale. To reduce her anxiety, withdraw the support in increments.

2. If your child has significant learning deficits and you conclude that you cannot help her without "buying into" her learned helplessness, consider hiring a professional tutor or an educational therapist. Alert the tutor to your child's propensity to become dependent and urge him to use his best judgment about when it is appropriate to provide help and when it is appropriate to insist on independent work. Establish a goals checklist for work completed independently at home (see **Goals,** page 84). Entrenched resistance by your child to becoming more self-reliant should be assessed by a qualified mental health professional.

LEARNING DISABILITIES

Estimates about how many children have learning disabilities vary from 3 percent to 25 percent of the school population. The variance reflects the fact that the diagnostic standards used to define a learning disability and to identify struggling students vary. The lower percentage indicates highly selective criteria and includes only those children with *specific* and significant learning deficiencies. The higher percentage includes children with less severe and/or *nonspecific* learning problems (see **Underachievement,** page 312, and **Atypical Learning Problems,** page 16).

The identification issue is further complicated by a wide range of common diagnostic labels, including *learning disability, learning different, dyslexia, perceptual dysfunction, attention deficit disorder, attention deficit hyperactivity disorder, decoding deficits, sensory-motor dysfunction,* and *minimal brain dysfunction.* Despite differences in diagnostic criteria, terminology, and explanations about why children struggle, most educators agree that early intervention is vital if academic and psychological damage is to be prevented.

Although there is general consensus about the value of early diagnosis and treatment, many school districts erect a formidable barrier to early intervention: they insist that students be a minimum of two years below grade level in reading or math to qualify for special help. As it is impossible for a kindergartner or first-grader to be two years below grade level, the youngster is forced to flounder until his problems are considered sufficiently debilitating to qualify him for help.

Many school districts have other highly selective criteria. Some require a significant discrepancy in the subsection scores on an IQ test or a significant discrepancy between a child's IQ and his scores on standardized achievement tests (nationally administered skills tests—see **Performance on Standardized Tests,** page 212, and **Understanding Diagnostic Test Results,** page 316). The required IQ discrepancy may range from twenty points in one district to twenty-six points in another. Children with a low average IQ and poor academic skills are also usually excluded from learning assistance because they are considered to be functioning at an academic level consistent with their intelligence. The same rationale could also prevent a dyslexic or chronically inattentive child with a low average IQ from receiving help. (IQ tests are believed by some educators to be culturally biased, and the tests are generally not used to determine special education eligibility of minority students. See **IQ Test Scores,** page 130.)

Federal and state law stipulates that students manifesting symptoms of learning disabilities must be diagnostically tested. Federal law 94-142 also stipulates that if a learning disability is identified, the student must be provided with remedial help. In theory every child suspected of having a learning disability is referred to the school psychologist for testing. In practice many "gray area" youngsters with subtle to moderate learning deficits are never tested. Students with atypical, intermittent, or enigmatic problems that are considered nonincapacitating are rarely admitted to resource programs. This practice is not a callous conspiracy on the part of insensitive school districts but a classic example of misguided priorities and of limited supply being overwhelmed by excessive demand.

Too little money and too many children have produced a battlefield mentality where beleaguered school psychologists and administrators practice educational triage. The "seriously wounded" are helped, and the "walking wounded" are sent back to the front line untreated. Unfortunately, their untreated "minor" wounds have a disturbing tendency to become "infected" and debilitating.

Because state and federally mandated guidelines are subjectively interpreted and selectively applied, the standards for admission to learning assistance programs vary greatly from state to state, from district to district, and even from school to school within the same district. One school psychologist may be willing to bend the rules and admit a child with moderate problems into a remedial program, while another in a neighboring district may be unwilling or unable to bend the rules because the program is full and there is already a long list of children with more serious learning deficits waiting to be admitted.

It is popular today for educators, psychologists, columnists, and politicians to express alarm about the "at risk" students. The statistics are indeed frightening. In some high schools 50 percent of the students fail to graduate. Other youngsters are pushed through the system and are educated in name only. Despite deplorable skills, many of these semiliterate teenagers are awarded diplomas. Unfortunately, most of these teenagers will discover after graduation that they cannot compete for decent jobs in a highly technological marketplace that is seeking motivated, conscientious, goal-directed workers with good skills and efficient work habits.

The warning signals of learning problems include letter and number reversals (common in kindergarten but more serious in first grade), poor concentration, inaccurate reading with word and letter omissions and transpositions, poor reading comprehension, math deficiencies, impulsiveness, overactivity, memory deficits, poor motor coordination, illegible handwriting, chronic sloppiness, and difficulty following written or verbal instruction. Inefficient decoding of sensory data is the common denominator in most of these problems. Children who struggle to decipher and recall written and spoken words and symbols are destined to suffer in school. Because their sensory *input* is garbled, their *output* (performance in class and on tests) is also garbled. Parents who disregard their child's learning deficits in the hope that the problems will disappear of their own accord are placing their child at serious educational and psychological risk (see **Psychological Problems and Psychological Overlay,** page 239).

The need to become directly involved in the educational process is compelling if you conclude that your child needs help and is being denied this help or if you conclude he is not being adequately served by his learning assistance program. Becoming actively involved, however, can be intimidating, especially if you are confused about technical jargon, unsure about your prerogatives, and uncertain about what steps to take. Logic dictates that the more informed you are about the issues, the better prepared you will be to ask penetrating questions of the school personnel who are working with your child, critically evaluate your options, and make astute decisions. (See **Communicating with the School,** page 35, and **Conferencing with School Officials,** page 39.)

Because the quality of learning assistance can vary significantly, it is vital that you monitor your child's progress closely. One school may have a superb program, while another in the same district or in a neighboring district may have an abysmal program.

As a general rule superior resource programs address the underlying causes of a child's learning disability. Less adequate programs focus on crisis intervention and on helping children complete their assigned class work and homework. This "get the child through the day" approach rarely eliminates the source of a learning problem but rather is designed to teach children how to cope and compensate. Schools committed to this approach assume that your child will *never* completely overcome his learning problems. If you are unwilling to accept this rationale, you must become an activist who fights for better programs in your local school district, or you must provide private learning assistance for your child. The alternative is to do nothing and allow your child to struggle, become demoralized, give up, and shut down.

SUGGESTED CORRECTIVE STRATEGIES

In School

1. (ES) To obtain specific information about your child's learning deficits, ask his teacher(s) to complete the following checklist. The inventory describes many common symptoms of learning disability. Your child need not manifest all or even most of the symptoms to be a candidate for remedial assistance. A significant pattern of "yes" responses is a warning signal that your child should be diagnostically evaluated. (For more detailed information about learning problems, see *Learning Disabilities and Your Child* and *Kids Who Underachieve* included in the Resource List.)

STUDENT EVALUATION

Academic

	YES	NO
Poor reading comprehension	——	——
Difficulty with phonics	——	——
Reversals	——	——
Inaccurate reading	——	——
Difficulty with math computational skills (addition, etc.)	——	——
Poor handwriting	——	——
Inaccurate copying (from blackboard or at desk)	——	——
Difficulty understanding math concepts	——	——
Difficulty working independently	——	——
Sloppy work habits	——	——
Difficulty with spelling	——	——

	YES	NO
Difficulty with written language arts (essays/syntax, etc.)	____	____
Poor organizational skills	____	____
Poor planning skills	____	____
Incomplete projects	____	____
Difficulty following verbal instructions	____	____
Difficulty following written instructions	____	____

Behavior

	YES	NO
Short attention span	____	____
Difficulty following directions	____	____
Overactive	____	____
Impulsive	____	____
Fidgety	____	____
Distractible	____	____
Accident-prone	____	____
Forgetful	____	____
Daydreams	____	____
Slow in completing tasks	____	____
Excitable	____	____
Unpredictable	____	____
Disturbs other students	____	____
Chronic procrastination	____	____
Chronic irresponsibility	____	____

(continued)

	YES	NO
Coordination		
Gross motor coordination deficits (sports, etc.)	——	——
Fine motor coordination deficits (drawing/ handwriting, etc.)	——	——
Clumsy	——	——
Awkward	——	——
Poor balance	——	——
Right-left confusion	——	——
Fear of physical activities (climbing, sports, etc.)	——	——

Your level of concern about this student (please circle):

Extreme   Moderate   Minimal   None

2. (J/HS) To obtain information about a student in junior or senior high school, ask each teacher to complete the applicable sections on the following student evaluation checklist, opposite. You will note that this inventory is less comprehensive and is formatted differently because teachers in upper-level courses rarely get to observe their students as extensively as teachers in elementary school.

3. If deficits are indicated, discuss the problems with your child's teacher. A pattern of general deficiencies or a specific, severe deficit in one or more areas indicates that there should be an assessment by the school psychologist or by an independent education psychologist (see **Parents' Rights,** page 201).

4. If you believe your child's assistance program is weak or if he is not improving after a reasonable period of time, you must be prepared to intervene. You may need to explore other remediation strategies with the resource specialist, engage a private tutor (ideally a specialist in correcting learning problems), or enroll your child in a private learning assistance

STUDENT EVALUATION

Code: *1 = Poor   2 = Fair   3 = Good   4 = Excellent   5 = Not Applicable*

General Performance: All teachers please complete this section

_____ General self-concept

_____ Effort

_____ Behavior

_____ Concentration

_____ Organization

_____ Completes assignments on time

_____ Works independently

_____ Keeps up with class

_____ Neatness

_____ Class participation

_____ Test performance

_____ Attitude

Academic Performance: Please complete section pertaining to your subject

English/Language Arts:

_____ Correct grammar usage

_____ Punctuation

_____ Spelling

_____ Expository Writing

_____ Vocabulary

_____ Comprehension

_____ Creative writing

_____ Term papers

Most Recent Test Grade: _____

Most Recent Quarter Grade: _____

Math:

Working at grade level? Yes ____ No____ Approximate level: _____

_____ Understands concepts

_____ Applies concepts

_____ Computational skills

_____ Abstract reasoning

(*continued*)

STUDENT EVALUATION, CONTINUED

Math: (continued)

———— Accuracy   ———— Recall

Most Recent Test Grade: ————   Most Recent Quarter Grade: ————

History: *Science:*

———— Notetaking   ———— Notetaking

———— Outlining   ———— Outlining

———— Understands concepts   ———— Understands concepts

———— Can identify key   ———— Can identify key
　　　information   　　　information

———— Recall of information   ———— Recall of information

———— Term papers and reports   ———— Term papers and reports

Most Recent Test Grade: ————   Most Recent Quarter Grade: ————

Foreign Language:

———— Vocabulary   ———— Verb conjugations

———— Grammar rules   ———— Declensions (Latin)

———— Conversation   ———— Vocabulary gender

———— Completes assignments   ———— Studies adequately

All Teachers:
Your level of concern about this student's performance (please circle):

　　　　Extreme　　　Moderate　　　Minimal　　　None

program. The alternative is to allow your child to fall further and further behind, which could have catastrophic consequences.

At Home

1. Discuss identified problem areas with your child and brainstorm solutions to specific problems. If there are several deficit areas, you may need to establish remediation priorities. You may decide to concentrate on math first and then work on vocabulary skills. You may conclude that you can provide the necessary academic assistance for your child, or you may conclude that private tutoring or educational therapy is required.

2. Refer to the Table of Contents and to specific entries for strategies and suggestions about how you can help your child at home.

LISTENING IN CLASS

Youngsters who can listen attentively and assimilate information when their teachers speak have a distinct advantage over those who are inattentive. During the typical school day students are bombarded with thousands of spoken words. Those who don't listen in class miss important instructions about how to complete an assignment and explanations that clarify a science concept or math procedure (see **Following Verbal Directions,** page 78). Their work seldom conforms to the teacher's guidelines and is typically incomplete and improperly done. Poor listeners do not follow along when their classmates read aloud, and when it is their turn to read, they cannot find their place. The net effect is a continual state of confusion, academic inefficiency, and poor school performance.

As children progress through school, the need for listening skills increases significantly. In most high schools students are exposed to hours of lecture each week. Teachers who lecture often rationalize that they are preparing their students for the realities of college, where good notetaking skills are vital to academic survival. They expect youngsters to record pearls of wisdom and play back the information verbatim on tests. Few of these teachers would admit that it is simply *easier* for them to read their own notes to their classes than to interact actively, creatively, and dynamically with their students.

Chronic listening problems may be attributed to several sources. Some children have difficulty filtering out distractions and focusing because of attention deficit disorder (see page 5). Others have auditory memory deficits (see page 22) and cannot retain what they hear. Children with auditory sequencing deficits have problems remembering verbal information in the proper sequence. All of these perceptually based conditions can undermine the ability to listen attentively.

A child's preferred learning mode can also affect his ability to listen. The child who is a visual or kinesthetic learner is at a significant disadvantage if his teacher's preferred teaching style is verbal. If the child is unable to adapt to her style, he is destined to struggle and suffer.

Until fundamental changes are made in teaching philosophy and methodology, children with poor listening skills will have to accommodate themselves to a verbally oriented system. They must develop the ability to discipline themselves to listen attentively, to take notes from lectures, focus when the teacher gives instructions and communicates information, and recall what the teacher has said. Those who cannot master these basic survival skills are destined to become increasingly discouraged and demoralized.

SUGGESTED CORRECTIVE STRATEGIES

In School

1. (ES) If you suspect your child is not listening in class, discuss your concerns with the teacher. Sometimes simply moving a child's desk closer to the teacher's desk can be an effective remedy. This proximity could allow the teacher to monitor your child more closely and provide immediate feedback to your child when his mind is wandering.

2. (ES) If your child is in grade 1–3, you might suggest in-school strategy 3 under **Attention Deficit Disorder,** page 5. There are two potential problems with this strategy: The teacher may not agree to make the extra effort to monitor and modify your child's behavior, and the other children in the class may also want to participate in the behavior modification program. If the teacher is willing, the system can be used with the entire class, although obviously the procedure cannot be allowed to interfere with teaching.

3. Ask the teacher or counselor if he or she would be willing to monitor your child to make certain he is properly recording assignments.

4. If your child is manifesting symptoms of attention deficit disorder, auditory memory, or auditory sequencing problems (for specific symptoms, see pages 5 and 22), request that he be evaluated by the school psychologist, resource specialist, or speech and language specialist. If a deficit is confirmed, highly effective remedial methods can be used to remedy these conditions. (Refer to the corrective strategies for specific problems.) If your child qualifies for learning assistance, the resource specialist should also be able to monitor your child to make certain critical verbal information has been processed and understood.

At Home

1. Discuss substantive, engaging subjects at the dinner table. Encourage your child not only to express his ideas but also to listen attentively to the ideas of others. Engaging your child in a daily ritual of examining issues that affect his life promotes the development of not only good listening skills but also quality communication skills.

2. (ES) Play a game in which you give your child a series of verbal instructions. The instructions might direct your child to a "hidden treasure." After giving the directions, ask your child to repeat them to you. Then have him follow the directions. ("I have hidden a spoon in the house. If you follow my instructions, you will be able to find it. Go into your bedroom. Make a quarter turn to the right. Go six steps forward, heel to toe. Make a quarter turn to the left and start searching.") The complexity of the instructions should be increased in increments. (You may also need to demonstrate what a quarter turn to the right and a heel-to-toe step are.) Your goal is to improve your child's listening skills, memory, and confidence. You want to set your child up to win, so be patient and gear your instructions to your child's age and ability. With practice your child's auditory skills will improve and his negative mind-set about his listening capability should slowly dissipate.

3. Do a project with your child that he will enjoy. Patiently give him a controlled amount of instructions and ask him to repeat the instructions before proceeding. ("Glue the green strip of paper in front of the drawing of the house and glue the gray paper walkway so that it leads to the front door. Then glue the fence around the house.") Be prepared to repeat the instructions if he needs to hear them again. Be patient. Children who have poor listening skills need practice before they can realistically be expected to overcome the problem.

LOGIC

Logic is a requisite to solving problems, understanding concepts, evaluating issues, making predictions, and communicating ideas effectively. Students who capitalize on their ability to reason have a distinct advantage in college-oriented and advance placement classes. They also have a distinct advantage when they take competitive exams for admission to college and graduate school. Because logic is a key component of IQ tests, students with good reasoning skills usually receive high scores on these exams (see **IQ Test Scores,** page 130).

The workplace also rewards logical thinking. Employees who can identify, analyze, and solve problems are eagerly sought and quickly advanced.

On the most basic level, logic is linked to fundamental cause-and-effect principles (see **Disregard of Consequences,** page 50). The anecdote about touching a hot stove and discovering that it burns is a classic example of logic in action. Although many animals can also make this basic cause-and-effect connection, human beings are unique in their ability to make logical associations from both *direct* and *indirect* experiences. They can read a book or hear a story about someone else touching a hot stove and draw conclusions, make predictions, and use their insights to guide their actions.

Critical Thinking (see page 42) and **inferential reasoning** (see **Reading Comprehension,** page 250) are extensions of logic. Achieving students continually use their critical thinking skills to probe, associate, and evaluate issues. Such a child might conclude: "Kids who are into drugs act weird, get bad grades, and get in trouble. I won't take drugs, because I don't want to be like them." The child with good reasoning skills doesn't need to experience drugs first-hand to reject them. The same child can also use logic to assess situations and issues where information can be inferred but is not necessarily stated: "My friends are taking their raincoats and umbrellas to the football game. There must be a reason. Maybe they know something I don't know."

Although intelligence is clearly a major factor in a child's ability to apply logic, think critically, and solve problems, many highly intelligent children do not use their reasoning powers to full advantage, and they suffer setbacks they might otherwise have avoided. Their failure to think logically and their disregard of consequences cause them to function below their potential and, in some cases, to make egregious errors in judgment.

Youngsters who repeatedly miscalculate and show poor judgment often share two other distinguishing traits: They do not plan effectively, and they do not think strategically (see **Smart Thinking,** page 275). In cases of chronic self-sabotaging behavior, underlying psychological factors must also be considered. Children who continually "self-destruct" require professional counseling.

Logic is the turbocharger in your child's intellectual propulsion system. Systematic instruction and practice, feedback, and support are vital if this turbocharger is to function at peak performance. Each time you encourage your child to analyze issues and problems encountered in everyday life and develop logical solutions, you are helping her refine her reasoning skills. These skills will serve her throughout her life.

The fact that logic and language are processed in the left hemisphere of the brain and that feelings, intuition, and artistic responses are processed in the right hemisphere has received a great deal of publicity in recent years. This phenomenon has encouraged some educators to differentiate "left-brained learners" from "right-brained learners." Many of these educators argue that our educational system would be far more effective if teachers would adjust their instructional methods to their students' preferred and natural learning modality rather than requiring students to adjust to the teacher's preferred modality. Contending that our schools prioritize left-brain logic and language at the expense of right-brain artistic and creative functions, they argue that right-brain learners are often treated unfairly and their talents are often unacknowledged.

Although it is true that most schools emphasize left-brain skills, the currently popular left brain/right brain differentiation is misleading. No child is exclusively right-brained or left-brained. Children continually use *both* hemispheres of their brain at the same time. The artistic child must be able to plan a project, and the child with scientific aptitude must be able to draw a diagram.

Providing opportunities for students to develop logical thinking skills *and* artistic and creative skills should be an integral component of any well-conceived educational program. Although students with natural left-brain or right-brain abilities should be encouraged, acknowledged, and affirmed for their talents and accomplishments, their learning environment ideally should stimulate and challenge them in *all* modalities if they are to develop their full range of intellectual, artistic, creative, and emotional resources.

SUGGESTED CORRECTIVE STRATEGIES

In School

1. If you suspect your child is having difficulty thinking logically, confer with her teacher. Specific questions you might ask include:

■ Does my child have difficulty making reasonable predictions?

■ Does my child have difficulty perceiving how concepts and issues are related?

■ Does my child have difficulty perceiving the progression of sequential ideas?

■ Does my child have difficulty drawing reasonable conclusions and inferences from given information?

■ Does my child use non sequiturs (conclusions or inferences that do not follow from the premises or evidence) when expressing ideas verbally or in writing?

Some teachers may have difficulty answering these questions because they have not perceived the connection between logic deficits and your child's difficulties in class. If the teacher feels she cannot answer the questions, suggest that she observe your child more closely and report back to you later. Should she find that your child does appear to have difficulty with logic, request supplemental materials that your child could use at home to improve his skills in this area. Classroom materials designed to improve logic are included under **Thinking** in the Resource List at the back of the book.

At Home

1. **(ES)** Create logic games to play with your child that encourage him to make reasonable associations and develop plausible responses to "mind teasers." For example:

■ "Boy Scouts are taught how to make many different types of knots. Why would some people want to learn this skill? How many possible uses for different knots can you think of?"

■ "The light from the most powerful spotlight could never reach the moon, because it is 250,000 miles away. An extremely powerful laser beam, however, could conceivably reach the moon. Why do you think this might be possible?"

■ "Predict what would happen if atmospheric conditions caused all radio and TV transmissions to break down for three days."

If creating your own logic games proves too difficult, find out what is available at your local teacher supply store. To locate other materials and books written at your child's developmental level that are specifically designed to develop logical thinking, consult the librarian at your local library. Your local toy store may also have logic games. Your child's teacher or the school resource specialist may be able to recommend (and perhaps lend) materials to you. (See Resource List, pages 343–344.)

2. Refer to the cause-and-effect activities described under **Smart Thinking,** page 275. These suggested interactive exercises are directly applicable to developing your child's logical thinking.

MAINSTREAMING AND SPECIAL DAY CLASSES

Federal law requires that students who are officially identified as learning disabled be assigned to special assistance programs (see **Parents' Rights,** page 201). These programs range from small self-contained classes that students with serious learning problems attend for the entire day to part-time learning assistance programs that children with less severe learning problems attend for a portion of the day. When children participate in part-time resource programs (RSP classes), the procedure is called *mainstreaming.* Full-time programs are generally described as *special day classes.*

After a child is referred by the teacher or the Child Study Team (see page 111) to the school psychologist for diagnostic testing, an IEP conference (see **Individual Educational Program [IEP],** page 126) is scheduled to discuss the test results, examine the child's specific academic deficits, and develop a plan for correcting the identified problems. Factors that influence the recommendation made during the IEP include the severity of the child's learning problem, district resources, class availability, and the district's special education philosophy. Because the number of students participating in mainstreaming and special day classes is limited, each student can theoretically be provided with highly individualized, intensive remedial assistance.

Special day classes are intended to provide a safe haven while children receive intensive academic assistance. Students who cannot possibly meet the academic demands of the regular classroom are insulated from the embarrassment, frustration, demoralization, and feelings of inadequacy that can undermine their self-confidence and motivation.

Although, in theory, segregating learning disabled students in self-contained classes makes sense, the practice can also pose risks. In junior and senior high school these classes are sometimes used as "warehouses" for children with serious educational, emotional, and behavioral problems. Older students may have attended special day classes since elementary school, and their unresolved learning problems often spawn a wide range of nonadaptive, ego-protecting behaviors. If other students in the class manifest the same behaviors, an antilearning environment may develop. Students who are initially motivated when they begin the program may mimic these behaviors and become unmotivated.

Special day classes also pose other risks:

- The program may be intellectually stultifying.

- The teacher may be trained inadequately or "burned out."

- Students may not be pushed adequately to catch up.

- The curriculum may be poorly conceived.

- The class may not be homogeneous and may contain children with learning problems and children with emotional problems.

- The students may never be taught the requisite academic skills for successful reintegration into the mainstream.

- Children may become permanent "second-class" students with severely limited academic and vocational options despite having average to superior intelligence.

Some educators believe that the potential value derived from segregating seriously learning disabled students in special day classes is more than offset by the monumental problem of ultimately reintegrating these youngsters successfully into the educational mainstream. They argue that students can become so dependent on the small teacher/student ratio that even after their learning problems have been ostensibly remediated, they will have great difficulty adjusting to the psychological and academic demands of regular classes, which are less nurturing and less individualized (see **Learned Helplessness,** page 152).

Special day classes can also produce social problems. Children in self-contained programs are often misunderstood and may even be ridiculed by the other students on campus. Their special status can cause the segregated children to feel "defective" and to conclude that their situation is hopeless. Some youngsters consider placement in special programs to be conclusive evidence that they are retarded, despite the fact that retarded children are placed in other programs. Once special day students become demoralized and give up, the probability of their prevailing over their learning problems is significantly reduced.

Concern about the liabilities of self-contained programs has prompted many schools to mainstream as many students as possible. Students in pullout resource programs spend a specified amount of time each day (or in some cases every other day) with the resource teacher, reading specialist, or speech and language therapist. This specialist focuses either on remediating the underlying learning deficits or on helping students catch up and keep up with their classes. The severity of the learning problems and the specialist's availability will determine the frequency and duration of the pullout sessions. The resource specialist may choose to use remedial materials or to help the students with their class work. After the session the RSP students return to their regular classroom.

Ironically, children may be penalized for participating in an RSP program (see page 70). Some classroom teachers hold their students strictly accountable for all class work missed while they are with the resource specialist. This creates a "Catch 22" situation: students are penalized with poor grades if they do not receive assistance, and they are penalized with poor grades for missed work when they do receive help.

Classroom teachers who consciously or unconsciously resent students being pulled out of class and who direct their resentment at the students are myopic. Although their objective should be to help these children resolve their learning problems these teachers seem primarily intent on having every student complete all the material being taught. For them, requiring learning disabled students to finish a math worksheet seems more important than whether these students actually learn how to do the problems. Inflexible, insensitive teachers not only cause unwarranted stress and embarrassment, they also cause learning disabled children to resist participating in the learning assistance program.

To resolve the "Catch 22" situation, some school districts are now sending their resource specialists and teacher aides into the regular classrooms to provide on-site help. Although this practice eliminates the problem of pulling children from their classes, the effectiveness of the approach has yet to be fully documented.

The value of any remedial program hinges on the skills, personality, insight, and skills of the teacher (see **Evaluating Special Education Programs,** page 70). Mainstreaming programs and special day classes can be successful when the teachers implementing these programs are talented, perceptive, affirming, creative, and motivating. With effective assistance and first-rate teachers, most learning disabled children can acquire the needed academic skills and self-confidence to prevail in school.

SUGGESTED CORRECTIVE STRATEGIES

In School

1. The objective of any remedial program is to help your child overcome his learning problems. If he is in a self-contained class, review the goals for the program, teaching philosophy, instructional methods, and projected timetable for your child's reintegration into the mainstream. Do not pressure the teacher into giving you an unrealistic target date. You do not want your child to be mainstreamed before he is ready. On the other hand, you should want him to be reintegrated into regular classes when he is ready. You will need to monitor his progress and remain in touch with his LH (learning handicap) teacher. In some cases children with severe learning problems may need to remain in a self-contained program for their entire education.

2. If your child is being mainstreamed, carefully review with the resource specialist and classroom teacher the objectives of the remediation program. Examine the IEP document (see **Individual Educational Program [IEP],** page 126). Discuss how you might provide additional support at home and how you should monitor your child's work. Also discuss what criteria should be used to evaluate your child's progress.

3. If you feel that your child is being penalized because he is being taken out of class for assistance, express your concerns to the teacher and the resource specialist. If you cannot resolve the problem, involve the principal in the discussion. Being intolerant about missed class work defeats everyone's objective, which is to get your child up to grade level and functioning efficiently and effectively in school (see **Conferencing with School Officials,** page 39).

At Home

1. Monitor your child's progress carefully. This monitoring is necessary whether he is in a self-contained classroom or in a resource program.

2. Once your child's learning deficits have been identified, you may want to provide additional help at home in these areas. Refer to entries

under specific deficits for applicable suggested corrective strategies.

3. If you are not satisfied with your child's progress in the resource program or self-contained class, consider hiring a tutor or enrolling your child in a supplemental private learning assistance program. You must be realistic, however. Don't expect instant progress, especially if your child has significant learning problems. Your child's progress in school may be slow, despite a first-rate learning assistance program. At some point you must trust your intuition. If you feel more assistance is necessary, seek help outside the system.

MATH

The starting point in correcting a child's math problem is to figure out where and why the child is stuck. Is he struggling because he does not understand fractions (**a conceptual deficit**) or because he has difficulty performing specific mathematical operations such as subtraction or multiplication (**a computational or operational deficit**)? A child who has chronic math problems probably has deficiencies in both areas.

Assigning additional practice sheets or requiring a confused child to recite the multiplication tables ad nauseam will not resolve a conceptual problem. Although the child must ultimately learn the multiplication tables by rote, drilling number facts without addressing his underlying confusion is at best a stopgap measure. In the long run math mastery hinges on understanding the concepts.

Math skills must be developed sequentially. Children must be able to multiply to solve division problems, and they must understand part/whole relationships to solve fraction problems. Youngsters who don't understand the basic concepts may be able to do some problems correctly, but they usually hit a "brick wall" at some point. They may forget how to do problems they had supposedly already mastered, or they may be unable to make the transition from arithmetic to algebra or geometry. Their conceptual deficits will invariably come back to haunt them as they proceed into upper-level math courses.

In some cases math deficiencies are linked to perceptual decoding deficits. Reversing number sequences (*79* perceived or written as *97*) or confusing *6* with *9* cannot help causing computational errors (see **Dyslexia**, page 58). The child who has difficulty copying numbers from his textbook (**near-point copying**) or from the chalkboard (**far-point copying**) or who misaligns his columns when adding, subtracting, or dividing is also going to make mistakes, even if he understands the underlying concepts.

Children with concentration deficits are also at risk when they do math (see **Attention Deficit Disorder,** page 5). Their inattentiveness to details may cause them to disregard the minus sign and add when they should subtract. Children with ADD also typically do poorly on homework assignments and tests where precision is required.

Most children of normal intelligence can master basic arithmetic. Although addition, subtraction, multiplication, and division involve aspects of rote memory, children who understand how numbers "work" have much less difficulty learning their number facts; ultimately they will find higher-level math less challenging than those who have memorized the number facts without understanding the underlying conceptual principles that govern the computational operations.

SUGGESTED CORRECTIVE STRATEGIES

In School

1. If your child has math problems, request that a diagnostic math test be administered to identify his specific deficits. This test should indicate whether the problem is computational or conceptual (or both). It should also reveal if your child is reversing or misaligning numbers when he does computations (see **Dyslexia,** page 58, and **Inaccurate Copying,** page 113). The teacher or resource specialist can then employ teaching strategies designed to remediate the specific identified deficits. For example, **manipulatives** (units such as pennies, cubes of different sizes, or Popsicle sticks) can be used to help your child understand how numbers function. **Fraction tiles** can be used by teachers to explain part/whole relationships. These tactile and visual props can be an invaluable resource for helping a child who is confused about basic math concepts. A method called *touch math* can also be very effective.

2. The teacher's classroom observations can provide feedback about the origins and symptoms of your child's math problems. For example, your child may have difficulty adding numbers involving decimals, but he may understand decimal concepts and how to add. If he makes "silly" computational mistakes when adding or forgets to insert the decimal point, he probably needs more directed practice. Extra homework sheets may be appropriate. If his problem is inattentiveness or sloppiness, you and the teacher may need to design a creative incentive program to encourage neatness and accuracy. If he is confused about *how* to add whole numbers or does not understand what decimals are, he needs help with the concepts. The Math materials in the Resource List at the back of the book may prove effective.

3. A child who is seriously deficient in math needs learning assistance. In some cases the classroom teacher may be able to provide this assistance before or after class. If your child has serious or chronic math problems, he may need the help of a trained resource specialist who can identify where he is stuck and systematically and sequentially remediate the deficits. Math problems can be as debilitating as reading problems, and you must be your child's advocate if he is falling behind. Testing and remediation are essential. (See **Parents' Rights,** page 201.)

At Home

1. (ES) Behavior modification techniques can be effective in helping a child who understands the concepts but makes silly mistakes because of inattentiveness. Set up a program that gives your child points for each problem he does accurately and legibly. A prize, an award, or even money could be the incentive. It may be sufficient to say simply: "These problems need to be recopied so that they are more legible. Let me show you how I would like them to look." Once he does a neat, legible set of problems, photocopy the page and put it in a plastic sleeve. When subsequent work is sloppy or illegible, show your child the facsimile in the sleeve and insist that the current work be as neat and legible as the assignment he did previously.

2. (ES) If your child has computational problems, ask the teacher to provide appropriate supplemental practice materials. If the class is working on long division, but your child has not mastered his multiplication tables, the practice sheets should focus initially on multiplication. If he doesn't understand the concept of multiplication, he will need help in this area. If you feel you cannot explain math concepts to your child, request that the school resource specialist or the teacher do so. Once the concepts are understood, flash cards can be used to drill multiplication facts. Make the sessions fun by creating games! ("Let's play Monopoly, but before anyone can throw the dice, he has to solve a math problem from this stack of cards.") You might also create incentives for your child ("Let's see how many of these problems you can get. You can earn a point for each correct answer. When you get twenty points, we can go out for an ice cream cone"). Other incentives might involve long-range goals ("For each complete times table you can do, you'll receive five points toward winning the radio-controlled car"). Points earned for math proficiency can be combined with points derived elsewhere, such as from doing chores. Repeatedly praise your child for his accomplishments and keep the sessions short. If he is having an "off" day, stop! You can always come back to it later. You will need to rely on your judgment and intuition to determine if your child has mastered a concept. Ask the teacher to tell you when your child has mastered adding fractions or dividing with decimals. Children often need several exposures before they truly learn something. Do not expect "closure" (complete mastery) after each session. You want your child to have positive associations with math and working together.

3. (J/HS) Helping older students with math problems can be challenging for parents. You may have forgotten how to solve certain algebraic equations or how to prove theorems in geometry, or you may lack the patience to explain the concepts and operations to your child. If you cannot get help from the teacher or resource specialist, you will need to consider hiring a tutor. Ask the teacher to recommend someone who is qualified and effective.

4. (ES) If you don't feel comfortable making up your own math games, visit your local teacher supply store. Examine materials such as flash cards, number fact cards, workbooks, and videos that address the deficits identified by the teacher. If you have difficulty working with your child in a tutorial capacity, ask about fun math games you could play together or computer software that focuses on the deficits. Again, make the sessions enjoyable. If your child struggles, provide emotional support and communicate positive expectations. Specific materials you may want to examine are included in the Resource List at the back of the book.

5. (ES) Think of ways to integrate math into family interaction and games. You might, for example, see who can add 977 and 341 faster, with you required to do the problem in your head and your child allowed to use paper and pencil. Start with problems you know your child can do and give your child a handicap (you begin five seconds after he begins) if necessary. You want him to succeed, so be patient and supportive if he makes a mistake ("By next week I bet you'll have no difficulty with these subtraction problems. You're getting better all the time, and with some more practice you'll be dynamite!"). Your goal is to reduce your child's anxieties about math as well as to improve his skills. As he begins to improve, make the problems more difficult. You might say the remainder of a problem is 927 and he has to figure out any minuend and subtrahend that will produce that remainder. The simplest answer, of course, would be $928 - 1$, but you could increase the difficulty by requiring that the minuend be at least five digits and the subtrahend at least four.

MEMORIZING INFORMATION

Our educational system has traditionally rewarded students who can recall prodigious amounts of verbal and written data. Remembering this information is a relatively easy task for some but excruciatingly painful and demoralizing for others.

The motivated child with poor memory skills may devote hours to studying math facts, vocabulary definitions, historical dates, spelling words, grammar rules, Spanish verb conjugations, chemical symbols, or biology phyla, only to discover at exam time that he cannot recall vital information. Because he does not understand that intelligence and good memory are not synonymous, he may simply conclude he is "dumb" (see **IQ Test Scores,** page 130).

A child with poor recall may be highly creative, intuitive, inventive, artistic, articulate, or analytical but struggle to recall math facts or memorize data that seem irrelevant. The child's selective abilities underscore the fact that intelligence is a multifaceted phenomenon. Unfortunately, many of the more creative manifestations of intelligence are rarely affirmed in traditional schools.

The kinesthetic learner, for example, is at a particular disadvantage in schools that do not offer classes in art, mechanical drawing, drafting, or shop. He may be able to create a magnificent three-dimensional art project or take apart an engine and reassemble it "by touch," but he may struggle to learn French vocabulary words or grammar rules. In spite of his superior mechanical, spatial, and artistic aptitude, he will pay a high price for his inability to conform to a data-oriented educational system. His frustration and feelings of inadequacy could permanently warp his perceptions about his own talents and capabilities. (For more information on alternative learning strategies, see the Resource List at the back of the book.)

Teachers who base their assessment of a child's ability primarily on the retention of data generally give A's to students who do well on timed math tests, who spell accurately, who can recall historical dates, and who can remember chemical formulas. Children with exceptional visual memory skills are often described as having "photographic memories" and are held in awe by their teachers and classmates. The analogy is accurate. The child who takes visual "pictures" of what he is learning and who can see words and numbers in his mind invariably has less difficulty remembering information than the child who attempts to imprint information using other modalities (see **Visual Memory,** page 326).

When he needs to recall information for a test, all he has to do is scan the "photos" (see **Grades,** page 89, and **Spelling Problems,** page 283).

The realities of a traditional education make it strategic for children to develop their visual memory skills irrespective of their own preferred learning modality. Although auditory and kinesthetic learners should certainly capitalize on their natural learning style (see suggestions below), acquiring effective visual memory techniques can make their study time more productive and their test-taking experiences less traumatic. Students who can utilize a wide range of learning and study methods invariably do better in school than those who draw on more limited resources.

SUGGESTED CORRECTIVE STRATEGIES

In School

1. If your child is having difficulty memorizing information, the teacher may be able to recommend specific techniques that will facilitate memorizing number facts, vocabulary definitions, or grammar rules (see suggestions under **Visual Memory,** page 326, and **Auditory Memory,** page 22, and suggestions in the "At Home" section below).

2. If your child has severe memory deficits, ask that he be evaluated by the Child Study Team (see page 111 for definition), school psychologist, or resource specialist. If significant visual or auditory memory deficits are revealed, request that learning assistance be provided in these deficit areas (see **Parents' Rights,** page 201, and In-dividual Educational Program [IEP], page 126).

At Home

1. Try an experiment with your child. Select fifteen relatively difficult vocabulary words and their definitions. Your child should not be familiar with the definitions of these words. Group the words randomly into three lists. On the first evening, have your child learn one list of the words visually. Have your child write out the definitions several times and study the material silently. Urge him to form mental pictures of what the words mean (e.g., an image of a "vulnerable" person). Then give him a quiz. The next evening, ask him to recite the definitions from the second list aloud.

Encourage him to make an audio tape in his mind (e.g., a "buoyant" cork floating as waves lap against it). Spend the same amount of time discussing the words and give your child a quiz. On the third night, have him dramatize the words and definitions from the third list. Encourage him to play the role of someone who is, for example, "parsimonious." Ask your child which learning system seems best and compare the results of the quizzes. Your child's preferred learning style may be visual, auditory, kinesthetic, or a combination. Encourage him to use his preferred style when he has to study and memorize. Emphasize that learning is easier if he studies actively rather than passively. Explain with concrete examples what this means. You might make a distinction between one who tries to learn to play baseball by watching someone else play and one who learns by actually playing the game. Urge your child to get involved and be creative when he studies and is attempting to memorize information. If he is an auditory learner, have him pretend to give a lecture containing the information he must learn. By talking aloud, he can capitalize on his preferred learning modality. A kinesthetic learner might choose to trace his spelling words in modeling clay spread onto a large cookie tray, trace the words on fine sandpaper, or manipulate the letters from a Scrabble game. Urge him to be creative and inventive when studying and to use the system that works best for him.

2. Explain to your child that although he should use his preferred learning style, certain types of information lend themselves to being learned visually. Being able to take a visual picture and see a fact or spelling word can be an important test-taking tool. For ideas about how to develop your child's visual memory skills, see the suggested corrective strategies under **Spelling Problems,** page 283, **Visual Memory,** page 326, **Auditory Memory,** page 22, **Vocabulary,** page 329, and **Nonphonetic Words,** page 191.

MONITORING HOMEWORK

The conscientious child who can work independently and efficiently needs little or no supervision when doing homework. The child who chronically procrastinates, does the minimum possible, submits late, incomplete, and inaccurate assignments, and disregards the effects of her actions is, however, a candidate for more intensive parental monitoring (see **Inadequate Study Time,** page 116, **Time Management,** page 308, **Disregard of Consequences,** page 50, **Working Independently,** page 332, **Incomplete Assignments,** page 121, and **Procrastination,** page 235).

Children with learning problems obviously need more supervision than children with good academic skills. The temptation to avoid work and procrastinate can be very appealing to a frustrated, demoralized child. The child may prefer to delude herself that if she doesn't really try, she can't really fail (see **Learning Disabilities,** page 157, **Psychological Problems and Psychological Overlay,** page 239, **Negative Attitude Toward School,** page 188, **Effort and Motivation,** page 63, **Fear of Failure/Success/Competition,** page 74, **Anger and Frustration,** page 1, **Self-Esteem and Self-Confidence,** page 266, **Bouncing Back from Setbacks and Learning from Mistakes,** page 30).

Poor study habits can also force parents to become more actively involved in monitoring their child's homework. A child who does not establish goals and priorities, plan ahead, record assignments, attend to details, take notes, follow instructions, identify and remember important information, and anticipate what her teacher is likely to ask on a test is waving a red flag. If left to her own devices, she could capsize academically (see **Goals,** page 84, **Study Skills,** page 292, **Planning Ahead,** page 222, **Recording Assignments,** page 258, **Underachievement,** page 312, **Attention to Details,** page 12, **Memorizing Information,** page 182, **Time Management,** page 308, and **Inadequate Study Time,** page 116).

Assistance must be provided for students with learning or study skills deficits. Before you can reasonably expect your child to relinquish her counterproductive behaviors and develop a more responsible work ethic, she must have the requisite skills and she must believe she can do the assigned work. She also must clearly and unequivocally understand your position on effort, responsibility, and commitment (see **Behavior and Performance Guidelines,** page 26). As she begins to achieve and becomes more competent and confident, she should require less supervision.

Be aware that the decision to monitor your child closely is not without risks. If your child concludes she is being constantly scrutinized, she may become anxious, resentful, and resistant, *or* she may become emotionally and academically dependent on the extra attention. The risk of dependency increases if you take "ownership" of her problems and attempt to correct every mistake she makes (see **Learned Helplessness,** page 152, and **Self-Esteem and Self-Confidence,** page 266).

SUGGESTED CORRECTIVE STRATEGIES

In School

1. If you and the teacher believe your child has academic deficits, she should be referred to the Child Study Team (see page 111) and diagnostically evaluated by the school psychologist. If this evaluation reveals deficiencies and your child clearly lacks the requisite skills to do her homework, you must insist that learning assistance be provided (see **Parents' Rights,** page 201). Request that her assignments be modified so that she can complete them within a reasonable time frame and with minimal help and that her work be graded flexibly until she can catch up with her class.

At Home

1. (ES) If you are to supervise your child effectively at home, you must have information about her strengths and weaknesses. Ask her teacher to complete the **learning disabilities checklist** (elementary school, page 160, and junior/senior high school, page 163).

2. (ES) Ask the teacher to take a minute each day to fill out the daily performance checklist on page 187. This will tell you whether your child is completing her homework and studying adequately.

3. (J/HS) Junior and senior high school teachers may feel that students in the upper grades should be responsible for doing their work and should not have to be monitored by parents. Therefore they may not be willing to complete the daily performance checklist. If you feel your child is not sufficiently responsible to work independently, discuss your concerns with the teachers, the counselor, and/or the assistant principal. Ideally, they will be able to create an acceptable monitoring/feedback system.

DAILY PERFORMANCE CHECKLIST

Second Grade and Above

Code: *1 = Poor   2 = Fair   3 = Good   4 = Excellent*

	MON.	TUES.	WED.	THURS.	FRI.
Completes assignments					
On time					
Neatly					
Handwriting					
Keeping up with class					
Effort					
Behavior					
Comments					
Parents' initials					

Establish realistic daily performance goals and keep a weekly tally of points your child earns. She could work for a specific reward when the agreed-on performance goal is achieved. You must factor your child's academic skill level into the equation. If she has poor fine motor or spatial skills, you cannot expect her handwriting to improve immediately (see **Handwriting,** page 106).

For more monitoring ideas, see relevant suggestions under **Disorganization,** page 46, **Inadequate Study Time,** page 116, **Time Management,** page 308, **Procrastination,** page 235, **Working Independently,** page 332, **Smart Thinking,** page 275, **Planning Ahead,** page 222, **Incomplete Assignments,** page 121, **Distractions While Studying,** page 55, **Goals,** page 84, **Priorities,** page 228, and **Preparing for Tests,** page 225.

NEGATIVE ATTITUDE TOWARD SCHOOL

There is a direct correlation between a child's attitude toward school and the amount of success or failure he is experiencing. The child who is achieving academically is going to enjoy school more than the child who continually receives poor grades and negative feedback about his attitude and effort from his parents and teachers. The constant battle to survive in school invariably produces frustration, discouragement, resistance, anger, and self-protecting behavior (see **Learning Disabilities,** page 157, **Underachievement,** page 312, **Atypical Learning Problems,** page 16, **Effort and Motivation,** page 63, **Psychological Problems and Psychological Overlay,** page 239, **Bouncing Back from Setbacks and Learning from Mistakes,** page 30, and **Self-Esteem and Self-Confidence,** page 266).

The child who dislikes school may either suffer in silence or loudly proclaim his unhappiness to anyone who will listen. He may blame himself for his poor performance and conclude that he is "dumb," or he may blame others for his plight and feel victimized. The classic litany of rationalizations and complaints includes "The teacher is boring," "The work is stupid," "The teacher is unfair," and "Why do I have to learn things I'll never use?"

Learning problems can obviously be a primary source of unhappiness in school. When a child discovers he cannot do the work, he will try to protect himself from feeling inept and worthless. He may procrastinate, refuse to complete his homework, become helpless, or simply give up (see **Learned Helplessness,** page 152).

A negative attitude toward school may also be symptomatic of underlying emotional or family problems. Troubled children rarely understand why they are unhappy or depressed, and lacking conscious awareness of their underlying motives, they may conveniently attribute their problems to a poor teacher or a boring curriculum. By complaining they can vent their inner turmoil, express their anger, and deflect attention from the issues that are truly causing their pain. They may sabotage themselves, become manipulative, or choose other unhappy, angry children for friends (see **Peer Pressure,** page 209). These passive aggressive behaviors are guaranteed to make their parents' lives miserable and can be a powerful weapon in the hands of an angry child (see **Psychological Problems and Psychological Overlay,** page 239, **Anger and Frustration,** page 1, **Guilt,** page 101, **Fear of Failure/Success/Competition,** page 74, **Self-Esteem and Self-Confidence,** page 266, and **Disregard of Consequences,** page 50).

Identifying the source of your child's unhappiness about school is the first step in reorienting his negative attitudes. If he has learning problems, the specific deficits must be identified and treated before you can realistically expect any attitude changes (see the learning disabilities checklists on pages 160 and 163). Once your child begins to achieve in school, his negative attitudes should change. As his self-confidence improves and his expectations change, he will no longer need to protect himself by complaining (see **Effort and Motivation,** page 63, **Keeping Up with the Class,** page 134, **Monitoring Homework,** page 185, and **Working Independently,** page 332).

Children who are wrestling with emotional or family problems require counseling. If the psychological issues causing their unhappiness and counterproductive behavior are compounded by learning problems, these youngsters must also be provided with learning assistance in school and/or private educational therapy. In some cases this educational therapy may be provided concurrently with counseling. Extremely angry, resistant children with entrenched self-sabotaging behaviors, however, may need to receive counseling *before* they will allow themselves to respond positively to a learning assistance program.

Although learning assistance may improve school performance, it should not be considered a surrogate for counseling or psychotherapy when a child has emotional problems (see **Psychological Problems and Psychological Overlay,** page 239). Chronic unhappiness rarely disappears of its own accord. In most instances a child's attitude and school performance will continue to deteriorate if his underlying problems are not addressed. For this reason it is vital that the appropriate support systems be established *before* a child shuts down academically and emotionally.

SUGGESTED CORRECTIVE STRATEGIES

In School

1. Ask your child's teacher if she believes his negative attitude about school is linked to learning problems (see the learning disabilities checklists on pages 160 and 163). If she thinks that underlying skills deficits may be causing or contributing to the problem, request that your child be evaluated by the Child Study Team (see page 111) or school psychologist (see **Parents' Rights,** page 201). Help from the resource specialist will improve your child's skills and self-confidence, and this in turn should improve his attitude.

2. If your child cannot do his class work or homework, ask the teacher to reduce the difficulty level and the quantity of the assignments until he can catch up. Putting a child in a hopeless situation is guaranteed to produce demoralization.

3. Discuss your concerns about your child's attitude with the school counselor, psychologist, principal, or vice principal, and request suggestions about how to identify and deal with the factors responsible for the negativity.

At Home

1. If your child has academic deficits and does not qualify for learning assistance in school, you will need to provide help at home. Even if he does qualify for help from the resource specialist, this may not be sufficient to guarantee that he will be able to catch up. Supplemental tutoring, educational therapy, or enrollment at a private learning center may be required to change negative attitudes about school.

2. If you suspect your child's attitude problems are linked to emotional or family issues, request a referral to a qualified mental health professional from your pediatrician or the school psychologist. Counseling should be provided before the negative attitudes become entrenched and before your child has established a pattern of sabotaging himself in school.

3. If your child's negative attitudes about school do not appear to be linked to underlying emotional problems, use the **DIBS** method (page 233) to help him identify the specific issues that may be causing him to dislike school. The method will also encourage him to become actively involved in finding solutions to his own problems.

NONPHONETIC WORDS

Some youngsters find it relatively easy to recognize and pronounce such nonphonetic words as *should, laugh, drought, thought,* and *buoyant.* Others find this task nightmarish (see **Phonics,** page 217). Each time they encounter a previously learned nonphonetic word, they appear to be seeing it for the first time. This inability to associate the visual appearance of a word with its pronunciation usually creates formidable barriers to reading fluency.

Diagnostic testing usually reveals that children who struggle to read nonphonetic words have **visual memory deficits** (see page 326). These deficits can also produce significant spelling problems (see page 283). Innovative methods for teaching children how to imprint visually have proven highly effective, and these methods are described below.

SUGGESTED CORRECTIVE STRATEGIES

In School

1. (ES) If your child is not using the **Dolch** list (words grouped according to their level of difficulty; see Resource List), suggest that the teacher have him use the list to improve his recognition of nonphonetic words. The list incorporates many of the common words children are expected to be able to read at each grade level. Your child might put five words from the list onto flash cards each day and memorize them. The procedure can also be reinforced at home (see following).

2. Encourage your child to make a list of difficult nonphonetic words he encounters when reading. These words should also be placed on flash cards and studied using the visual imprinting method described below.

At Home

1. A highly effective technique for helping your child remember sight words and for developing visual memory skills involves encouraging children to imagine their eyes are a camera. They then take a "picture" of a difficult word, keeping the "shutter" (their eyelids) open until they can see the word clearly in their mind. First have your child write each word on an index card, using colored pencils or felt pens. If he wishes, he can even write the individual letters of each word in different colors. Have him hold the card slightly above eye level. The word should be held directly in front of his nose, slightly to the right, or slightly to the left of his line of vision.

Encourage your child to experiment and determine which position produces the best results. Looking up (straight ahead, to the right, or to the left) will help your child imprint information visually, as the eyes naturally go upward when information is being visually accessed and represented. Have him study the word until he thinks he knows it. Then have him close his eyes and see if he can still "see" the word in the colors he has cho-

sen. If he can't, have him open his eyes and study the word again. Once he can see the word in his mind's eye, have him spell it aloud to you. Then have him write it. Follow this procedure for five to ten words and then give a review quiz. Urge him to close his eyes and visualize the words when taking the actual test in school or when writing a difficult word in a report. This technique can also be used for improving spelling skills (see page 283) and for remembering number facts (see **Math,** page 178), definitions, historical dates, and chemical formulas. (See illustration, page 286.)

2. Have your child use the preceding technique with the difficult words on the **Dolch** list or the **Key Word Inventory** (see "Phonics" in the Resource List at the back of the book). You might set up a reward system, such as a penny for each word mastered, to be used for a special present.

NOTETAKING

Good notetaking skills are a vital component in the school success formula. Students who cannot effectively identify and record key information from textbooks, lectures, and class discussions will find themselves severely handicapped in upper-level classes.

Some students figure out how to take good notes on their own, but most require systematic instruction. The general neglect of formal notetaking instruction in American education can often be traced to a series of flawed assumptions and to miscommunication. Many elementary school teachers assume that students will naturally figure out how to take notes. Others assume that students will be taught notetaking skills in junior high school.

Teachers in the upper grades generally have a different set of assumptions. They expect students entering seventh grade to know how to take notes and consequently devote little or no time to teaching the skill. As a consequence, millions of children never master this requisite to effective studying and learning.

When taking notes, students must extract, distill, and link important information. The procedure also forces them to think about and evaluate what they are studying. This active involvement produces superior learning, enhanced comprehension, and improved retention (see **Critical Thinking,** page 42, **Passive Learning,** page 205, **Memorizing Information,** page 182).

Successful students realize that their notes will help them understand and remember what they are studying. Although notetaking initially requires extra time, the procedure can dramatically reduce the total amount of study time they must spend to do a first-rate job. Instead of having to reread an entire chapter several times, they can simply review their notes (see **Smart Thinking,** page 275).

The nuts and bolts of good notetaking are not mysterious. Students must learn how to:

- Identify main ideas and details

- Understand information and concepts

- Record key data using a consistent format

- Use their notes effectively while preparing for tests

The ideal time to teach children notetaking and note utilization skills is in elementary school, *before* counterproductive study habits become firmly entrenched and *before* poor grades cause demoralization and lowered expectations. Teachers who begin the instructional process in fourth, fifth, or sixth grade provide students with an invaluable resource that they can use throughout their education.

Because notetaking skills are often taught mechanically, it is common for students to develop profoundly negative associations with the procedure. Some teachers simply write their own notes on the chalkboard and require their students to copy them. Although this may provide a model for "good" notetaking, it is also mind-numbing. By doing all the work and thinking, the teacher encourages passive thinking and learning. Children become scribes and quickly learn to dread the boring ordeal.

Students who perceive notetaking as a useless exercise intentionally designed by their teachers to make their lives miserable usually become resistant. This reaction is unfortunate, for notetaking doesn't have to be boring or painful. Creative teachers can actually make the procedure relevant, interesting, and enjoyable by demonstrating how the skill can be mastered easily and applied immediately to preparing for the next history or science test.

Passive learners are the most resistant to spending the initial extra time and effort required to take good notes. Conditioned by a poor track record, they refuse to accept that any procedure could improve their grades, make learning easier, and significantly reduce the total amount of time required to do a first-rate job of studying (see **Disregard of Consequences,** page 50).

Notetaking is only one component in an effective study plan. Students must also learn how to make effective use of their notes. They must train themselves to ask questions about what they have written down. They must connect important facts to underlying concepts, and they must relate what they are currently learning to what they have already learned. Taking notes and reviewing them mindlessly do not constitute quality studying and active learning. Good students use their notes as a springboard for delving into the substance of what they are studying. This process produces mastery.

Notetaking should not be confused with outlining. Many children dislike outlining because the method appears contrived. Whereas outlining is a highly formatted and formularized method for organizing and recording information, notetaking is less structured. Both procedures can help children "digest" and retain information, and in the appropriate contexts both can be powerful study tools. Outlining can be especially useful in preparing reports and making oral presentations. As a general rule, notetaking should be taught before outlining is.

Children who begin to take and use notes effectively usually see a demonstrable improvement in their schoolwork (see **Grades,** page 89, and **Reading Comprehension,** page 250). As they begin to recognize the connection between good grades and good notes and realize that notetaking will produce desirable payoffs, their resistance to spending the initial extra time usually disappears.

SUGGESTED CORRECTIVE STRATEGIES

In School

1. Ask your child's teacher if notetaking skills are being taught. If the teacher indicates that the skills are not taught formally, diplomatically express your concerns and present reasons why you feel that this vital skill should be an integral part of the curriculum.

2. Discuss with the teacher the strategy you are using at home to help your child learn how to take and use notes effectively (described in the "At Home" section below). Ask her for feedback and for suggestions about how to help your child achieve mastery.

At Home

1. Create an emergency telegram. For example, "Water pump broken

Flagstaff. Two days fix. Send $250 Flagstaff Hotel 123 Main St." Create scenarios in which you and your child send telegrams with only the important information included. Practice editing the telegrams to eliminate superfluous words such as *a, an, the,* etc. Explain that writing notes is like sending a telegram that costs $1 per word. You need to include enough words to be able to understand the content, but you also need to minimize the unnecessary words. Make the process of creating and editing the material fun. The subject matter can be serious or nonserious.

2. Pretend you are a news broadcaster. Describe a current event (for example, a flood in the Midwest). Have your child apply the previous skills and practice writing down only the key information. After you have finished, review your child's notes and discuss his rationale for including certain facts and information. Then have him use his notes and pretend to be the broadcaster. Do not be highly critical. Your child's skills will improve with practice. Make the session fun, short, and nonstressful. If your child enjoys the process, he will be less resistant and more willing to use the skills.

3. Teach your child common abbreviations such as *p.* = page, *ex.* = exercise, *w* = with, *thru* = through. Encourage him to use as many abbreviations as he can, but emphasize that he must be able to understand his own abbreviations. You might also have him practice a simplified form of speed writing that leaves out most of the vowels (e.g., "U mght also hv hm prctc a smplfd frm of spd wrtng tht lves out mst of th vwls"). Explain that these abbreviations can save time when taking notes from a textbook and can also help him quickly record key information from his teachers' lectures. You might show him a format that will simplify his notes. If, for example, your child read a section in his science textbook about lasers, he might take the following notes:

Lasers invntd 1954
2 Types: synthtc rby crstals & gas
Rglr lght tumbls
Lser lght strght lne

Your child will obviously need to practice notetaking and will need several exposures to the abbreviation method before he masters the procedure. Remember to make the notetaking practice sessions fun and to praise your child repeatedly.

4. An alternative to the standard notetaking method is called *mind-mapping* or *chunking*. This method encourages students to represent information graphically. Your child would read a section in his textbook and then create a graphic picture or a word diagram that represents what he remembers. (Examples of the mind-mapping method can be found under **Reading Comprehension,** page 250.) Your child would then reread the material and expand his mind map by adding more details. Urge your child to be as creative as he likes. Artistic, playful embellishments are great, and the more the better. You want your child to have positive associations with this technique. Encourage the use of colored pens or pencils, as this will make the process more enjoyable and artistic and will help your child retain a visual/mental picture of the information. If your child wishes, he may read the article a third time, and as he reads he can add more details. This active involvement makes learning painless. It is perfectly acceptable to draw a picture of a laser, draw arrows, and put information in small boxes.

5. Have your child "read" his mind map and tell you all he has learned about lasers. Then have him put his mind map aside and tell you all he can remember. This verbalization process will reinforce memory and allow your child to utilize the auditory modality to supplement the visual and kinesthetic modalities.

6. Some children prefer the standard form of notetaking and others prefer the mind-mapping method. Other children may prefer to alternate or use both systems concurrently. It is perfectly acceptable for your child to jury-rig his own system. If he is required to use the format his teacher uses, however, he should be prepared to adapt to her specific formatting instructions.

PARENT-TEACHER CONFERENCES

Periodic conferences are vital links in the parent-teacher communication chain. When these meetings function as intended, they can provide you with an important update about your child's academic strengths and weaknesses and with vital information about her behavior, motivation, and effort. The meetings also serve as an early warning system. The teacher can alert you to specific problems such as letter and number reversals; poor reading comprehension; incomplete, late, or sloppy assignments; difficulty following instructions; concentration deficits; or inadequate studying. You and the teacher can then examine specific assistance strategies and coordinate your efforts in school and at home.

A good parent-teacher conference will inform you if your child is having difficulty in French because she is not memorizing her verb conjugations, if she is struggling in history because she is not taking good class notes, or if she is getting poor grades in English because she is not carefully proofreading her essays. These conferences, however, should not focus exclusively on deficiencies. Your child's talents and accomplishments should also be identified so that you can acknowledge and affirm her for these achievements.

Unfortunately, parent-teacher conferences are often little more than a formality in which a great many nonsubstantive platitudes are exchanged. If you believe that your child's teacher is not providing precise, meaningful information or specific suggestions about how your child can resolve problems, *you* must take responsibility for focusing the conference.

Because many classroom teachers receive little or no formal training in identifying learning problems, they may be tempted to attribute your child's academic problems to misbehavior, laziness, immaturity, or a poor attitude. These explanations are usually inadequate and misleading. Relatively few children are developmentally or physically immature. Misbehavior, laziness, and a poor attitude are generally the *symptoms* and not the *source* of a learning problem. To use these labels to describe an inattentive, unmotivated child who cannot keep up with her class obscures the true causal factors, which may involve attention deficit disorder (see page 5), dyslexia (see page 58), or an auditory memory dysfunction (see page 22). Unfortunately, improper identification of problems can prevent or delay vital intervention and remediation.

General, amorphous descriptions of your child's behavior are of little value. Observations such as "He's misbehaving," "He's not keeping up," "His reading is poor," "He's creating a disturbance in class," and "He's having trouble with math" may be accurate, but they do not help you identify and resolve the underlying issues. To get more information, you might respond to these statements as follows: "In what specific ways is he misbehaving? Why do you think he is manifesting these behaviors? Why is he not keeping up with the class? What specific reading deficits does he have? What does he do that creates a disturbance in the class? Is he having difficulty with math concepts or math computations, and what can be done to address these problems?"

The more specific the teacher feedback, the more productive the conference will be. A child with a minor reading problem may simply require basic tutoring. A child with a serious reading problem will probably need more comprehensive learning assistance (see **Learning Disabilities,** page 157). If you accept meaningless platitudes from the teacher, you cannot make intelligent choices or be certain your child is receiving the appropriate help.

You must have information if you are to help your child resolve his problems. You must be prepared to ask incisive questions. The teacher may not be able to answer all of these questions, but he will realize that he must monitor your child closely.

Although a little knowledge can be dangerous, no knowledge can be disastrous. The more you understand about your child's problems, the more intelligently you can assess your options and the more effectively you can contribute to the remediation process. Poorly identified learning problems and skills deficits are a ticking time bomb. Deficits that may seem relatively benign during first or second grade can explode in third or fourth grade.

The efficacy of parent-teacher conferences increases when you and your child's teacher are on the same wavelength. Putting the teacher on the defensive or implying he is incompetent will only succeed in creating an adversarial situation that is not in your child's best interests. You must make every effort to be reasonable, sensitive, and respectful. If communication breaks down and the differences cannot be resolved, you should confer with the principal or assistant principal (see **Conferencing with School Officials,** page 39). Should the disagreements prove irreconcilable, request that your child be placed in another class.

SUGGESTED CORRECTIVE STRATEGIES

In School

1. If you suspect that your child may have learning problems, ask his teacher to fill out the student evaluation checklists on pages 160 and 163. These checklists will help you identify specific deficit areas and will provide you with precise feedback about how your child is functioning in the classroom. If your child is in a special education program, a second form should be completed by the special education teacher. Once your child's deficits are identified, ask the teacher and/or resource specialist for supplemental remedial materials for home use. An outside agency, tutor, or educational therapist working with your child can also derive important information from this completed form. The information will help focus the remediation program, facilitate the selection of teaching strategies, and encourage the establishment of specific improvement goals.

2. Use the student evaluation checklists to focus subsequent parent-teacher conferences. You might say, "You indicated on the checklist you completed two months ago that my daughter's handwriting is illegible. Have you seen any improvement?"

At Home

1. Discuss the teacher's feedback with your child in terms she can understand. Use your discretion about showing your child the completed forms. You may want to give your child selected feedback, but you should first ask the teacher if he has any objection to your sharing this information. The teacher's evaluation of your child can be very important if your child is denying that she has problems in school. Brainstorm with your child how she can resolve the specific deficits that have been identified during the conference. For example, if she is not concentrating in class, you might ask her to suggest ways in which she might take more responsibility for paying attention (see **Attention Deficit Disorder,** page 5). She might also have valid ideas about how to improve her reading. Your child's active involvement is vital. (See **Smart Thinking,** page 275, for brainstorming strategies and other appropriate entries in this book for suggestions about how to resolve specific academic deficiencies and behavior problems.)

PARENTS' RIGHTS

The rights of children who require special education services are mandated in the Education for All Handicapped Children Act of 1975 (PL 94-142) and later amendments. This law requires that schools:*

1. provide a free and appropriate public education to all handicapped children, which includes special education and related services to meet their unique educational needs

2. provide handicapped children with an education in the least restrictive environment on the basis of individual needs

3. guarantee to each handicapped child an unbiased, valid assessment in a mode of communication normally used by the child.

4. provide parents the opportunity to be involved in the educational decision concerning their child

Each state supplements and amplifies PL 94-142 with its own educational codes, and counties and local school districts then superimpose their own local guidelines and policies. In California, for example, the state provides a specific timeline for testing a child and developing an individual educational program (see page 202).

Although state and local guidelines cannot, in theory, supersede federal statutes, in reality these codes play a major role in determining how federal law is interpreted and implemented. Some states, counties, and districts apply the federal law quite creatively, which may have the effect of circumventing the intent of the law.

Parents who agree to enroll their child in a special education program may discover a disconcerting lack of consistent quality in the programs offered in

---

* This information is derived from *Child and Parental Rights in Special Education*, a manual published by the California State Department of Education.

Procedure	Deadline for Completion
Written referral	15 days
Assessment plan & informed consent	At least 15 days
Assessment team meeting	50 days (not to include days in July and August)
Development of IEP & implementation	Immediately
Review	Annually or on request

different schools, districts, counties, and states. The program in one school may be excellent, while the program in another school in the same district or in a neighboring district may be inadequate.

Most school districts do not permit families to "shop" for the best remediation services. Although parents may be convinced that a particular program or teacher in another district or even in another school within the same district might best serve their child's needs, districts generally discourage inter- and intradistrict transfers. In most instances children qualifying for special education are enrolled in either a resource (RSP) program or a self-contained LH (learning handicap) class (also referred to as a special day class) at their local school. Some districts, however, may assign children with learning problems to special magnet schools.

You are justified in expecting that your child will be provided with quality remedial assistance, and you have a compelling responsibility to speak out when the local program is inadequate, poorly conceived, or poorly taught. As is the case in most bureaucracies, "the squeaky wheel gets the grease." Unfortunately, the deficiencies in a school's special education program may not be easily remedied. This is especially true when districts are poorly funded, have an entrenched, threatened, and unenlightened administration, or are staffed by inadequately trained special education personnel.

If you are wrestling with the decision to become embroiled in a confrontation with the school system, you must be guided by your intuition. If you conclude your child's needs are not being met and the classroom teacher, resource specialist, LH teacher, school psychologist, or principal cannot allay your concerns, the next step is to bring the issues to the attention of the district superintendent. You should balance any trepidations you might have about approaching this "luminary" with the realization that the superintendent is a public servant whose salary is paid with your taxes. If the superintendent cannot resolve the problems to your satisfaction, you can then exercise your federally mandated rights and file a formal complaint.

If you believe your child is being unfairly denied special education services, you may formally contest the decisions of the local school district. The U.S. Constitution and federal and state laws and regulations guarantee due process. You have the right to request a formal and impartial hearing to resolve disagreements about special education programs and services. The hearing process ensures that federal and state-mandated rules and time frames are followed. Local school districts are required to provide specific information about the hearing procedure.

STEPS FOR DUE PROCESS

1. *You can submit a written request to the superintendent of public instruction for a due process hearing.* If both parties agree to mediation, the conference must be scheduled and completed within fifteen days of the date the hearing request is filed. The hearing officer mediating the disagreement must be from outside the local school district. The hearing process generally must be completed within forty-five days, although exceptions are permitted if both parties agree. You can have access to any documents in your child's educational records, and you can be represented at the meeting by a private educational or clinical psychologist, educational therapist, psychiatrist, child advocate, or attorney who understands the academic issues and is familiar with the appropriate federal, state, and local codes. You can also refuse to place your child in any recommended program.

2. *If a school district refuses to participate in the hearing (this is unlikely) or you disagree with the decision rendered, you may appeal to the court.* Your attorney may also advise you to file a lawsuit if your school district is unresponsive to your reasonable requests. These are obviously expensive and time-consuming last resorts.

3. *You can file a complaint with the local or state superintendent that alleges that your child's school is in noncompliance with federal and state law.*

If you find yourselves in conflict with your school district, request a copy of the district's parents' rights manual. This manual, which districts are legally mandated to make available, will spell out the criteria for qualifying for diagnostic testing, the time frames for providing testing, the standards for admission to special education programs, and grievance protocols.

The decision to confront a local school district and create an adversarial situation should hinge on the urgency of your concerns. Your child's academic and vocational future and emotional well-being may hang in the balance. Although the prospect of having to confront the school district may be unpleasant, the alternative—reluctant acceptance of a flawed education program—could be disastrous for your child. You are your child's most important advocate, and you must be willing to take a stand when a stand is clearly required.

PASSIVE LEARNING

Passive learners may spend a great deal of time doing their homework, but they are simply going through the motions of studying. Because their primary concern is to complete their work quickly and effortlessly, studying translates into little more than mindlessly turning the pages of their textbooks. Mastery is seldom a priority.

Passive learners rarely establish personal goals, challenge themselves, hone their talents, or knock down the barriers that impede their progress. Because they are complacent and lack pride and self-confidence, they are usually content to submit incomplete, shoddy, or late work. They memorize facts without understanding the significance of the information and do not look beneath the surface at the underlying issues and concepts. Their inefficient study habits and superficial learning inevitably have a disastrous effect on their comprehension, retention, and test performances.

In some cases passive learning reflects poor teaching. Students become cerebrally anesthetized when they are subjected to mind-numbing lectures and required to memorize and regurgitate facts ad nauseam. An endless stream of mimeographed handouts and repetitive drilling can dull the brain of even the most highly motivated child.

Diagnosed and undiagnosed learning problems can also cause children to learn passively (see **Learning Disabilities,** page 157, **Atypical Learning Problems,** page 16, and **Underachievement,** page 312). Struggling children often acquire nonadaptive, counterproductive behavior as a defense against failure and feelings of frustration, inadequacy, and futility. Although some students with learning problems continue to study diligently, many simply give up. The chances of shutdown increase significantly when the academic deficits are disregarded or are inadequately treated. Students who feel overwhelmed by seemingly insurmountable obstacles have three basic options: They can grit their teeth and continue to plug away, they can express their frustration and anger by acting out, or they can withdraw into a shell and become passive. By not investing themselves emotionally in the learning process, they consciously or unconsciously rationalize that they are not really failing because they are not really trying.

Ironically, some passive learners are conscientious and highly motivated. They spend a great deal of time doing homework, but their efforts are scattered and nonproductive because they do not know how to study effectively.

The starting point in helping your child become an active learner is to identify *why* she is learning passively. If she has learning deficits, these deficits must be diagnosed and treated. If she does not establish personal performance goals, she must be encouraged to work toward specific, realistic, and desirable payoffs (see **Goals,** page 84). If you suspect psychological or family issues are causing her to learn passively, she must be evaluated by a competent mental health professional.

If your child does not know how to study or manage time properly, you can help her acquire these vital skills. Every child of normal intelligence can learn how to study more effectively and efficiently. With systematic instruction your child can learn *how* to activate her brain, *how* to manage her time, *how* to get organized, *how* to ask incisive questions when she reads and studies, *how* to identify key information, *how* to remember facts, and *how* to anticipate what is likely to be on tests (see **Study Skills,** page 292, and related entries).

Most children enter kindergarten with a ravenous intellectual appetite. Those who lose this natural enthusiasm are waving a red flag. Unless focused academic assistance and guidance are provided, a pattern of intellectual lethargy could persist throughout their lives.

Like unused muscles, unstimulated minds quickly atrophy. Parents who conclude their child is unmotivated and unenthusiastic about learning have justification for concern and a compelling obligation to stoke their child's intellectual furnace at home. The child who is content to coast mindlessly through school will also probably be content to coast mindlessly through life.

SUGGESTED CORRECTIVE STRATEGIES

In School

1. Ask your child's teacher to evaluate his motivation and behavior. Can he do the required work? (If he cannot, he should be tested by the school psychologist.) Does he appear depressed, withdrawn, or insecure? (If he does, he should be evaluated by a mental health professional.) Does he cave in when he encounters challenges? Does he give up when he experiences a setback or makes a mistake? Is he chronically lethargic or sleepy? (If he is, he should be examined by a physician.) Is he passive even when the material being presented is interesting? If your child appears to be manifesting symptoms of underlying educational or psychological problems that neither you nor the teacher feel competent to address, consult with the school psychologist, resource specialist, and your family physician.

2. The antidote for passive learning is to stimulate students and engage them intellectually and emotionally. Effective teachers encourage children to establish short-term and long-term goals, show them how to plan, help them understand the rationale for learning what they are being asked to learn, and demonstrate the practical application of the skills and information being taught. These are important steps in the process of encouraging active learning. If your child is learning passively, discuss your concerns with her teacher. Ask if she would be willing to work with your child on goal setting and strategic planning. Diplomatically inquire if there are ways to help your child appreciate the relevance of the skills and information being taught. It would be nonstrategic and counterproductive to make the teacher feel you are blaming her for your child's passivity. Your goal is to encourage her to make your child's educational experiences as stimulating as possible.

At Home

1. By intentionally creating opportunities for learning together, you can play a vital role in developing your child's enthusiasm for learning. An exploratory hike in the woods, a visit to the library to research a topic, a trip to a marsh to observe wildlife, an excursion to a planetarium or an aquarium, and a discussion about current events at the dinner table are important catalysts in producing active thinking and learning.

2. Encourage your child to think about *what* she is learning and studying and *why* she is being asked to learn this material. Ask thought-provoking questions such as "Why do you need to know how to do fraction problems? Let's look at a cake. Would you prefer to eat one-eighth of the cake or one-fifth?"

3. Determine your child's preferred learning modality (auditory, visual, or kinesthetic) and her preferred thinking mode (logic, feelings, concepts, or information) and encourage her to use her natural talents and preferences. Rely on your observations, the teacher's observations, and your child's own perceptions of how he learns best. (See *In Their Own Way* and *Frames of Mind*, included in the Resource List at the back of this book, for a discussion of learning styles and preferences.) Make the material as relevant as possible. For example, you might say that a child learning important historical dates is like a quarterback learning the plays, a dancer learning steps, or a violinist learning scales. If your child likes soccer, encourage her to imagine herself doing drills before a game (e.g., Constitution 1789/ articles 7/ amendments 22). Have her practice learning number facts or chemical formulas in the same way. If your child is an auditory learner, urge her to pretend she must give a speech that contains the information she must learn for her next science test. Have her practice giving the speech to an imaginary audience or to you. By hearing herself recite the information, she will be better able to remember it. The goal after sufficient practice is for her to give the speech without looking at her notes. This will indicate that she has understood and mastered the material.

4. Share your own enthusiasm for learning with your child. Do projects together that involve research or planning, and have her actively participate in the investigation process. For example, you might involve your child in the process of selecting a vacation destination and in planning what to do, where to stay, and how to get there. Discuss the pluses and minuses of driving versus taking a plane or a train. Model how you critically evaluate options and choices and encourage your child to do the same. Ask questions about the material your child is studying (e.g., "Why did Lincoln want to prevent the South from seceding?") and urge her to ask questions. Then, after providing some guidance, have her search out the answers. Remember to affirm and acknowledge her progress!

PEER PRESSURE

Children usually seek friends who share their attitudes, values, feelings, and life experiences. Successful students gravitate to other successful students, and athletes generally associate with other athletes. Students who like acting or rock music pick friends who share these interests. This principle also applies to children who are struggling academically. They typically select friends who are also struggling.

The collective energy of a peer group—whether positive or negative—affirms the self-perceptions and values of individual members. The effects of this group dynamic are especially evident in the case of students with serious learning problems who have been enrolled in special day classes for years. To protect themselves from feeling inadequate or different, these students often band together, isolate themselves from the mainstream, and develop their own interests, values, and social system. Their shared attitudes, learning deficiencies, and defense mechanisms serve as a refuge from academic demands they cannot meet (see **Learning Disabilities,** page 157, and **Psychological Problems and Psychological Overlay,** page 239).

When peer groups manifest negative energy, nonadaptive behaviors often become the standard for social acceptance by the group. Teenagers who have been in a no-win situation for years may express their frustration and anger by acting out, shutting down, resisting help, or becoming demoralized. In extreme cases they may vent their despair in destructiveness, drinking, drugs, vandalism, or theft (see **Disregard of Consequences,** page 50, and **Smart Thinking,** page 275).

Although struggling students generally seek friends who share their frustration and discouragement, there are exceptions. Some youngsters who do poorly in school remain motivated and choose friends who are successful. If, however, the gap between their performance and that of their achieving friends widens, these friendships may not endure. The contrast in performance levels may become too threatening and demoralizing.

As your child matures, his peer group's value system will have an increasing impact on his own values, especially if your child is highly impressionable or insecure. Although your conviction that your child's friends are reinforcing negative attitudes and behaviors will trigger anxiety and a desire to intervene, direct attempts to influence selection of friends often triggers resistance, resentment, and unpleasant showdowns. Under these circumstances a consultation with a skilled counselor or therapist would be a more strategic response. Ideally, the counselor will be able to help your child examine his feelings and confront the underlying issues that are influencing his attitudes, behaviors, values, and choice of friends.

Before your child can realistically be expected to develop a more positive self-image and faith in his ability to prevail in school and in life, he will need to resolve the internal conflicts that are causing his counterproductive behavior (see **Anger and Frustration,** page 1, and **Self-Esteem and Self-Confidence,** page 266). If he has learning or study skills problems, the deficits must be identified and remediated (see **Parents' Rights,** page 201). As your child begins to feel better about himself, he will probably choose friends who also have positive feelings about themselves, and your concerns about his peer group will disappear (see **Fear of Failure/Success/Competition,** page 74).

SUGGESTED CORRECTIVE STRATEGIES

In School

1. If you're concerned about your child's choice of friends, talk to his school counselor or principal and request suggestions about how to handle the situation (see **Conferencing with School Officials,** page 39). If your child is getting into trouble in school because of his associations with particular children, intervention is more urgent. Realize that the school has *no* authority to prevent your child from associating with other children on campus unless the group is considered a gang or is breaking the law, violating school codes, or causing disruptions. Many schools have recently enforced dress codes that specifically ban gang colors on campus.

At Home

1. A child's need for a sense of identity, comradeship, and group acceptance and affirmation can be compelling. For an insecure child the desire to find like-minded friends and to find a refuge in a world that may be perceived as hostile is often consuming. The group may become the child's surrogate family. If your child is struggling, he may so intensely identify with his friends that he will vehemently resist your suggestions that he disassociate himself from the group. Deciding what situations you can handle effectively at home and what situations require counseling demands a judgment call. The intensity of his group identification and his choice of friends must be factored into your assessment. If your child is refusing to listen or to look at the issues and is clearly on a collision course with reality, you will obviously need professional help. If the situation is less urgent, you might want to experiment with the **DIBS** method described on page 233. This approach may help your child examine issues and develop specific solutions to the underlying problems that may be causing him to identify with a peer group that is generating negative energy and counterproductive behaviors and attitudes. If you decide that you do need to consult a therapist, ask your pediatrician, family physician, or school psychologist for a referral.

PERFORMANCE ON STANDARDIZED TESTS

Standardized tests are designed to determine your child's level of achievement in specific skill areas. To obtain comparative statistical data and establish national norms, the tests are administered to large numbers of children of the same age and at the same grade level throughout the country. This process is called *standardization*. Below is a facsimile of typical data produced by standardized achievement tests.

The raw scores represent the total number of correct answers that a hypothetical fourth-grader had on the test. The stanine score is a statistical representation of the correct answers on a scale from one to nine and indicates the child's performance relative to the other hundreds of thousands of children who took the exam. The percentile score is another way of statistically ranking a child's performance relative to other children taking the test. In this hypothetical case,

FACSIMILE TEST RESULT REPORT

	RAW SCORE	STANINE	PERCENTILE	GRADE EQUIVALENCY
Reading Comprehension	27	4	46	3.7
Vocabulary	32	5	48	3.9
Math Concepts	37	6	54	4.3
Math Computations	35	5	50	4.0

out of every hundred children of the same age and grade level taking the test, the child scored higher in reading comprehension than forty-five children and lower than fifty-three children. (The ninety-ninth percentile is the highest statistical score that one can receive on a standardized test. A child who scores at the fiftieth percentile is considered to be approximately at grade level.) The tests usually also indicate how a child compares to children in the same geographical area. The norms on some tests are so specific that they can indicate how students attending private schools compare with other students who also attend private schools (see glossary of common testing terms under **Understanding Diagnostic Test Results,** page 316).

The standardized testing procedure is currently being closely scrutinized by educators for several reasons. Some believe that the tests do not adequately measure students' skills. Others argue that many important skills are not evaluated on the tests. There are also educators who contend that parents, administrators, teachers, and the media place far too much importance on the test results. They point out that the performance ratings of principals and local, county, and state superintendents are often based primarily on their students' test performance. To improve scores, some school districts are exerting intense pressure on teachers to prioritize teaching those skills that will be covered on the tests. This pressure to teach to the tests is causing sound educational philosophy, important educational objectives, and good teaching procedures to be subverted.

The previous arguments notwithstanding, standardized tests and comparative scores do provide valuable information that teachers, school psychologists, and resource specialists can use to identify students with deficient skills. The fourth-grader who takes a standardized exam in the second month of fourth grade (4.2) and receives a score of 3.2 (third grade, second month) in reading comprehension is comprehending one year below grade level. Ideally, such a child would be targeted for learning assistance.

It is both ironic and sad that one of the most valuable applications of standardized test scores—the identification of children requiring remedial help—is being disregarded by many fiscally troubled school districts. Although the learning deficits of a child testing one year below grade level *should* be addressed, assistance is rarely provided when a student's skills are less than *two* years below grade level (see **Learning Disabilities,** page 157, **Underachievement,** page 312, **Individual Educational Program [IEP],** page 126, and **Mainstreaming and Special Day Classes,** page 173). In many schools children in the gray area slip through gaping holes in the diagnostic screen and muddle through twelve years of school. These children qualify for help only when their problems become incapacitating. By this point the educational and psychological damage may already be irreversible (see **Underachievement,** page 312).

Children scoring below the norm (usually below the 50th percentile) may have specific or nonspecific academic deficits that range from subtle to severe. The deficits may be attributable to poor teaching, learning problems, family problems, emotional problems, and/or environmental factors. Although test performance can be skewed by test anxiety and distractibility, the scores generally offer a relatively reliable profile of students' skills. Children who test below grade level on standardized tests, who receive poor grades on teacher-designed tests, and who struggle in class are prime candidates for more extensive diagnostic testing.

The current testing procedures may be inadequate, and the way in which test scores are utilized may be flawed, but reality dictates that children learn how to accommodate themselves to the testing system. Students will be required to take standardized tests throughout their education. Those who want to go to college, win scholarships, select training programs in the military, go to graduate school, pass professional and vocational licensing exams, and earn promotions must figure out how to get the best possible scores on these tests. (*Please note:* Students with *documented* learning disabilities can apply to take untimed college entrance exams [SATs]. Consult your child's school counselor for details.)

SUGGESTED CORRECTIVE STRATEGIES

In School

1. If your child is scoring more than one year below grade level, request a diagnostic evaluation by the school psychologist or resource specialist. If your child doesn't qualify for assistance, you may need to provide tutorial support at home (see **Reading Comprehension,** page 250, **Spelling Problems,** page 283, **Math,** page 178, etc., for specific remediation strategies). If you feel the problem requires professional assistance, consider hiring a tutor or enrolling your child at a private learning center.

2. If she has difficulty with the test-taking procedure because of concentration deficits, anxiety, or visual accuracy deficits, ask her teacher or resource specialist if your child can take some practice tests to improve her confidence and reduce any phobias, fears, or procedural problems she might have. If appropriate, she might take some of these practice tests at home (see additional suggestions below).

At Home

1. If your child's scores on standardized tests are not consistent with her performance in class, test anxiety or test phobia could be the culprit. Some children "tense up" when taking tests (see **Test Anxiety,** page 304). Showing your child some basic relaxation techniques could reduce this stress factor. Suggest that she close her eyes and that she see herself confidently taking the test and doing well on it. Urge her to *imprint* the success picture in her mind. This preview, which requires only a few seconds, can significantly lessen the anticipatory panic some children experience while waiting for a test to be handed out. Also urge your child to close her eyes for several seconds and take two or three deep breaths before starting to answer the questions. This breathing procedure should help her relax and reduce her anxiety. The key is for your child to program herself with positive expectations (see **Test Anxiety,** page 304). You may also want to refer to the books included in the Resource List at the back of the book for more suggestions.

2. Children with concentration problems usually also have difficulty with standardized tests. If your child forgets to leave a blank line on her answer sheet when she cannot answer a question, she will mark all subsequent answers in the wrong place. Her scores will also be skewed if she becomes distracted while taking the test. There are no "quick fixes" for concentration problems. Discuss with your child the value of concentrating while taking tests. Explain the importance of matching the correct line on the answer sheet to the question she is answering. You might brainstorm together how she could discipline herself to focus on this important detail. Ask the teacher for a blank answer sheet or make one up yourself to make the demonstration more relevant. The teacher might even be willing to give you a standardized test at your child's grade level that has subsequently been updated and is no longer being used by the school district. You could use this to practice the procedure for accurately filling out a test booklet or an answer sheet. Demonstrate how placing one answer on the wrong line can cause all subsequent answers to be wrong. Then experiment with ways to make sure the answer sheet is marked accurately. Your child might, for instance, cover all but the line she is working on with her test booklet and move the edge down one line each time she answers a question (see **Attention Deficit Disorder,** page 5, and **Attention to Details,** page 12, for a description of the symptoms of concentration problems and for suggestions about how to improve her concentration accuracy).

3. If your child has a tracking problem (reads inaccurately and loses her place), she will probably have a difficult time filling out her answer sheets properly. Because her eyes move erratically, she will tend to lose her place and will be at a significant disadvantage when taking standardized tests and marking answer sheets. The practice procedure described above could be very beneficial (see **Dyslexia,** page 58, and **Inaccurate Copying,** page 113, for a description of visual tracking problems and for suggestions about how to improve your child's visual accuracy).

PHONICS

During the last thirty-five years educators and textbook publishers have debated the pluses and minuses of teaching children to read phonetically or by sight. The phonics method teaches children the sounds of individual letters and combinations of letters and has them use these sounds to decode words. Advocates of this approach contend that children who can apply phonics rules and conventions possess an invaluable tool they can use to read most words in the English language.

Proponents of the sight approach contend that many words in our language do not conform to consistent phonetic rules (see **Nonphonetic Words,** page 191). Because of these exceptions, they argue that reading should not be taught phonetically. They also argue that the process of sounding out each word is cumbersome and reduces reading speed. When teachers carefully control the difficulty level of newly introduced words and provide ample practice, most children can quickly learn to recognize by sight most words with ease and quickly achieve reading fluency.

Children who have no underlying perceptual deficits (see **Dyslexia,** page 58) can learn to read using either the phonetic or the sight method and can usually decipher and remember most words after one or two exposures. Only the most difficult words require extra effort. Most of these natural readers will rarely remember as adults how they were taught.

In contrast, poor readers never forget their struggle to decipher words. These children are typically found in the lowest reading groups in their classes. For them reading aloud is a nightmare. The embarrassment they experience each day may cause permanent emotional scars and could trigger a profound aversion to reading that may persist throughout their lives. Unfortunately, many poor readers often erroneously conclude that they are "dumb."

The instructional pendulum currently appears to have swung back from the sight reading approach emphasized in many textbooks during the 1970s and early 1980s to a phonetic approach, and most elementary school reading programs now incorporate this method. The phonics method involves two steps: word attack and blending. Children attack (sound out) each phoneme and then link or blend this phoneme to subsequent phonemes.

Problems with phonics are usually linked to specific decoding deficits in one or more of the following areas: visual tracking (seeing words accurately and perceiving syllables in the proper sequence—see **Dyslexia,** page 58), visual memory (remembering what is seen—see page 326), auditory discrimination (hearing the difference between sounds—see page 19), or auditory memory (remembering what is heard—see page 22). These deficits are primary symptoms of a learning disability and can erect formidable obstacles for children irrespective of the reading method the teacher selects. Chronic inaccurate reading that involves letter, word, and number reversals, letter and word omissions, and transpositions is symptomatic of dyslexia.

As a general rule children with reading problems respond best to a phonetic approach. Because of the previously mentioned phonetic exceptions, however, these children will need to learn to recognize some words by sight (e.g., *two, could, lieutenant, rough, buoyant, although*).

Children with significant reading and decoding problems may have difficulty with both the phonetic and the sight methods. During the last twenty years many innovative techniques have been developed to help these children. The methods usually involve multisensory instruction in which children are taught how to utilize alternative learning modalities to compensate for their deficits (e.g., Orton-Gillingham method, Slingerland method, neurological impress method, neurolinguistic programming, Lindamood Auditory Discrimination in Depth Program). Talented teachers, resource specialists, tutors, and educational therapists who encounter students with significant and resistant reading problems will experiment with different approaches until they find one that works (see **Dyslexia,** page 58, **Auditory Discrimination,** page 19, **Auditory Memory,** page 22, and **Visual Memory,** page 326, for a description of some of the methods referred to above).

SUGGESTED CORRECTIVE STRATEGIES

In School

1. (ES) Ask your child's teacher to alert you if she observes that he is struggling with phonics. If he is having difficulty, ask if she can provide additional help in class or assign supplemental materials for use at home. (Remedial classroom materials are included in the Resource List at the back of the book.)

2. If the teacher indicates that your child has problems with phonics, request that he be evaluated by the school psychologist or resource specialist to determine if he has a perceptual dysfunction. If the tests reveal auditory memory, auditory discrimination, visual memory, visual tracking, word attack, and/or blending difficulties, request that the resource or reading specialist provide remedial assistance (see **Parents' Rights,** page 201, and refer to the entries that describe your child's specific deficits).

At Home

1. (ES) Ask your child's teacher to indicate your child's current reading level and ask her (or the librarian) to suggest interesting and appropriate books or materials that you and he might read together. These materials should initially be slightly *below* your child's "comfort" reading level. Read a sentence to your child and then ask

him to read the same sentence. This modeling procedure is intentionally designed to set your child up to read more successfully. Patiently help him sound out challenging words. Be supportive and affirming. Use a pencil eraser or your finger to divide the word into syllables. (Your ultimate objective is for your child to divide words into syllables on his own.) Once your child can sound out the word, help him blend the syllables together. Have him write difficult words on index cards for later review.

2. (ES) Set up a system in which each difficult word that your child can read at the end of the session is worth a point, with the points to be applied to an agreed-on reward such as a special toy or a trip to the zoo. For each word he can still read at the end of the week, he could be given bonus points. As your child's reading fluency develops, increase the number of sentences that you read before he begins to read.

3. (ES) When it seems appropriate, experiment by *not* reading the sentences first. Recognize that by not modeling how to read the sentences you are withdrawing a security blanket. Remove the blanket slowly and be sensitive if your child becomes anxious. As he progresses, slowly increase the difficulty of the materials. Ask the teacher to reassess your child's reading level periodically. Don't be surprised if he struggles with words he has already seemingly mastered. Children with reading problems frequently need many exposures to words before they achieve mastery. If you find yourself losing your patience, quit for the day. If you chronically lose your patience, do not work with your child. Hire a tutor or enroll your child at a private reading center. Communicating frustration or anger will only compound your child's negative associations with reading and further undermine his tenuous self-confidence. To admit that you cannot be your child's tutor is *not* an admission of your failure as a parent!

4. (ES) Ask the teacher to lend you a copy of the Dolch list, which contains words grouped according to grade level. With some creativity you and your child can make a game out of learning these words. For example, put the words on flash cards and award points for every word your child identifies. Or write a clue on the back of each card that tells where a small prize—such as a cookie or a dime—is located. Each time your child can read a word, turn over the card and help him read the clue. After he has enough clues, he can look for the prize. Another graded list you might find useful is the Key Word Inventory (see the Resource List at the back of the book). Other supplemental remedial reading materials that focus on developing phonics skills that you might

want to examine at your local teacher supply store or order directly from the publisher are also included in the Resource List.

5. (J/HS) Years of struggling often cause teenagers with basic phonics problems to become very sensitive about their reading deficits. Because they feel inadequate and vulnerable, they may deny they have a problem despite overwhelming evidence to the contrary. Penetrating this defensive wall can be very challenging. Your child might agree to let you help him read a popular teen or music magazine. You might offer to buy him a subscription to *Mad* or *Sports Illustrated* and, if he agrees, you could spend ten minutes each evening reading it together, using the techniques described above. Don't be surprised, however, if your teenager refuses your help. You cannot force him to accept assistance. Assure him that if he decides later that he wants help from you or a tutor, it will be available. He may be more receptive if you explain that practice is essential to improving performance in any endeavor. Be patient, supportive, and affirming. Suggest that he make a list of difficult words and use the Dolch list or the Key Word Inventory (see above) to supplement that list.

6. If your child is enrolled in a remedial program, periodically consult with the resource specialist to coordinate your efforts, assess progress, and identify problem areas. If your child does not qualify for help in school and you feel assistance is necessary, you may want to assert your rights to the school authorities (see **Parents' Rights,** page 201). If you believe your child requires more help than the school can provide, consider hiring a qualified tutor or enrolling your child in a private reading or learning disabilities center.

PLANNING AHEAD

As children progress into the upper grades, their academic success hinges increasingly on their ability to plan and organize effectively. To write a first-rate history term paper, they must allocate time for library research, taking notes, checking footnotes, preparing a bibliography, writing a first and final draft, editing and proofreading. If they are studying for an exam, they must budget time to reread the assigned chapters in their textbooks, review their notes, and answer practice test questions (see **Time Management,** page 308, and **Preparing for Tests,** page 225).

Conscientious students face a classic dilemma: a seemingly infinite number of obligations and limited time and energy. In addition to their academic responsibilities, these students must find time for chores, paper routes, Scout meetings, piano lessons, part-time jobs, and after-school sports. Youngsters who cannot juggle these commitments are going to experience stress and, perhaps, marginal grades (see **Smart Thinking,** page 275, **Preparing for Tests,** page 225, and **Grades,** page 89).

One of the distinguishing characteristics of the good student is that she *anticipates* what must be done to complete her assignments successfully. She establishes goals and priorities (see pages 84 and 228), creates a study schedule, and develops a practical strategy for attaining her objectives. This procedure requires focused effort, efficient use of resources, and an appreciation for the principles of cause and effect (see **Disregard of Consequences,** page 50). The ability to plan effectively usually produces rewards that justify the extra effort: good grades, pride, self-confidence, and free time.

Children who do not plan ahead are typically in a constant crisis. They do not finish their homework. They leave their book reports to the last minute. They put off studying until the night before an exam. Their grades predictably suffer, and the resulting frustration and demoralization invariably have a negative impact on everyone in the family (see **Procrastination,** page 235, **Incomplete Assignments,** page 121, and **Inadequate Study Time,** page 116).

Children who get into the habit of planning do so automatically and unconsciously. They make a mental checklist of things to do for an excursion to the beach. They think about what they want to pack for a vacation. They realize that long-term projects, such as writing a term paper involving many steps and components demand more careful planning. Before beginning they list the required steps and target dates, and they check off each step when it is completed.

If you want your child to acquire good planning skills, you must provide repeated opportunities for her to practice the procedures. Once she realizes that planning will make her life easier, allow her to attain her goals, and create more free time, she will integrate planning and organization into her daily modus operandi without having to be coerced by you or her teachers. The payoffs will be her incentive, and in time the procedure will become a firmly entrenched habit.

SUGGESTED CORRECTIVE STRATEGIES

In School

1. If you conclude your child has not developed good planning skills and you believe other students in his class may not have either, ask the teacher if she can incorporate planning activities into the curriculum. The students could systematically plan a field trip, a class party, or a community service project. They might also cooperatively develop a plan for studying for a science final exam or for writing a term paper, with all students encouraged to use the plan. Each student could then privately compare his or her test results with previous test results.

At Home

1. Encourage your child to take the following steps:

■ Apply planning skills to real-life situations (e.g., "What steps must be planned for the picnic?"—see **Goals,** page 84, **Priorities,** page 228, and **Time Management,** page 308).

■ Experiment with different types of plans (e.g., "Let's create a schedule, a flowchart, and a check-off list and see which works best").

■ Analyze why certain plans are more successful than others (e.g., "The plan for fixing your bike didn't work. What went wrong?"—see **Smart Thinking,** page 275, **Disregard of Consequences,** page 50, and **Problem Solving,** page 231).

■ Incorporate planning into different contexts (e.g., "What needs to be packed for the camping trip?").

2. For more specific suggestions about how to develop your child's planning skills, refer to **Disorganization,** page 46, **Goals,** page 84, **Priorities,** page 228, **Inadequate Study Time,** page 116, **Procrastination,** page 235, **Recording Assignments,** page 258, **Smart Thinking,** page 275, **Time Management,** page 308, **Problem Solving,** page 231, and **Preparing for Tests,** page 225.

PREPARING FOR TESTS

Children who know how to prepare efficiently for exams represent a relatively small and elite minority. Many children never learn fundamental test preparation principles. Convinced in advance that they will "bomb" the test, their expectations of disaster usually become self-fulfilling. These children frequently become test phobic (see **Test Anxiety,** page 304).

In preparing for exams, students must be able to identify important information, develop a system for comprehending and recalling this information, and anticipate what questions their teachers are likely to ask. Test-wise students search for patterns in previous tests and make note of their teachers' clues and comments. This detective work helps them identify what their teachers consider important (see **Smart Thinking,** page 275, **Study Skills,** page 292, **Identifying Important Information,** page 110, **Visual Memory,** page 326, **Auditory Memory,** page 22, and **Memorizing Information,** page 182).

Test-wise students also figure out—through trial and error—how they learn best, and they adjust their study procedures to their preferred or natural learning style. The child who learns best visually would create graphic mental pictures (see **Visual Memory,** page 326). A kinesthetic learner might design flowcharts, put data on index cards, or use three-dimensional physical props, models, and other manipulatives. An auditory learner would probably recite information aloud or subvocalize the information so he can hear it in his mind (see **Auditory Memory,** page 22). This utilization of natural talents and preferred learning styles is vital to being able to recall information.

Some educators might recoil from the suggestion that students be encouraged to "psych out" their teachers, but the accuracy of their test-taking "radar" is one of the features that differentiates successful students from less successful students (see **Smart Thinking,** page 275).

The first step in helping your child develop more effective test preparation skills is to determine if he has any underlying academic deficiencies. Learning disabilities, specific skills deficits (e.g., poor reading comprehension), and inadequate study skills (e.g., poor notetaking or chronic disorganization) can obviously undermine any child's test preparation efficiency (see **Learning Disabilities,** page 157, **Underachievement,** page 312, **Atypical Learning Problems,** page 16, and **Study Skills,** page 292). Family and emotional problems can also have a direct impact on test performance* (see **Psychological Problems and Psychological Overlay,** page 239).

If you conclude your child has no underlying learning problems and has simply never been taught how to prepare for tests, it is vital that he acquire these skills. Knowing how to prepare effectively for tests is one of the most important academic resources your child can possess.

SUGGESTED CORRECTIVE STRATEGIES

In School

1. If you suspect there are other children in your child's class who do not know how to prepare adequately for tests, diplomatically suggest to the teacher that test preparation procedures be taught to the entire class. The teacher might announce that a test will be given on a specific date and might identify the material that will be covered (e.g., Chapter 3, Units 1–3, in the science textbook). The class could then brainstorm a strategy for preparing for the test. After the discussion the steps could be written on the chalkboard (e.g., read the assigned material, take notes, review class notes, make up practice questions). Each child would then write in his or her notebook the grade he or she is aiming for on the test. (This should not be announced publicly.) The class could create a priority list of tasks that need to be done and could design a study schedule (see **Planning Ahead,** page 222 and **Time Management,** page 308). The children would then break up into small groups and study together (cooperative learning). Ideally, these groups should be comprised of "good" students and "poor" students so that the better students could serve as models for their less successful classmates. The students in each group should ask each other questions and make up a practice test. The groups might exchange their practice tests. The procedure could be used by the class to prepare for several tests. The objective is for students to practice and internalize the procedures so that they become automatic.

At Home

1. Ask your child what material in his textbook and notes is likely to be

---

* This process of systematically ruling out potential causal factors to determine the actual source of a problem is called *differential diagnosis.*

covered on the next test. Review his previous tests with him. Work together to make up a practice test. (To do so, you will need to review the assigned material.) Take turns asking each other questions. If your child cannot answer a question, look up the answer together. Be careful not to sound judgmental or disappointed and do not unwittingly create the impression that you are competing with your child. Be sure to point out that even with this preparation there is no guarantee that he will "ace" the test. The objective is for you to model effective test preparation techniques. If he does not get a good grade on the test, analyze together what went wrong. The ability to learn from mistakes and bounce back from setbacks is vital in developing your child's emotional resilience and analytical thinking skills.

Once your child appears to have mastered basic test-preparation procedures, begin to withdraw from your supportive role. It is important that your child not become dependent on your help (see **Learned Helplessness,** page 152).

2. Encourage your child to make up practice tests whenever possible. Explain that by doing so he will begin to think like a teacher and that this will help him anticipate what is likely to be on the next test.

For more suggestions, refer to **Goals,** page 84, **Disorganization,** page 46, **Inadequate Study Time,** page 116, **Monitoring Homework,** page 185, **Notetaking,** page 193, **Planning Ahead,** page 222, **Priorities,** page 228, **Smart Thinking,** page 275, **Memorizing Information,** page 182, and **Time Management,** page 308.

PRIORITIES

Successful students realize they must rank their responsibilities in order of importance and urgency (see **Smart Thinking,** page 275, and **Goals,** page 84). They may not always be consciously aware that they are creating a hierarchy, but they intuitively apply prioritization principles whenever they are faced with tasks that require careful planning and execution.

The ability to establish priorities is a requisite to strategic planning, effective time management, and efficient study skills. Successful students define their long- and short-term goals, and their strategy for achieving those goals incorporates a logical order for doing the necessary interim steps (see **Planning Ahead,** page 222, and **Time Management,** page 308). They realize that getting an A on their weekly Spanish quiz significantly improves their chances of getting the A they want in the course, and they consequently make studying for the quizzes a higher priority than watching their favorite sitcoms on TV.

The need to establish priorities often forces children to make difficult choices. Forgoing an afternoon playing basketball in favor of studying for a biology exam demands self-discipline. The child who is willing to suspend immediate gratification is clearly prioritizing the long-range payoff—a good grade on the test. This future-oriented thinking is a primary trait that differentiates the achieving child from the underachieving or nonachieving child.

The abilities to prioritize, plan (see page 222), manage time (see page 308), and establish goals (see page 84) are intrinsically linked. Strategic youngsters intuitively recognize that these skills are vital to attaining the payoffs they covet. The systematic application of the procedures helps them focus their physical and intellectual energy and creates productive order in their lives. In contrast, less strategic children are usually overwhelmed by challenging assignments and projects because they cannot develop a practical plan for moving efficiently from point A to point B to point C (see **Problem Solving,** page 231, **Planning Ahead,** page 222, and **Learned Helplessness,** page 152).

The ability to rank academic responsibilities is vital in upper-level classes. A high school student may have a science term paper due in three weeks, a French mid-term due in three days, and math problems due the next day. If he does not know how to organize these tasks and responsibilities, he is clearly at risk academically.

SUGGESTED CORRECTIVE STRATEGIES

In School

1. If you feel your child and his classmates have not been properly taught how to establish priorities, discuss this issue with the teacher. Elementary and junior high school teachers may be more receptive to taking "valuable time" away from basic academic instruction to teach this skill than high school teachers. Perhaps if you diplomatically propose how the principles of prioritization can be integrated into content area instruction, upper-level teachers might be more willing to teach the skill. As a class activity students might list the steps involved in writing a term paper and number the steps in the order of priority. When broaching these issues, you must realize that some teachers may consider your suggestions inappropriate. Many high school teachers would argue that students should *already* know how to prioritize by the time they enter ninth grade. This is true, of course, but it is also true that many children have not mastered this fundamental skill. Be prepared for negative reactions and resistance to your suggestions. Consider in advance how you might best discuss the issues and re-

spond to objections without alienating or antagonizing the teacher.

2. (ES) You might suggest to your child's teacher that she have the class plan a field trip or a class party. Children could brainstorm the steps and make up a list of tasks and responsibilities in logical order of priority.

At Home

1. The first step in teaching your child how to prioritize is to demonstrate how establishing priorities can make life easier and free up time for enjoyable pursuits. Suggest that your child have a party and that he be responsible for planning it. Brainstorm the steps involved and the tasks that must be completed. List the food and party favors that need to be purchased. Have him rank the tasks and purchases in order of priority. Discuss his reasons for his ranking. Have him commit to completing specific tasks by specified dates once his list of priorities is established (see **Goals,** page 84, **Planning Ahead,** page 222, and **Time Management,** page 308).

2. Play prioritizing games with your child. Have him imagine the following scenario: "You are on a big boat that hits a submerged reef. The captain tells you the boat will sink in ten minutes. Let's list the things you might put into the lifeboat and then number the list in the order of greatest importance or priority."

3. Review the steps in writing a research report or term paper. Have your child list all of the tasks and number them in the appropriate sequence. This order can vary somewhat. The bibliography might be the last step or one of the last steps. Library research, notetaking, and writing a first draft would obviously be at the top of the list, and final proofreading would obviously be done after the last draft is written.

4. With your child's active participation, create a list of steps required to get into college, make the Olympic hockey team, win an award at the 4-H Club, or earn a black belt in karate. Have her number the steps in order of priority or importance. The goal of these activities is to make the prioritization procedure an ingrained habit that your child will use automatically whenever she confronts a challenge or a problem.*

---

* See *Getting Smarter* and *Smarter Kids,* included in the "Study Skills" section of the Resource List at the back of the book.

PROBLEM SOLVING

Children must learn how to handle problems if they are ultimately to become fully functional, independent adults. A child who cannot deal with occasional teasing or an argument with a friend and who cannot cope with challenges, setbacks, mistakes, and occasional criticism or rejection is clearly vulnerable.

Some children are intuitive problem solvers. They also make mistakes and suffer setbacks, but they overcome these glitches because they have discovered how to break problems down into manageable parts. Their mastery of this "divide and conquer" principle allows them to avoid the "wheel spinning" characteristic of youngsters who become overwhelmed whenever they are confronted with a complex, challenging problem (see **Smart Thinking,** page 275).

Observing a child with natural problem-solving skills can create a false impression. The child may appear to respond so effortlessly that she seems to be operating without a strategy. Like a well-trained gymnast who reacts automatically and does not appear to be thinking about the complexity of her routine, the effective problem solver is not always consciously aware of her own analytical process. Although she may take some shortcuts, she nevertheless uses the following classic five-step problem-solving procedure:

1. *Collect the data.* **("It's obvious that I'll have to do a great deal of library research to write this report.")**

2. *Compare the data with what is already known.* **("The report is similar to the one I wrote first semester. I'll have to take notes on index cards, write down quotations and footnotes, organize the index cards, write my first draft, edit, write a final draft, proofread at least two times, and do a bibliography.")**

3. *Develop a plan that utilizes the data effectively.* **("The teacher described the specific steps for formatting the report in the handout. I'll check off each step after I complete it.")**

4. *Implement the plan.* ("I'll begin my library research tomorrow. I'll complete the first draft by next Tuesday and the final draft by the following Thursday. It will be ready by the Friday due date.")

5. *Determine if the plan works and develop an alternative plan if it doesn't.* ("If I fall behind schedule, I'll have to make adjustments. If I have problems, I'll talk to the teacher or ask my mother for help.")

Children who utilize this analytical method have a distinct advantage over their less strategic-minded classmates. They think tactically, establish goals, and consider the pluses and minuses of their decisions and actions. They learn from mistakes, bounce back from setbacks, and make expedient adjustments to the existing conditions. They link cause and effect and apply "divide and conquer" principles. When handling problems and challenges, they persevere. They achieve. They radiate self-confidence.

For complex psychological reasons, some parents feel they have a responsibility to insulate their child from problems. They may attempt to take ownership of every challenge or difficulty their child encounters, or they may try to "run interference" and deflect every potential glitch or upset. This need to offer constant protection from life's realities usually signals that the parents are excessively fearful or that they need to be in control. Their behavior can have disastrous psychological implications and deny their child vital opportunities to develop her own problem-solving resources. Overly protected children rarely become independent, self-sufficient adults and rarely acquire healthy self-esteem (see **Learned Helplessness,** page 152, and **Self-Esteem and Self-Confidence,** page 266).

SUGGESTED CORRECTIVE STRATEGIES

In School

1. If your child is not solving problems effectively, ask the teacher if the entire class might benefit from learning how to break down problems into manageable pieces. Students could use the five problem-solving steps to deal with a range of issues that affect the entire class. They might work together (cooperative learning—see **Studying with Friends,** page 296) and practice applying the steps and developing problem-solving strategies. For example, the class might examine how a complex, difficult assignment could be completed by the due date. The procedure could be reinforced by having students solve specific aspects of the problem individually and then share and compare their solutions with their classmates. Students who struggle in this area could be teamed with children who possess intuitive problem-solving abilities and could model their modus operandi.

2. Not being able to identify problems accurately is a major barrier to problem solving. Children often confuse the *symptoms* of the problem with the *source* of the problem. The following DIBS Problem-Identification/Problem-Solving Method can be applied to a wide range of problems encountered in class:

Define:
> Teacher: "I have a problem. When I leave the classroom, work stops and many of you begin to misbehave."

Investigate:
> Teacher: "Let's look at what is causing this problem. Any ideas?"
> Students: "Letting off steam." "Some kids like to misbehave." "We never get to talk to each other in class." "It's fun to get away with something."

Brainstorm:
> Teacher: "Let's brainstorm as many ideas as we can to solve my problem."
> Students: "Three minutes each period of free talk time." "An honor system in which everyone behaves and is quiet when the teacher leaves the room." "A class monitor who will report children who misbehave."

Select:
> Teacher: "Let's select one or two ideas to try out, and we'll see if the solution works. How about three minutes of free talk time if the class completes the work that was assigned?"

The DIBS method can be applied whenever the entire class or an individual student in the class is experiencing a problem. Issues might include teasing, cheating, sharing responsibilities, etc. The key to making the system work is to identify the problem accurately and to identify who "owns" the problem. This type of strategic problem solving can provide youngsters with a powerful tool for dealing with life's inevitable upsets. (See *Smarter Kids,* included in the Resource List at the back of the book.)

At Home

1. The following guidelines will help your child acquire effective problem-solving skills:

- *Link the problem-solving process with real-life situations.* ("How can you get your older brother to stop teasing you?")

- *Encourage experimentation with different strategies.* ("Could you try to walk away when he teases you? Could you ask him to stop without getting angry?")

- *Encourage critical assessment about why some strategies are successful and some are unsuccessful.* ("The approach you used apparently has not worked. Any ideas about why it didn't work? Do you think your brother understands that you truly want to end the teasing and that you are also willing to make some changes in your behavior?")

- *Encourage the analysis of strategies described in school materials.* (E.g., "Why did General Washington's plan for winning the war prove effective?")

- *Encourage incorporation of strategic skills into personal planning.* (E.g., "If I want Dad to let me spend the weekend at my friend's house, I'd better get all my chores done by Friday.")

2. Encourage your child to apply the DIBS method to difficulties encountered in school and at home. For example, she could use the system to find a solution to the following problems: a sibling who borrows her possessions without asking, a fight with a friend, a dilemma about how to do something with a friend and find time to study for a test or do assigned chores, or a friend who is lying, stealing, or revealing secrets. Remember that it is often hard for children (and adults!) to define a problem accurately and differentiate it from the symptoms and causes of the problem. Much practice is required before a child might be able to say "I'm upset because I think my friend Megan lied to me!" rather than "I'm mad because Megan is dumb!" (For additional suggestions, see **Smart Thinking,** page 275, and **Critical Thinking,** page 42.)

PROCRASTINATION

The child who chronically procrastinates will invariably generate stress and unpleasantness that affects everyone in the family. Although the child's exasperated parents may believe the behavior is intentionally designed to torment them, the actual explanation is usually more complex.

Procrastination can generally be linked to one or more of the following underlying factors:

- Poor academic skills

- Poor time management skills

- Inadequate goal orientation

- Disorganization

- Disinterest

- Poor study skills

- Laziness

- The desire for negative attention

- Low self-esteem

- Inadequate appreciation of cause-and-effect principles

Like their adult counterparts, children usually procrastinate when they want to avoid unpleasant, boring, difficult, or time-consuming jobs. Repeated negative school experiences must inevitably damage self-confidence, undermine motivation, and cause phobic reactions to homework and studying. Youngsters with learning problems can be especially adept at evading their schoolwork. By procrastinating, a struggling child can temporarily deflect his pain and frustration. If he has a reading problem, he will probably put off reading a book for his book report until the last minute. If he has language arts deficits, he will avoid writing his science term paper, and if he has concentration problems, he will avoid academic tasks that require focused, sustained effort (see **Language Arts [Essays and Reports],** page 141, **Time Management,** page 308, **Planning Ahead,** page 222, and **Attention Deficit Disorder,** page 5).

Avoiding schoolwork can be an appealing path of least resistance to a demoralized child. The excuses, rationalizations, and complaints that the work is boring or irrelevant are obvious defense mechanisms designed to protect the child from feeling inadequate and hopeless. By procrastinating, he can pretend that the work doesn't exist. Denial serves as his last line of defense.

Some children procrastinate because they are not in the habit of establishing personal goals. These children typically learn and think passively and are usually described by their exasperated parents and teachers as lazy and unmotivated. Lacking a sense of purpose and direction, they are content to coast through school and life in cerebral neutral (see **Goals,** page 84, **Passive Learning,** page 205, and **Underachievement,** page 312).

Procrastination may also be linked to a poorly developed appreciation of the principles of cause and effect. Children who don't consider the consequences of their actions usually deny the obvious connection between their poor performance in school and their irresponsible behavior (see **Disregard of Consequences,** page 50, and **Behavior and Performance Guidelines,** page 26).

Low self-esteem and poor self-confidence can also cause children to procrastinate. The insecure child who is terrified by the prospect of failing and having to confront his deficiencies may feel unconsciously compelled to avoid challenges and responsibilities. He may rationalize his behavior with such excuses as "The teacher didn't assign any homework," "I did it in school," "Don't worry; I'll get it done," and "It's boring!" After convincing himself that the self-deceptions are true, he will deny all evidence to the contrary. The illusion that everything is okay inevitably shatters when he gets his report card.

Procrastination may also be linked to poor study and organizational skills. A child may have good basic academic skills but may not know how to plan projects, prioritize steps, and budget time. Her late and incomplete work reflects the fact that she does not understand how to create order in her life (see **Study Skills,** page 292, **Planning Ahead,** page 222, **Disorganization,** page 46, **Priorities,** page 228, **Incomplete Assignments,** page 121, and **Time Management,** page 308).

In some cases chronic procrastination is symptomatic of emotional or family problems. A depressed, angry, or resentful child may use nonadaptive behavior as a weapon against his concerned parents. This weapon can be especially potent when his parents highly value conscientiousness, effort, punctuality, and achievement. The child who resorts to this form of passive aggression because he feels that this is the only way he can safely vent his unhappiness and anger or get attention requires professional counseling.

SUGGESTED CORRECTIVE STRATEGIES

In School

1. If you recognize that your child is procrastinating, explore strategies with the teacher that might motivate him to get his work done. Elementary school teachers are usually more than happy to work with parents on correcting their students' self-defeating behavior. Junior or senior high school teachers may be less willing because they see far more children each day and have less time to devote to individual students. Moreover, many teachers in the upper grades feel that it is the student's responsibility to get his work done and that they are not obligated to "spoon feed" children who procrastinate. If you point out to the teacher the underlying causes for your child's counterproductive behavior and suggest a collaborative effort to reorient your child, the teacher may be more willing to cooperate, assuming the plan does not require a great deal of extra work on the teacher's part.

2. To help you monitor your child, ask the teacher to complete a daily assignment monitoring checklist. The school may already have such a checklist. If not, use the one on page 187. Modify the checklist so that it focuses on your child's particular behavioral deficits.

3. If you believe your child is procrastinating because of specific academic or study skills deficits, ask that he be evaluated by the Child Study Team (see page 111 for definition) or the school psychologist. If he does not qualify for testing or assistance, you may need to consider private tutoring, educational therapy, or enrollment at a private learning center (see **Learning Disabilities,** page 157, **Underachievement,** page 312, and **Atypical Learning Problems,** page 16).

4. (J/HS) If your child is chronically procrastinating in school, a conference with his guidance counselor is critical. Counselors constantly deal with this problem, and they often have a systematic method for monitoring and motivating students who procrastinate. Many high schools, however, do

not have such programs and are rather cavalier about providing support for underachieving, unmotivated students. If this is the case at your child's school, you may need to seek the counseling services of an independent therapist. Ask your pediatrician, family physician, or the school principal for a referral.

At Home

1. If it is apparent from the teacher's feedback, report cards, and your own observations that your child has acquired the habit of procrastinating, you must attempt to identify the reasons for the behavior. Your response to a child who procrastinates because of poor academic skills should be different from your response to a lazy or passively aggressive child. The student evaluation forms on pages 160 and 163 will help you determine if your child has underlying academic deficits or a specific learning disability. If you are able to identify specific deficits, refer to the appropriate entries in this book for suggested corrective strategies.

2. If your child is procrastinating because he does not establish goals or does not know how to think tactically, prioritize, manage time, or plan ahead, refer to these entries for specific suggestions.

3. Helping your child create a study schedule is vital if he chronically procrastinates. These guidelines will provide structure and should significantly improve your child's schoolwork. Actively involve your child in the process of creating the study schedule. With the teacher's input you may decide that seventy-five minutes should be the average study time each evening. Encouraging your child to participate in the process of designing his schedule and having him commit to the times when he agrees to study is a critical part of the process of empowering your child. This active participation encourages responsibility, produces less resistance and resentment, and discourages passive learning. Establish the parameters, but be prepared to compromise when appropriate (see **Time Management,** page 308, **Priorities,** page 228, **Goals,** page 84, **Monitoring Homework,** page 185, and **Learned Helplessness,** page 152).

PSYCHOLOGICAL PROBLEMS AND PSYCHOLOGICAL OVERLAY

Children perceive and respond to their world on two levels: the neurological and the psychological. These two levels overlap, and problems in one area often trigger problems in the other.

The dyslexic child who cannot read accurately or remember what she is reading is experiencing difficulty on the neurological (sensory) level of perception (see **Dyslexia,** page 58). If she becomes increasingly frustrated and demoralized and concludes the school battle is hopeless, her confidence, desire, and motivation will erode. She may simply tolerate school, or she may hate it. As her frustration mounts and her self-confidence deteriorates, she may compensate for her feelings of inadequacy by acting out, giving up, retreating into a defensive shell, or becoming resistant, hostile, irresponsible, or manipulative. The sensory dysfunction has now spilled over onto the psychological level of perception. Emotional problems and counterproductive behaviors that are caused by a learning disability are described as *psychological overlay*. The more serious a child's learning problems are, the greater the risk of psychological overlay.

Just as sensory processing problems can cause emotional problems, so too can psychological problems cause learning problems. An angry, depressed, insecure, or guilt-ridden child will probably have difficulty concentrating, following her teacher's instructions, or reading accurately. Her inner turmoil may also manifest itself as hyperactivity or careless mistakes.

Failure can be addictive. Children who experience a steady diet of embarrassment, frustration, reprimands, and demoralization often become habituated to negative payoffs. The coping mechanisms they use to protect themselves from feeling worthless—irresponsibility, procrastination, laziness, denial, blaming, acting out, passivity, and daydreaming—offer no real protection and simply guarantee continued poor performance. Struggling children do not, of course, recognize this obvious irony.

Children continually compare their accomplishments with those of their classmates. Even five-year-olds are keenly aware of how they rate on the performance scale. "Smart" kids do well and are praised by their teacher and parents. "Dumb" kids get into trouble. Their teachers get angry at them, and their parents are disappointed in them. These conclusions may be simplistic, but they are essentially accurate. Unfortunately, feelings of worthlessness often persist throughout life, with grave emotional, academic, and vocational consequences.

Differentiating the symptoms of an underlying psychological problem from the symptoms of psychological overlay can be difficult. Parents who are confused about what is causing their child's unhappiness or chronic self-defeating, inappropriate behavior have two basic options: They can hope the problem will correct itself or they can seek help.

Psychological problems and psychological overlay rarely disappear of their own accord, and smart parents will consult the school psychologist, a private educational psychologist, or a mental health professional for an accurate diagnosis. Children with psychological problems require counseling or psychotherapy, and children with psychological overlay require educational therapy or tutoring. Although the symptoms of psychological problems and psychological overlay may appear to change as children mature, the underlying issues, if untreated, will persist and could become increasingly entrenched and debilitating. Not seeking help when the need for help is clearly indicated can have catastrophic consequences for the child and the entire family.

SUGGESTED CORRECTIVE STRATEGIES

In School

1. Ask the teacher if he believes your child's unhappiness or counterproductive behavior is being caused primarily by school difficulties or by other psychological factors. Be prepared for the possibility that he may not be able to answer this question. Also discuss your concerns with the school psychologist, who can administer diagnostic tests that will reveal if your child has learning problems and/or underlying psychological problems.

2. (ES) If it is the consensus of the school personnel that your child's frustration, nonadaptive behaviors, and counterproductive attitudes are attributable primarily to her learning problems (psychological overlay), request that she be provided with learning assistance (see **Parents' Rights,** page 201). If she is already in a resource program, and her skills and behavior are not improving, request a meeting with the school psychologist, resource specialist, and classroom teacher. You should use this meeting to define specific academic and behavioral objectives and to explore innovative strategies for achieving these objectives. For example, if your child is acting out on the playground because she is frustrated academically, you should develop a coordinated plan to reduce the frustration and modify the unacceptable behavior. You might design a simple checklist that the teacher could complete each day to let you know when your child has misbehaved. If your child is clearly struggling academically, the quantity and difficulty of the work she is expected to do could be reduced. When she misbehaves, she could have a special time-out area. At the end of the time-out she might complete a simple questionnaire that asks if she is ready to return to the playground and is willing to abide by the behavior guidelines. She could check off the specific changes she agrees to make (e.g., no talking in class, completing her work, no back talk, no complaints).

At Home

1. The following inventory is designed to help you differentiate the more serious symptoms of psychologi-

---

PSYCHOLOGICAL DANGER SIGNALS

Disorganized Thinking

Lack of orientation (time, place, and people)

Delusions (persecution, grandeur)

Sensory distortion (auditory and/or visual hallucinations)

Nonadaptive Behaviors

Social withdrawal (seclusiveness, detachment, inability to form friendships, excessive sensitivity, unwillingness to communicate)

Tantrums

Superstitious activity (motor rituals that must be performed before doing a task)

Extreme mood changes

(continued)

Excessive fantasizing

Phobic reactions (fear of people or germs)

Fixations (excessive and exclusive interest in something)

Suicidal tendencies

Chronic explosive anger or hostility

Depression

Excessive fearfulness

Excessive anxiety

Chronic manipulative behavior

Chronic bullying

Chronic lying

Chronic stealing

Chronic need to control others

Physical Dysfunctions

Bed-wetting (in older children)

Incontinence (in older children)

Repeated stomachaches (also symptomatic of a physical problem)

Sleep disturbances

Children manifesting any of the behaviors described above are at risk, and treating their psychological needs must take priority over treating their learning problems. (In many cases emotional problems and learning problems can be treated concurrently.) The longer parents wait to provide help, the more debilitating the emotional damage may be.

cal problems from the symptoms of psychological overlay (behavior produced by a learning problem). If you identify these red-flag symptoms, you should have your child assessed by a mental health professional.

2. Psychological overlay caused by learning problems usually produces less extreme symptoms than those described on the preceding list. The symptoms include frustration, anger, acting out, resistance, resentment, low self-confidence, denial, blaming, laziness, procrastination, and irresponsibility. Refer to specific entries in this book for suggestions about how to deal with these behaviors. Unfortunately, making an accurate diagnosis is complicated by the fact that some symptoms of psychological overlay are also symptomatic of psychological or family problems. If you are unsure about the source of your child's symptoms, consult the school psychologist or a private mental health professional. Unlike underlying psychological problems, psychological overlay will often disappear when children begin to succeed in school. Should your child's nonadaptive behaviors and attitudes persist despite the best efforts of his teacher and resource specialist, you will need to seek outside professional help such as educational therapy, family counseling, and/or psychotherapy.

3. Children who have psychological overlay usually suffer from low self-confidence (see **Self-Esteem and Self-Confidence,** page 266). Encourage your child to develop her talents in nonacademic areas (such as dance, gymnastics, art, karate). Accomplishments in these areas can be an important source of confidence and pride that offsets the trials and tribulations that your child is experiencing in school.

PUNCTUATION

The rules of punctuation have tormented students throughout the ages. Today these rules are generally applied more flexibly, and some teachers do not require their students to follow all of the traditional conventions for punctuating compound sentences, introductory prepositional phrases, series, and restrictive and nonrestrictive clauses. Despite this liberalization, children can expect to encounter teachers who require strict adherence to the rules.

In junior and senior high school, most teachers insist that their students apply the basic rules of punctuation in their expository writing, especially in English classes. Students who learn the rules and use them consistently are on safer ground than those who disregard them or use them inconsistently.

You can show your child that learning punctuation rules does not have to be an irrelevant, painful, mind-numbing experience by being creative and by making the process interesting and challenging. Punctuating an essay correctly can be made into a contest in which your child pits his skills against the rules in much the same way that he pits his skills against a game of Nintendo. Once he becomes convinced he can win the contest handily, he will be less resistant to the procedure.

SUGGESTED CORRECTIVE STRATEGIES

In School

1. If your child's teacher is concerned about your child's punctuation, ask her to specify the particular rules that are problematic for him. Perhaps she can suggest supplemental materials that might be used in school and/or at home to reinforce the rules and improve mastery. If your child is hav-ing a great deal of difficulty, ask the teacher if she can provide individualized help after class.

2. Ask the teacher if she wants you to check your child's work to find punctuation mistakes. Some teachers do not want parents to proofread homework assignments and reports. If you do check over your child's work, you may need to review the rules yourself.

At Home

1. Make two photocopies of a page from a newspaper or book. Count up all the punctuation marks. Set one copy aside and carefully "white out" *all* the punctuation marks on the second copy. Photocopy this page again, then go through it with your child and discuss where some of the commas, periods, quotation marks, etc., should be placed. You might say: "The word *and* in this sentence is followed by a second subject. This indicates a compound sentence. You must put a comma before *and* because the rule says that a compound sentence (two independent clauses) joined by the conjunction *and, or,* or *but* requires a comma." Tell your child how many punctuation marks were on the original, and see how many he can replace. The more practice, the better, but know when to stop for the day! "Overkill" can trigger resistance and resentment. If you're enjoying yourselves, repeat the activity several times. Follow the same procedure with written work your child has *already* submitted. Count the original punctuation marks, white them out, photocopy the report, and then go through

it. Compare the number of punctuation marks in the original with the second version. If you find that you lack the skills or patience to work with your child, consider hiring a qualified tutor.

2. When helping your child proofread assignments, don't simply insert missing commas, colons, and quotation marks. Explain *succinctly* why the punctuation is needed.

3. If you feel insecure about punctuation rules and find the previous activity a bit threatening, go to a teacher supply store and request material specifically designed to reinforce punctuation rules. Materials you might want to review are included in the Resource List at the back of the book.

4. If your child is having difficulty remembering what a conjunction or an adverb is, encourage him to use his visual memory skills. He might, for example, visualize a cherry tree with two cherries hanging from stems that form an inverted letter *V.* The fork that joins the cherries could be associated with the conjunction. Each cherry would be a noun and could also be the subject of an independent phrase. Your child could then see the cherries *fall* (the verb) "to the ground" (the prepositional phrase).

READING ALOUD

Oral reading ability is one of the major criteria elementary school teachers use to evaluate academic achievement. Students who can read accurately, fluently, and with proper intonation are affirmed and rewarded. Those who lack these skills become acutely aware of their deficiencies each time they are asked to read aloud. If their experiences are traumatic, the embarrassment can produce feelings of inadequacy, reading phobias, and emotional scarring.

To read well, your child must acquire skills in phonics, word attack, blending, and visual tracking. He must also be able to recognize nonphonetic words (e.g., *rough*), anomalies (e.g., *psychology*), and common foreign words (e.g., *colonel, buoyant, faux pas, demitasse, crochet, lieutenant*—see **Nonphonetic Words,** page 191).

There are two basic approaches to teaching children to read. The most common is the phonetic or "sounding out" method (see **Phonics,** page 217). This method teaches methods for attacking words that conform to consistent rules of spelling and pronunciation. Children use the rules to sound out the individual phonemes (or syllables) and then blend the sounds together to form words.

The second method encourages children to learn words "by sight." Utilizing visual memory skills (see page 326), students continually add to the storehouse of words they are able to recognize by their appearance. Practice, of course, is essential, and most students require several exposures to more difficult words before they can immediately recognize them.

Because of the many phonetic anomalies in the English language, many teachers integrate both phonics and sight recognition in their instructional strategy. Children sound out words that conform to standard phonics rules and memorize those that do not.

Poor visual tracking (seeing letters, words, and syllables accurately) can make reading aloud a nightmare for a child. To read efficiently, the child's eyes must be able to scan smoothly from left to right (ocular pursuit). If his eye muscle control is deficient, he may transpose letters or omit letters, syllables, words, or even phrases when reading. Static tracking problems usually manifest themselves as letter and/or number reversals (*b* is perceived as *d*, or *q* is perceived as *g*). The child may also have up/down reversals (*6* is perceived as *9*, or *n* is perceived as *u*). Kinetic tracking problems usually manifest themselves as flipped words (*was* is perceived as *saw*, and *bad* is perceived as *dab*). When tracking problems are chronic, the condition is usually referred to as *dyslexia* (see page 58).

Children with oral reading problems may also have difficulty hearing the difference between sounds (*e* may be perceived as *i*). Intensive phonetic discrimination training has proved to be very effective in improving the oral reading of children with auditory discrimination problems (see page 19).

Stress can also interfere with oral reading fluency. Shy children may become quite anxious when asked to read aloud. If they also have reading problems, their fear of making mistakes may cause them to make errors, which in turn will intensify their stress and insecurity. Developing a creative strategy to reduce the fears of shy children (e.g., having them practice reading aloud privately to the teacher *before* class) is vital. These children clearly require extra affirmation.

SUGGESTED CORRECTIVE STRATEGIES

In School

1. If your child stumbles, falters, and/or reads aloud inaccurately, and the teacher feels that she cannot remediate the problem in class, request that he be evaluated by the school psychologist, reading specialist, or resource specialist. It is relatively easy to identify specific reading deficits involving phonics, word attack, blending, and/or visual tracking. If deficits are identified, request that your child be provided with remedial assistance. Once he is tested and assigned to a resource program, verify that the IEP (Individual Educational Program; see page 126) pinpoints his specific deficits and indicates the remedial methods that will be used to correct these problems. The IEP should also target specific short-term and long-term remediation goals and provide a general time frame for the remediation process. If the administration is reluctant to evaluate your child or provide assistance, ask to see the school district's parents' rights manual (see page 201). Your child's rights are protected by federal law, and you may need to assert these rights aggressively if diplomacy fails.

2. (ES) If your child is being traumatized by being required to read aloud in class, request that he be excused from doing so until he and the resource or reading specialist have made headway in correcting his reading problems. Embarrassment can be psychologically damaging and negate any advantage that might potentially be derived from extra oral reading practice time.

At Home

1. (ES) Your child must practice to improve his oral reading skills. If he has significant reading problems, he may be very sensitive and resistant. These defense mechanisms can usually be overcome if you are patient and supportive. Orchestrating positive associations with reading and communicating positive expectations are vital. Youngsters who see themselves making progress are generally less resistant and defensive. The following guidelines can make your reading sessions more enjoyable for you and your child:

■ Ask the teacher to indicate your child's current reading level. This can be obtained from standardized test scores (see page 212) or from the teacher's or resource specialist's observations.

■ Select reading materials from the library or bookstore that are slightly below your child's current reading level. Ask the teacher or librarian to recommend appropriate books, then involve your child in the selection process. Choose materials that your child finds interesting. (This may be difficult if your child is reading at basic primer level.) Explain to your child that he should choose "easy" materials at first. As he progresses, he can select more challenging books.

■ If your child has significant problems, slowly read a sentence or a portion of a sentence aloud. Have him follow along by pointing to each word as you read. Then ask him to read the same sentence. If he makes an error, use discretion in correcting him. You want to make reading aloud a pleasant experience, so be patient, supportive, and affirming. Acknowledge progress and brainstorm strategies for learning difficult or nonphonetic words (see page 191). Your child could make up his own personal flash cards of difficult words.

■ Quit for the day when either you or your child becomes restive or loses patience. Forcing your child to continue beyond his natural endurance will cause him to become resistant and resentful—ego-protecting mechanisms that may manifest themselves as chronic yawning, distractibility, hypersensitivity, or irritability. Realize that reading is difficult for your child and that his self-confidence is fragile. If his negative associations with reading are not changed, he will become phobic about reading.

■ The need to preread each sentence will not be necessary as your child's skills improve. Begin alternating reading paragraphs aloud. At some point your child will be ready to read the material aloud without having to alternate. If he prefers to continue the sharing procedure, let him do so. Acquiring positive associations with reading is the key that will ultimately produce proficiency and confidence.

■ Carefully control the progression to more challenging reading materials. Don't push your child too quickly. If you're going to build his self-confidence, you must orchestrate repeated opportunities for success.

2. (J/HS) Working with older students who have profound reading problems can pose a monumental challenge to concerned parents. If your child is resistent to your help or highly defensive, consider hiring a trained professional tutor who has had extensive experience working with teenagers who have reading problems.

■ Establish specific performance goals with your child; for example, "When you progress into third-grade reading materials, we'll celebrate by going out for a pizza."

READING COMPREHENSION

The process of teaching children to read is akin to constructing a building. Basic decoding skills—phonics, word attack, blending, and sight word recognition—form the foundation of the structure. Simple comprehension skills (understanding and remembering facts and details) comprise the lower floors, and advanced comprehension skills (drawing inferences, analytical thinking, and applying information) comprise the upper floors.

In grades K–2 the primary focus is on teaching children how to decipher written symbols. A child who has trouble with this task may be so exhausted by the effort that she may not have any intellectual energy left to think about what the words actually mean.

During the first three years of elementary school the concepts, issues, and information that children are expected to comprehend are relatively simple and uncomplicated. A child might read: "Human beings can survive several weeks without food and several days without water, but they can survive only several minutes without air." This information is easily understood, and the child can relate the data to her own observations and life experiences. As she progresses into the upper grades and her vocabulary and reasoning skills expand, the complexity of the material she is expected to comprehend will increase significantly.

In grade three the focus of reading instruction begins to shift. Decoding skills are still taught, of course, but children are now expected to understand, retain, and use the information they read. This shift from the basic decoding of words to the utilization and application of information is reflected in textbooks and reading materials that increasingly emphasize comprehension and vocabulary development.

On the most basic level of understanding, the *literal level*, a child *must be able to identify and remember facts and information.*

Literal statement: The man and his son picked up the toy sailboat and carried it to the pond.

Literal question: What did the man and his son do?

A ninth-grade reading comprehension test might contain the following:

Prior to the Second World War, Nazi Germany, which in allegiance with Nazi Italy was called the Axis, began to conquer surrounding countries in Europe. In 1939 Germany invaded Poland. This invasion convinced the English government that war with the Axis powers was unavoidable.

The invasion of which country convinced England that war with Germany was unavoidable?

a. Hungary b. France c. Czechoslovakia d. Poland

On the second level of understanding, the *inferential level,* a child must demonstrate that she can reason and apply logic (see page 169). To draw inferences, she *must make conclusions based on information that is implied but not expressly stated in the context of what is being read or discussed.* For example, she might read the following:

Inferential statement: The man and his son experimented with different lenses, different angles, and different aperture and speed settings as they tried to create the most pleasing visual effect.

Inferential question: What do you think they were doing?

The following inferential reasoning statement and question might appear on a fourth-grade comprehension test:

It hadn't rained for six months. The long drought was followed by a famine that caused great suffering for the farmers in the poor country. The famine was hardest on the young, the old, and the weak. Many

a. survived. b. became wealthy. c. ate. d. died.

The question probes the students' ability to infer from the context that famine is bad even though they may never have seen the word before and may not know its actual definition. The child who has difficulty with literal comprehension (remembering facts and information) also usually has difficulty drawing inferences.

On the highest level of comprehension, the *applicative level,* a child *must be able to use or apply information she reads or hears.*

Statement: As they experimented with their new laptop computer, the woman and her daughter discovered the remarkable speed with which it could solve complex math problems.

Applicative question: In what ways could the girl use the laptop computer in school and outside of school?

A high school student might find the following statement and applicative essay question on a biology test:

> There are six major disadvantages to using pesticides: They leave a residue; they can kill the plants they were designed to protect; they are difficult to apply evenly; they can disturb the balance of nature; they can cause pollution; insects can develop resistance to the chemicals.
>
> Write an essay that examines alternative crop-protecting methods that could reduce dependence on pesticides. Refer to the disadvantages of pesticides and explain and justify the rational for your alternatives. Incorporate information from your textbook, class lectures, and class discussions.

When students enter junior high school, they are expected to answer increasingly probing questions about the content and meaning of what they read and study. The pressure accelerates in high school. Although the capacity to comprehend, reason, draw inferences, and apply information is linked to intelligence, reading comprehension skills *can* be improved with systematic instruction (see **IQ Test Scores,** page 130). Students who are taught how to maximize their capacity to understand, remember, and utilize important information are rewarded with good grades and usually find themselves on a track leading to college and to challenging, rewarding careers.

In upper-level classes, especially in college preparatory classes, the capacity to remember literal information does not necessarily guarantee good grades. Most teachers demand insight as well as factual knowledge. They want their students to demonstrate that they can analyze, interpret, and critique what they read, and their tests are designed to measure these skills. (See **Critical Thinking,** page 46.)

Some children can decode words with ease but have difficulty comprehending. Research suggests that many of these students don't create mental pictures while reading. For example, they might read in a science textbook about the positive and negative ecological effects of building dams. The chapter may describe how tons of cement are poured to create the dam and how water is released and may examine how dams are used to control floods and improve farming. If the students cannot visualize the dam stretching across the river and cannot visualize how it is built or how it works, they will invariably have difficulty understanding and remembering the information.

Teaching your child to form mental images when reading and to verbalize these images can dramatically improve her reading comprehension skills. Methods for imparting these skills are described below.

SUGGESTED CORRECTIVE STRATEGIES

In School

1. Ask the teacher to pinpoint your child's specific reading deficits. Be forewarned that many classroom teachers—and especially junior and senior high school teachers—have had only limited training in diagnosing reading problems. They may recognize from standardized and teacher-designed tests that your child is not comprehending well, but they may not know how to specify the deficiencies that are causing the problem. High school teachers may be very expert in their academic areas but may not be able to identify specific reading deficits because they have not been trained to do so. The reading problems inventory on page 254 should help you and the teacher identify specific deficiencies.

2. If your child has basic visual decoding deficits characterized by inaccurate reading, letter and word reversals, omitted syllables and words, letter transpositions, and losing her place when reading, she will require assistance from a trained resource or reading specialist (see **Dyslexia,** page 58). Commonly used remedial materials specifically designed to correct visual tracking deficits are included in the Resource List at the back of the book.

3. If your child's comprehension is more than one year below grade level, ask the teacher to adjust the academic expectations to your child's skill level. Most teachers can make reasonable accommodation to the needs of their struggling students. You want your child to stretch, but you don't want her to become frustrated and demoralized by unreasonable demands, which can be psychologically damaging. To acquire the reading skills she needs to succeed in school, your child needs a focused, well-conceived remediation strategy and a concerted, cooperative effort from everyone involved in the remediation process.

4. Materials written at different grade levels that are designed to improve your child's reading comprehension skills are included in the Resource List at the back of the book.

READING PROBLEMS INVENTORY

	YES	NO
This student:		
Has difficulty with phonics	____	____
Has difficulty blending sounds together	____	____
Has difficulty with sight word recognition	____	____
Has difficulty reading accurately	____	____
Reverses letters, numbers, or words	____	____
Omits letters or syllables	____	____
Skips over words or entire lines	____	____
Has difficulty understanding and/or remembering literal information	____	____
Has difficulty understanding and/or remembering inferential information	____	____
Has difficulty understanding and/or using applicative information	____	____

If the teacher indicates that your child has problems in any of the areas described above, request that she be evaluated by the school psychologist, resource specialist, or reading specialist (see **Dyslexia,** page 58). If your request for testing is denied or deflected, request to see the district's parents' rights manual (see page 201).

5. If you suspect that your child is having difficulty creating visual pictures, ask her to describe something she has just read in a textbook. If she has difficulty, ask her teacher if there is anyone in the school trained in the Visualizing/Verbalizing Method (developed by Nanci Bell at the Lindamood Center in San Luis Obispo, California). This program is specifically designed to develop your child's comprehension skills. (If no one is trained in this method, refer to the suggestions under "At Home.")

6. If you suspect your child has inferential deficits, ask the teacher for his opinion. If he concurs, ask if he has materials that are specifically designed to improve this skill. (See the Resource List at the back of the book for suggestions.)

7. A systematic study skills program can help your child improve her applicative comprehension. If your child's school does not offer such a program, see the suggestions under "At Home" below.

At Home

1. If the checklist on page 254 indicates that your child has basic visual decoding problems, he will need specific help in these areas. Decoding errors, tracking problems, blending, phonics, and word attack deficits can create serious roadblocks to reading comprehension. Refer to the suggestions described under **Inaccurate Copying** (page 113).

2. When working with your child at home, remember to keep the sessions within ten to twenty minutes for younger children and twenty to twenty-five minutes for children in sixth grade and above. When your child (or you!) becomes frustrated or resistant, it's time to quit for the day!

3. If your child has inferential or applicative reading comprehension deficits, use real-life situations to examine potential consequences that are implied but not directly stated. (E.g., "She watched three hours of television and talked for at least an hour on the phone each evening. What kind of grades do you think she received on her report card? Why?" "He couldn't understand why the coach had benched him. He was the best shooter on the team. What could have caused the coach to bench one of his best players? How many possible reasons can you come up with?" See **Disregard of Consequences,** page 50.)

4. Read newspaper articles with your child and ask questions that encourage inferential and applicative thinking. (E.g., "What might have caused this car accident to occur?" "Why do you think they lost the football game?" "Why are so many people upset about the apartheid policy in South Africa?")

5. **(ES)** At your local teacher supply or educational software store, request parent-child interactive materials for developing comprehension skills (see Resource List).

6. If the teacher's completed inventory indicates that your child's decoding skills are satisfactory but that her comprehension skills are deficient, she may need your help in developing her ability to create visual associations. As you read together, periodically stop her and ask her to describe what she is reading in her own words. Use the following stimuli to encourage visualization: action ("Describe what is happening"), color ("Describe what colors you see when you think about this chemical process"), mood ("How do you think the Indians felt as they saw the settlers take over their land?"). If your child has great difficulty with visualizing, consider hiring a tutor trained in the Visualizing/Verbalizing Method. You may want to contact the Lindamood Center in San Luis Obispo, California, for a referral to a trained tutor in your area. You may also want to purchase *Visualizing and Verbalizing for Language Comprehension and Thinking* (see Resource List).

7. An alternative way to develop the capacity to form visual pictures and improve comprehension is to ask your child to draw a "mind map" or illustration as he reads. (This technique is also called *chunking*.) Let's assume your child is reading an article about lasers. Examine the two different mind maps that appear below. This method stimulates your child to think about what he is reading and to incorporate information he feels is important in a graphic representation. Comprehension and retention are significantly enhanced because your child is intellectually engaged in the reading process. Encourage him to use colored pencils or pens and to be as creative as he wants. This makes the process more enjoyable and stimulates more active participation. If your child omits facts that you think are important, discuss these facts. The

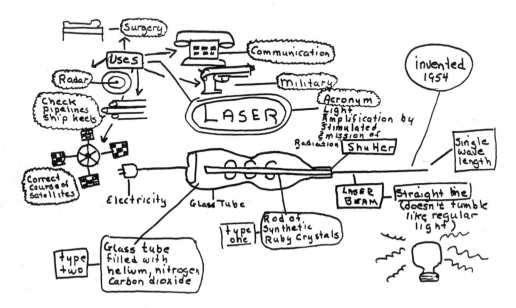

mind map doesn't have to contain every bit of information, nor does it have to be done exactly as you would do it. Be patient! You are opening new doors, and your child may be tentative and even resistant at first. You are asking him to *think* about what he is reading, and this may be difficult and threatening, especially if he has been in intellectual neutral. If he enjoys the method and practices it, his mind maps, comprehension, and retention will improve.

8. If your child continues to struggle with reading comprehension and does not appear to be responding positively to the strategies outlined above, consider hiring a private tutor who knows how to teach applied study skills techniques. Many reading and learning centers offer courses in study skills. Refer to *Getting Smarter* (see Resource List) for strategies designed to improve study skills and applicative comprehension deficits. Also refer to strategy 4 under **Critical Thinking,** page 44. If you take your child to a reading center, request that his specific reading comprehension deficits be identified. By using a procedure called *item analysis,* the reading specialist can analyze your child's incorrect responses and determine your child's specific deficits. Insist that the instructional materials and remediation strategy address the identified deficits. (*Please note*: Many teachers believe that basic decoding and comprehension deficits must be remediated before higher-level inferential deficits can be corrected. This position is logical, but there are teachers who prefer to work on decoding and comprehension skills concurrently.)

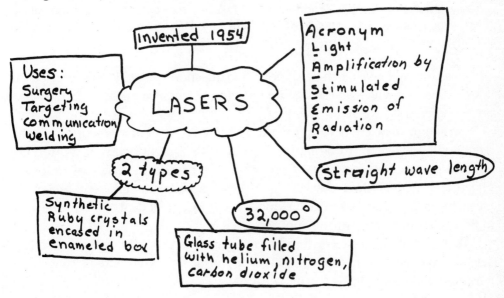

RECORDING ASSIGNMENTS

Students who do not properly record their homework assignments are setting themselves up for disaster. These children delude themselves that they can remember the details and play Russian roulette with deadlines, page and exercise numbers, and formatting directions. If they bother to write down their assignments, they do so haphazardly on whatever is available. The outcome is preordained. They miss deadlines, fail to complete assignments, forget to study for announced tests, and disregard important instructions. Their grades inevitably suffer. These children either do not recognize or choose to deny a basic academic cause-and-effect principle: Poor school performance is directly linked to irresponsibility (see **Smart Thinking,** page 275, and **Disregard of Consequences,** page 50).

It would be standard operating procedure for a sixth-grade teacher to announce orally or write on the chalkboard:

SCIENCE ASSIGNMENT

Answer questions 1, 3, 5, 7, and 9, page 51. Complete sentences. Skip line between answers. Name on the upper right-hand line and date below it. Due tomorrow. Quiz Friday.

The child who writes in her binder "Do questions page 51" has omitted vital information and will probably not do the assignment as instructed. She will also probably forget to study for the quiz.

Although some children figure out an effective system for recording assignments without having to be taught how to do so, most children require clear guidelines, practice, and supervision until the procedure becomes automatic. Those left to their own devices may never develop an efficient assignment recording system, and they are destined to spend a great deal of their time trying to figure out what they are supposed to do.

If your child is not recording her assignments properly, you need to teach her how to do so and monitor her carefully until she demonstrates that she has mastered and internalized the procedures.

SUGGESTED CORRECTIVE STRATEGIES

In School

1. Once you and your child have selected an effective format for recording assignments (the sample below or the teacher's own form), ask the teacher to initial your child's assignment sheet each day to confirm that

ASSIGNMENT SHEET

SUBJECTS	MONDAY	TUESDAY	WEDNESDAY	THURSDAY	FRIDAY
_____					
_____					
_____					
_____					
_____					
_____					
Due Dates **Subject:** **Tests** **Reports**					
Teacher's Initials					

she has properly recorded all of her homework.

2. (ES) If you believe your child's class might benefit from systematic instruction in how to fill out an assignment sheet, diplomatically suggest this to the teacher. Also suggest that children be monitored carefully until they have mastered the procedure. (Unfortunately, many high school teachers will not be amenable to this suggestion, because they probably assume—often erroneously—that their students mastered this skill in elementary school.)

3. Ask your child's teacher(s) to initial the following assignment monitoring form each day. Make copies of the form and have your child tape it to the inside cover of her binder so it will not be lost. (See a variation of this form under **Monitoring Homework,** page 185.)

At Home

1. Tell your child that you want her to record *all* of her assignments on the assignment sheet and explain why you are insisting on this procedure.

2. Make certain that your child has a specific place in her binder for her assignment sheet. The sheet should probably be the first page in her notebook.

3. Work out a system of abbreviations with your child to facilitate recording assignments (e.g., ex = exercise, p. = page, thru = through, cmplt = complete, d = due, rpt. = report, sci = science, Fr = French, Sp = Spanish). These abbreviations can be especially helpful when teachers verbally dictate assignments.

ASSIGNMENT MONITORING FORM

WEEK OF: _____

	MON.	TUES.	WED.	THURS.	FRI.
Completed assignments due today	*				
Submitted assignments on time					
Work not completed					

* Teacher's Initials

4. (ES) Have your child "read" her assignment sheet to you. Make certain she can decipher her own entries and understands what is due the next day. If she is having difficulty prioritizing specific tasks and managing time, refer to the appropriate entries that address these issues.

REPEATING A GRADE

Having a child repeat a grade is a major decision that is not to be taken lightly. In most instances the recommendation for retention originates with a teacher who is convinced that an academically deficient or developmentally immature child cannot possibly handle the material at the next level.

On the surface, the rationale for retention is quite logical: a second exposure to the course content, coupled with greater maturity, will improve a struggling student's skills and allow him to have a more successful school experience. Those who favor this remedy contend that any possible negative psychological effects are more than offset by the child's being able to keep up with his class and, perhaps, even excel.

Most children are retained in grades 1–4, although some may be held back in grades 4–6. In rare cases students may even be held back in junior or senior high school. The retention rate reflects not only a school district's philosophy about how best to handle struggling learners but also the district's available resources for dealing with students' learning problems.

Retention may be the only alternative when a child cannot do the required work and does not qualify for learning assistance. Depending on state code and school district procedures, the administration may insist that the child's parents acquiesce to the administrative decision, or they may leave the final decision up to the parents.

As states develop more stringent competency tests for high school graduation, arguments in favor of retention are heard with increasing frequency. Many districts are no longer willing to push students with poor skills through the system and argue that awarding diplomas to students with fifth-grade skills makes the diploma meaningless and disserves students who cannot possibly meet the demands of a competitive job market. Despite this supposed tightening of competency requirements, many states continue to graduate students from high school who are functionally illiterate.

High school students who cannot meet the minimum academic skills requirements to graduate have several options: They can repeat classes, take intensive remedial courses, attend summer school, graduate late, drop out of high school, or earn an equivalency diploma at some later date. Certain states permit students to enter the community college system and take courses without having graduated from high school. Students can use credit from these courses to fulfill their high school degree requirements.

The decision to retain a child does not always originate with the teacher. Some parents are convinced that their child lacks the developmental, emotional, or academic resources to handle the requirements at the next grade level and believe that retention will permit the child to review and master important skills. Other parents have very strategic and pragmatic reasons for wanting their child to be retained. They feel that greater maturity will provide a competitive advantage, produce a higher grade point average, and ultimately improve their child's chances of being admitted into a prestigious university.

If you are considering retention for your child, you should carefully weigh any potential advantages against the following potential disadvantages:

■ *Negative psychological impact:* Children may feel embarrassed, incompetent, and socially stigmatized.

■ *Disillusioning quick-fix solution:* The immediate academic or social crisis may be relieved, but retention rarely solves the underlying learning problems that could trigger major academic problems in subsequent years.

■ *Resistance to remaining in school:* Retained students may be unwilling to continue attending high school until they are nineteen.

Most educational therapists agree that repeating a grade may buy time but that the procedure will not remediate underlying learning deficits. Although some children are developmentally immature and unready for the next grade level, most students considered for retention are not actually immature but, rather, have specific concentration, perceptual, attitudinal, intellectual, or study skills deficits that prevent them from achieving academically. Labeling these children immature and recycling them without identifying and resolving their learning deficits only puts off "the day of reckoning."

Even if your child has only subtle learning problems, the deficits, if untreated, are like buried artillery shells that could explode with devastating impact in sixth, seventh, eighth, or ninth grade (see **Atypical Learning Problems,** page 16). Although retained children may do well for the first few months, or even for the next year or two, the initial advantages of retention frequently diminish as they progress through school. Using retention as a substitute for effective learning assistance could be a well-meaning but misguided tactic that ultimately leads to disillusionment.

SUGGESTED CORRECTIVE STRATEGIES

In School

1. (ES) If you observe your child falling further and further behind, ask the teacher to alert you if she is considering retention. Tell her you don't want any last-minute surprises.

2. If the school justifies retention by citing significant academic deficits, ask what specific alternatives are available for your child. If your child has not already been tested by the school psychologist, request an evaluation (see **Parents' Rights,** page 201). Discuss with the teacher and, if appropriate, the principal what will happen if the underlying deficits are not resolved. Inquire about the success rate when children with similar deficits were retained. Ask to speak with the parents of some of these children. Insist on remedial support from the resource specialist if specific learning disabilities are identified. (Getting assistance for children with nonspecific learning disabilities will be more problematic.) Discuss the social and psychological implications of repeating the grade and ask if any short-term counseling is

available to make the experience less traumatic.

At Home

1. (ES) If your child's teacher is strongly in favor of retention and you concur with this plan, begin to prepare your child well in advance. Tell your child that you want him to feel good about himself and his skills. Explain that some children need more time to learn at first but that later school becomes much easier. Your child will probably have concerns about losing friends, making new friends, and being teased. Children are keenly aware of their comparative abilities. Assure your child that repeating a year does not mean he is "dumb." Handling this issue incorrectly can have a profound effect on his self-concept, so allow your child to express his feelings; never dismiss them as silly.

2. If you are undecided about whether to retain your child, ask him how he feels about the idea. He may agree that it is a wise decision, or he may feel strongly that he doesn't want to be held back. Explore alternatives. Would he be willing to receive tutoring, educational therapy, or study skills help? Would he agree to put in more time studying? How could he organize himself and schedule his time more efficiently? Although you must make the final decision, having your child's input is important. If he is clearly denying the reality of his situation or is unable to make a commitment to an assistance program, you will have to make a unilateral decision about retention. Having your child repeat should be a last resort. If retention is necessary, you might want to consider having your child transferred to another school in the district to assuage possible social concerns. If he doesn't want to start over and make new friends at another school, his wishes should be respected. He will need a great deal of affirmation and emotional support during the transition. You will need to monitor him closely to make sure the same academic problems do not recur. A second retention at a later date could be disastrous and should not even be considered as an option.

3. Retention is not a magical cure for school problems. Although repeating the year may be all that is needed to get your child on track, it may be nothing more than a stopgap measure. If you believe your child needs learning assistance and the school is unwilling or unable to provide this help, you may need to seek private learning assistance from a qualified tutor or an independent learning center. (See **Parents' Rights,** page 201.) Whether or not your child is retained, you will need to monitor his performance closely and receive periodic progress updates from his teacher.

SELF-ESTEEM AND SELF-CONFIDENCE

Self-esteem is the composite of a child's feelings about herself and represents her unconscious assessment of her value as a human being. The foundation of self-esteem is formed before birth and is comprised of inherited temperament, intelligence, and aptitude. During the first four years of life additional building blocks are mounted on this foundation. These blocks represent family values, child-rearing practices, life experiences, reasonable and clearly communicated expectations, fair and consistently applied rules, and social relationships (see **Behavior and Performance Guidelines,** page 26). Love, security, appreciation, encouragement, and affirmation are the mortar that hold everything together. When the foundation is solid and the mortar is strong, children possess self-esteem and a sense of their own power, connectedness, and uniqueness.

Healthy self-esteem is impossible when a child is physically or emotionally abused, denigrated, compared with more successful children or siblings, given confusing double messages, caused to feel guilt and shame, or repeatedly allowed to fail or do work below her potential. The child who does not like or respect herself is fated to smash repeatedly against barriers throughout her life. Her negative feelings will distort her perceptions and judgment and undermine her motivation, effort, performance, perseverance, commitment, and resilience (see **Psychological Problems and Psychological Overlay,** page 239, **Fear of Failure/Success/Competition,** page 74, and **Guilt,** page 101).

The child with healthy self-esteem feels deserving of success. She enjoys challenges, delights in developing her talents, and revels in her accomplishments. In contrast, the child with poor self-esteem typically avoids goals and challenges. Because she feels unworthy, she lowers her expectations and performs consistently with these diminished expectations. She may even sabotage herself to make her achievement congruent with her poor self-esteem (see **Effort and Motivation,** page 63, and **Goals,** page 84).

Achievers do not necessarily have healthy self-esteem, and those with healthy self-esteem do not necessarily aspire to such traditional standards of success as money, power, or fame. Achievement may even become a substitute for self-esteem. Because achievement can create the illusion of self-esteem, parents must look beneath the surface in attempting to assess their child's true feelings about herself. A child who has confidence in her athletic ability may excel on the basketball court, but if she lacks self-esteem, she may feel inadequate in other areas of her life. In extreme cases, she may study inadequately, steal, cheat, or take drugs (see **Disregard of Consequences,** page 50, and **Negative Attitude Toward School,** page 188).

The deceptiveness of achievement is chronicled every day in the media, where countless stories describe successful actors, singers, musicians, lawyers, ministers, physicians, accountants, and business executives who self-destruct for seemingly irrational reasons. In virtually every case the aberrant behavior can be traced to intrinsically flawed self-esteem.

Because self-esteem and self-confidence overlap, the words are often erroneously used synonymously. The two terms, however, are not equivalent. Self-confidence certainly is an asset but it is not a substitute for self-esteem. A self-confident child may believe she can prevail over any challenge or obstacle. Despite her self-confidence and even bravado, she may actually have poor self-esteem and be quite insecure.

When a child's self-concept depends primarily on her ability to achieve or on the affirmation of others, her self-esteem is tenuous. A series of reversals could crush her. Setbacks and defeats, of course, can test the mettle and emotional resilience of any child. The child with good self-confidence and self-esteem may temporarily falter in the face of a failure, but her positive feelings about herself will remain intact (see **Bouncing Back from Setbacks and Learning from Mistakes,** page 30).

Some parents believe they can give their child self-esteem. Others believe that their child's self-esteem will grow in proportion to the attention or presents they lavish on her. These parents will ultimately discover, however, that self-esteem *cannot* be bestowed. It must be earned. Children gain self-esteem by solving problems, prevailing over challenges, handling frustration, and dealing with setbacks. They earn it by working hard, persevering, and thinking strategically. As they develop their talents and experience their own power, they will acquire increasing self-sufficiency and self-appreciation. These qualities are the benchmarks of good self-esteem (see **Smart Thinking,** page 275, and **Anger and Frustration,** page 1).

Parents may also mistakenly believe they can produce self-esteem by shielding their child from trials, setbacks, uncertainties, frustration, and unhappiness. The opposite is true. Their continual attempts to make their child happy and to protect her from every potential unpleasantness will most likely undermine her self-esteem. Children must develop their own survival skills. They must learn to deal with defeat, handle glitches, and neutralize obstacles and opponents. Allowing them to falter is an essential part of the process of preparing them to handle life (see **Learned Helplessness,** page 152).

Although you cannot *give* your child self-esteem, you can stimulate its development by:

- Encouraging your child to establish goals.

- Encouraging your child to challenge herself and improve her talents.

- Communicating to your child that she is expected to assume age-appropriate responsibilities (chores, homework).

- Guiding your child to the insight that *she* is responsible for her own happiness and for her own accomplishments in life.

- Providing academic and/or psychological support if underlying issues are preventing your child from developing self-esteem.

By allowing your child to grapple with a controlled amount of frustration, you're casting a vote of confidence in her. (This doesn't mean you should allow her to struggle in a hopeless situation where she clearly needs adult assistance.) Encouraging independence does not preclude you from being concerned and involved, providing assistance in a crisis, or helping your child sort out a problem and analyze the issues (see the **DIBS** method, page 233). As your child improves her problem-solving skills, she will acquire faith in her own abilities and her self-esteem will grow commensurately. (See **Working Independently,** page 332, and **Problem Solving,** page 231.)

SUGGESTED CORRECTIVE STRATEGIES

In School

1. (ES) If you conclude that your child lacks self-esteem and/or self-confidence and that her experiences in school are contributing to the problem, examine the matter with her teacher. If your child is struggling academically, brainstorm ways in which she might be given opportunities to improve her self-confidence. Perhaps she might be encouraged to do extra projects that use her natural artistic, musical, or athletic talents. Perhaps she could be named a class monitor or she could keep track of certain class records. School achievement does not guarantee self-esteem, but it is certainly a factor in the development of self-confidence.

2. (J/HS) Junior and senior high school teachers may not be so supportive of your attempts to orchestrate opportunities for your child to improve her self-confidence. These teachers see many more students each day than do elementary school teachers, and they are often concerned primarily about the content of their courses and their students' performance on tests. Although some good teachers may be willing to work with you on intentionally creating opportunities for your child to win in school, others may not be especially cooperative or even sympathetic. If this is the case, it may be more appropriate to discuss your concerns with the school counselor, school psychologist, or principal, who may be able to elicit the teacher's cooperation or recommend an evaluation by a therapist or social worker. (Some enlightened districts have social workers and therapists on staff.) Unfortunately, issues involving self-esteem and self-confidence are often not addressed adequately at the high school level. Parents who are unable to elicit cooperation will need to seek private counseling or educational therapy.

At Home

1. Although you cannot give your child self-esteem, you can create a home environment that encourages its development. Express love, create security and stability, establish reasonable standards and expectations, require your child to assume age-appropriate responsibility, express faith in your child's abilities, communicate honestly, define the family's values, be consistent, encourage the establishment of personal goals, intentionally orchestrate opportunities for success, encourage independence and self-sufficiency, permit her to experience a reasonable amount of frustration, provide emotional support and, when appropriate, academic support, and acknowledge and affirm her accomplishments. These ingredients significantly increase the probability that your child will feel secure, like herself, feel deserving of success, and perceive herself as worthy, powerful, and competent. Parenting classes offered at the local community center, YMCA, school district adult education department, or community college can help acquire practical strategies.

2. Chronic poor self-esteem is usually symptomatic of underlying emotional problems. The factors responsible for these emotional problems will need to be examined in counseling or psychotherapy. Serious self-esteem deficits will not disappear of their own accord. The child who dislikes herself and feels "bad" will most likely continue to feel this way throughout her life unless she receives help from a mental health professional. Even if she should become successful in school, she will probably derive limited enjoyment and satisfaction from her accomplishments. Providing help before her negative feelings become entrenched can be the best investment you can make in your child's future.

SLOW READING

Children read slowly for many reasons. Some have difficulty decoding letters and words (see **Dyslexia,** page 58). Others have been trained by their classroom teachers, reading specialists, and resource specialists to read ("track") every word carefully. These teachers may stop their students whenever they hear a mistake and insist that the child slowly sound out ("attack") each syllable and carefully combine the sounds ("blend") to form each word.

Teachers committed to the meticulous "track/attack/blend/correct" procedure usually offer two common rationales: (1) children who read imprecisely will continue to do so unless their errors are corrected, and (2) children must read accurately to comprehend what they are reading and to develop self-confidence (see **Reading Aloud,** page 246, **Reading Comprehension,** page 250, and **Phonics,** page 217).

Unfortunately, the syllable-by-syllable/word-by-word method can have negative consequences. Children who are continually corrected often become highly self-conscious and sensitive. They tend to compensate by significantly reducing their reading speed, and many continue to read slowly and laboriously long after they have overcome their reading deficits. The burdensome habit of sounding out words places them at a serious disadvantage in upper-level classes, where they are required to do a great deal of reading.

Slow reading is not limited to children with reading problems. In many schools even good readers are encouraged to read word by word. This practice is reinforced by the tradition of having students read aloud in class. For poor readers this exposure can be traumatic and humiliating. Their anxiety about making mistakes may cause them to read even more slowly.

The justification for having children read aloud is obvious. The procedure allows teachers to monitor progress, evaluate skills, and provide assistance. The downside is that children often become habituated to vocalizing or subvocalizing (hearing the words pronounced in their minds) even when they are reading silently. This inevitably slows down their reading speed. (Seeing a child move his lips while reading silently is the most telling sign that he is vocalizing the words.)

Hearing words in one's mind when reading can, of course, be one of life's most aesthetically pleasing experiences. The sounds of beautiful poetry or prose can be exalting. There are times, however, when students must be able to activate their reading turbocharger and complete their assignments quickly. This procedure is usually called *speed-reading*.

When students speed-read, they skim or scan sentences without being restrained by the need to subvocalize. They learn to assimilate and remember information visually without needing to hear the words in their mind. At first children may find skimming disconcerting because it contradicts how they've been taught. After years of indoctrination, the vocalization and subvocalization of words becomes a hard-to-break habit.

Are children truly reading when they are skimming the pages in their textbooks? The answer depends on one's definition of reading. Certainly youngsters can assimilate information by skimming, and the brain can be trained to recall visual data that are not subvocalized. One of the most important advantages of speed-reading is that it permits students to preview a chapter quickly and get an overview before actually studying the material. Children can also use the method to identify important information that they can later examine more carefully. The technique can be a very effective resource when they review for tests and do library research.

SUGGESTED CORRECTIVE STRATEGIES

In School

1. The first step in determining why your child is reading slowly is to ascertain if he has tracking, visual discrimination, blending, word attack, or phonics deficits (see **Phonics,** page 217, **Nonphonetic Words,** page 191, **Reading Aloud,** page 246). If you suspect that your child has decoding problems, ask that he be evaluated by the school psychologist or resource specialist to determine if he qualifies for help in school (see **Parents' Rights,** page 201). If your child is already in a reading assistance program, ask the resource specialist if one of her remediation goals is to help your child increase his reading speed. Be forewarned that the specialist may want to resolve the decoding problems *before* concentrating on increasing speed. It is likely that she is aware of the "Catch 22": If she attempts to improve your child's accuracy, she risks significantly reducing his reading speed. Most specialists stress accuracy over speed, at least during the initial stages of the remediation process.

2. If your child reads slowly and does not have decoding deficits, ask if the school offers a speed-reading course. Some schools offer this course as an elective, after-school, or summer program.

At Home

1. If your child has decoding deficits that reduce his reading speed, refer to the suggestions under **Phonics,** page 217, **Reading Aloud,** page 246, and **Dyslexia,** page 58.

2. Do an experiment with your child. Have him place his first two fingers together to use as a pacing device.

Have him quickly scan a page from one of his textbooks, encouraging him not to subvocalize. Tell him to pretend that his eyes are a camera and that he should try to take a quick picture. Play a game and see how many bits of information he can remember after one scan. Then have him scan the page again and give a verbal summary. Now you scan another page and give a ver-

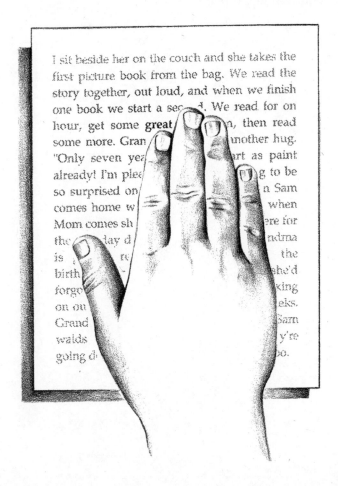

bal summary. Emphasize that the objective is not to remember everything but rather to get an overview of what is happening. When studying, he would read more carefully, possibly in conjunction with notetaking. Speed-reading takes practice, and breaking the subvocalization habit initially requires effort. Explain that skimming or speed-reading is appropriate only under certain conditions. You might say: "Skimming a unit in your textbook will let you know what the material is about. This overview will also give you a better idea about what you need to learn. Skimming can also be a great help when you review for tests. Reading the material carefully and slowly reading over your notes, however, are also important to effective studying."

3. (J/HS) If you conclude that your child's slow reading is chronic and is impeding his academic progress, consider enrolling him in a private speed-reading class. These courses are offered at learning centers in many metropolitan towns and cities.

SMART THINKING

A high IQ does not guarantee a "cake walk" through school or through life. To succeed academically, your child must be able to *use* her intelligence. This practical application of intelligence is the essence of smart thinking.

An important distinction must be made between smartness and intelligence. A highly intelligent child may be able to solve algebra problems in fourth grade, but she may have had two bicycles stolen because she was not smart enough to lock them to the school bike rack (see **IQ Test Scores,** page 130).

The smart child establishes goals, develops a strategy for getting from point A to point B to point C efficiently, calculates the odds, plans strategically, understands the principles of cause and effect, anticipates potential problems, bounces back from defeat, neutralizes obstacles, learns from experience, focuses her intellectual and physical energy on achieving her objectives, and figures out how to survive and prevail in a competitive world.

When confronted with a problem, the smart child asks herself, either consciously or unconsciously, five key questions:

1. **What am I trying to achieve?**

2. **What are the possible problems?**

3. **How can I get the job done?**

4. **How can I avoid mistakes?**

5. **How can I increase my chances of success?**

The child's analytical thinking process is an integral part of her responses to challenges. She may not always be aware of her thinking process, but her astute judgment calls confirm that her analytical thinking process is operating at full throttle.

Although the smart child realizes that the shortest distance between two points is a straight line, she also realizes that the path to her objective is not always direct. She will probably need to make some detours, and she will certainly need to make stops along the way. She realizes that short-term goals (e.g., a B+ on the next French test) are stepping-stones to achieving long-term goals (e.g., a good enough grade point average to be accepted at the Air Force Academy). If her objective is to become the starting pitcher on her softball team, she might spend hours pitching a ball through a tire suspended from a tree limb to improve her accuracy. She *voluntarily* commits the time and effort because she believes that this strategy will help her achieve the desired payoff.

Another characteristic distinguishes the smart child from her less successful classmates: She carefully considers the possible and probable consequences of her decisions and actions *before she acts* (see **Disregard of Consequences,** page 50). If she makes a mistake or suffers a setback, she assesses the situation and makes the necessary adjustments. The not-so-smart-thinking child does not learn from her negative experiences and consequently often makes the same mistakes repeatedly (see **Bouncing Back from Setbacks and Learning from Mistakes,** page 30).

The smart child is aware of what is happening around her and uses these observations and insights to guide her actions. If her history teacher has emphasized the civil rights movement, she will devote extra time to studying the relevant information as she prepares for her next test. She will also review her previous tests and quizzes and try to anticipate what questions her teacher is likely to ask.

The not-so-smart-thinking child responds very differently. She might forget to attach a bibliography to her history term paper, check over her math problems for errors, or review the new vocabulary before her French test. A smart child would be appalled by these "dumb" behaviors.

The seeming discrepancy between IQ (intelligence quotient) and "SQ" (smartness quotient) may be attributed to the fact that IQ tests are designed to measure a child's *potential* to succeed in school. The tests do not assess the practical application of intelligence, and they do not assess whether or not a child will choose to fulfill her intellectual potential.

Students who float through life intellectually anesthetized quickly become habituated to passive, ineffectual thinking. The long-term academic and vocational implications of this cerebral dulling can be disastrous. Teachers and employers do not reward passive thinking or mindless effort.

Parents have traditionally been responsible for teaching their children to think. Unfortunately, in our frenetic world many parents do not have the time or the inclination to teach their children how to apply their intelligence. These parents are too consumed with earning a living and paying the bills. Because they have renounced the responsibility to teach their children how to think, schools have tried to fill the void—with very limited success. Teachers are often too preoccupied with teaching the required academic curriculum and maintaining discipline to train their students how to think smart.

Our society is paying a high price for its myopic disregard for developing children's strategic thinking skills. More and more American children are making tragically flawed decisions. Despite the obvious risks they are smoking, driving while intoxicated, failing to practice safe sex, joining street gangs, taking and dealing drugs, and killing each other. They are also committing suicide in record numbers. The explanation for this frightening epidemic of poor judgment may well be as simple as this: No one is taking the time to teach them *how* to use their heads.

All children of normal intelligence can be taught to think strategically and can improve their analytical thinking powers. To achieve this objective, parents must create an environment at home—and teachers must create an environment in school—that encourages pragmatic thinking. With guidance, practice, acknowledgment, and affirmation, children can dramatically raise their "smartness quotient." Once they do, their potential for success in school and in life will improve dramatically.

SUGGESTED CORRECTIVE STRATEGIES

In School

1. If you suspect your child is not thinking smart in school, ask her teacher to complete the inventories that can be found under **Disregard of Consequences,** page 50, and **Bouncing Back from Setbacks and Learning from Mistakes,** page 30. The process should take approximately five minutes. The teacher may not be able to evaluate your child in all the areas, especially in junior and senior high school, where teachers see students in a limited context. Be diplomatic. Some teachers may feel you are "putting them on the spot." Others may resent being asked to spend extra time to complete the inventories. Explain that you sincerely want to help your child do better in school. To provide direction and assistance at home and to support the teacher's efforts in class, you need feedback about your child's performance and about any deficits that might be impeding her progress. (*Please note:* Some behaviors may appear on more than one checklist because they may be symptomatic of problems in different areas.)

2. Brainstorm with the teacher ways to work together to help your child overcome specific deficits iden fied on the inventories. See **Time Management,** page 308, **Goals,** page 84, and **Priorities,** page 228 for additional suggestions. Workbooks that address these issues include *Getting Smarter* and *Smarter Kids* (see "Study Skills" in the Resource List).

At Home

1. Complete the same checklist the teacher completed, to help you identify specific areas in which your child may not be thinking smart. Your observations may be different from those of the teachers, because you see your child in a different context. Some of the statements are not relevant for children in the lower grades of elementary school.

2. If you wish to define specific deficit areas even more precisely, complete the following attitude inventory. Also refer to checklists under **Bouncing Back from Setbacks and Learning from Mistakes,** page 30, and **Disregard of Consequences,** page 50.

3. Select relevant behaviors described in the Learning from Mistakes, page 33, Cause-and-Effect, page 52, and Attitude, page 278, inventories and create a checklist for your child to complete. Choose statements that she can understand and that are applicable to

ATTITUDE INVENTORY CHECKLIST

My child:	YES	NO
Seeks and accepts new challenges	____	____
Enjoys finding solutions to problems	____	____
Likes to test and stretch her limits	____	____
Has faith in her ability to succeed at whatever she undertakes	____	____
Takes pride in doing a first-rate job	____	____
Feels she deserves to "win"	____	____
Feels she is a valuable person	____	____
Feels she is intelligent	____	____

her level of maturity. Use her responses as a catalyst for discussion. Define one or two key problem areas (selecting too many to correct will overwhelm her) and explore possible solutions to these problems. Listen to your child! She may have excellent ideas about how to correct the problems. For example, she might suggest that she could make up a simple checklist to help her make sure she has completed all her homework. If she doesn't come up with any solutions, suggest ideas to her. For a more comprehensive treatment of how to develop smart thinking strategies, consult *Smarter Kids* (see the Resource List at the back of the book).

4. If your child is having difficulty with the principles of cause and effect, you might do an activity entitled "Possible and Probable Consequences."

Possible and Probable Consequences

What might happen if . . .

(ES) The oil level in the engine is too low.
Consequence:
Is this consequence *possible* or *probable*?

(ES) A child rides her bicycle at night without a light.
Consequence:
Is this consequence *possible* or *probable*?

(J/HS) A child jumps from a rock into a river without checking out the depth of the water and the speed of the current.
Consequence:
Is this consequence *possible* or *probable*?

(HS) You go to a party where the parents are not home, and kids are drinking beer on the front lawn.
Consequence:
Is this consequence *possible* or *probable*?

Make up more scenarios, keeping the tone upbeat and enjoyable and avoiding lecturing or sermonizing. Focus on discussing issues and examining your child's thinking and evaluative process. Offer your insights when appropriate, but don't expect your child to get it the first time you do this activity. Changing behaviors and attitudes, especially those that are entrenched, requires time and patience.

SPEECH DISORDERS

Children with speech disorders have difficulty pronouncing letters and words properly. Subtle speech disorders may take the form of relatively common articulation problems. The symptoms include omitting sounds (saying *at* instead of *cat*) or substituting one sound for another (*pag* for *bag*). Children may also distort words (e.g., *furog* for *frog*) or sounds such as the *r* and the *l*. Other symptoms include lisping, stuttering, stammering, and cluttering (extremely rapid, unintelligible speech). These disturbances in speech rhythm may be caused or exacerbated by physiological, genetic, or emotional factors. In extreme cases the child's communication may be incomprehensible.

There are many theories about the origins of speech disorders. Although most children with speech disorders are physically normal, approximately 15 percent have measurable physiological or neurological abnormalities. Research suggests that youngsters who stutter have a higher incidence of central nervous system dysfunction. Children born prematurely and those born of multiple births appear to be more predisposed to speech problems. Pinpointing specific causal factors is, however, controversial, and some authorities contend that there are no clearly defined causes.

In some cases interference in basic sound production can be linked to deficiencies in certain muscles or organs that produce sound. Some youngsters with speech disorders also have motor coordination deficits, developmental delay, and behavior problems. The behavioral implications may include resistance to help, rebelliousness, and acting out. These behaviors are psychological defense mechanisms that children with speech problems sometimes use to protect themselves from feeling inadequate and vulnerable.

Articulate skills are acquired sequentially. A three-year-old may say *wawa* instead of *water* because he has not yet acquired the ability to pronounce the *t* sound. This characteristic is not symptomatic of a speech disorder, and parents should not be alarmed. As the child matures, however, his articulation skills should improve. If the deficits persist, parents should consult their child's pedi-

ARTICULATION SKILLS

AGE	SOUNDS
3 years and 5 months	b, p, m, w, h
4 years and 5 months	t, d, g, k, ng, y
5 years and 5 months	f, u, s, z
6 years and 5 months	sh, l, th

atrician, who may refer the child to a speech pathologist for a comprehensive speech and language diagnostic evaluation.

Minor articulation problems often disappear by age eight or nine. The following chart indicates the approximate developmental stages at which children acquire specific articulation skills.

A four-year-old's difficulty pronouncing the *l* sound should not cause concern. A six-year-old, however, who cannot pronounce the *b* sound is manifesting an articulation problem and should be professionally evaluated.

Children who struggle to communicate intelligibly are often self-conscious, apprehensive, and insecure. If they are embarrassed or teased by other children, these experiences can undermine their self-confidence and warp their perception of themselves. Early intervention in the form of speech therapy is vital to avert unnecessary pain and trauma.

Although youngsters with serious speech problems are usually identified by their parents, teacher, or pediatrician and targeted for speech therapy in school, those with less severe deficits may slip through the diagnostic/treatment net. Perhaps these children have difficulty articulating only one or two sounds (e.g., the *r* sound), and their parents and teachers may assume that the deficits will correct themselves naturally. Some parents may even find certain articulation problems "cute." They may overlook chronic "baby talk," hoping that their child will ultimately outgrow the problem. This attitude will delay vital treatment.

You must be vigilant even if your child is receiving speech therapy in school. Because of limited speech therapy resources in many school districts, your child may be "bumped" out of the program before his problem is completely resolved. Be prepared to resist this cost-expedient action on the part of the school district (see **Parents' Rights,** page 201).

Because articulation problems become less cute as children mature and can create profound self-consciousness and ultimately affect career choices and advancement, early intervention is essential. Rebuilding a defeated child's self-image is far more challenging, time-consuming, heart-wrenching, and costly than early diagnosis and treatment.

SUGGESTED CORRECTIVE STRATEGIES

In School

1. If your child is having difficulty articulating sounds, *insist* that he be evaluated by the school speech therapist (see **Parents' Rights,** page 201). If he does not qualify for help or the program is full, consider private speech therapy. The classroom teacher does not have the specialized training to help your child. If she continually corrects him in class, she may unwittingly cause him to feel embarrassed, self-conscious, and inadequate.

At Home

1. Children with speech and language problems require specialized treatment from a trained speech pathologist. If your child is in a speech therapy program, ask the therapist if you should attempt to provide help at home. Do not continually correct your child's articulation errors. This would cause your child to become self-conscious and resistant and may trigger resentment and defensiveness. To protect himself, your child will begin to tune out your criticism. If the speech therapist feels you can help, ask for appropriate guidelines. Be patient! Articulation problems can be tenacious, and your child may not respond as quickly as you would like.

2. Ask the school speech therapist if there are tapes or computer programs that you can use to help your child at home. Specifically request materials that are fun. It is vital that you make your interactive sessions enjoyable.

SPELLING PROBLEMS

Millions of students are poor spellers. For some, weekly spelling tests are a nemesis. They conscientiously study their assigned words, and on the morning of the test they carefully review the words one last time with their mother or father. Then they take the test, and disaster strikes. A pattern of red marks on their graded paper confirms that they did not master many of the words they so diligently studied.

Other students have little difficulty memorizing words for spelling tests, but they cannot spell words correctly in their reports and essays. And finally, there are those unfortunate children who spell poorly in all contexts.

Spelling problems are usually attributable to two major sources: auditory discrimination deficits (hearing the difference between spoken sounds—see page 19) and visual memory deficits (being able to remember what is seen—see page 326). Children who cannot hear the difference between *band* and *bend* or who cannot see in their minds the spelling of nonphonetic words such as *receive* are prime candidates for becoming poor spellers. Although there are phonetic rules—*i* before *e* except after *c*—few children remember these rules when taking a test or writing a report.

Another characteristic of English contributes to spelling problems. Our language abounds with spelling exceptions for which there is no rule. *Alignment* is spelled with one *l*, whereas *alliance* is written with two, even though the words are pronounced similarly.

Spelling problems are also compounded by the fact that many common words are frequently mispronounced. For example, most Americans pronounce *prerogative* as *perrogative*. Because of this mispronunciation, the word is usually misspelled. There are many other examples of imprecise pronunciation. Little or no verbal distinction is made between words ending in *ant* (e.g., *reliant*) and *ent* (*talent*) or between words ending in *able* (e.g., *delectable*) and *ible* (*fallible*). The spelling challenge is compounded by an additional imprecision in pronunciation: *delectable*, for example, is often pronounced *dillectable*.

Another distinctive characteristic of the English language contributes to spelling confusion. Whereas the pronunciation of English has evolved, the spelling has not. Hundreds of years ago words such as *thought, through, fought, although,* and *rough* were pronounced precisely as they are spelled. (In Middle English the words were spoken with a guttural sound similar to German.) Because there is no longer a clear relationship between spelling and pronunciation, these words are now classified as nonphonetic and children are expected to learn them "by sight." Poor spellers quickly discover in first grade that there are innumerable examples of nonphonetic words in our language (*could* and *through* and foreign words such as *lieutenant* and *rouge*) that can make their lives miserable. Children, however, need not resign themselves to being incompetent spellers. The fundamentals of good spelling—the ability to discriminate the sounds of phonetic words and visualize the spelling of nonphonetic words—can be taught systematically. With good instruction and sufficient practice your child can learn to compensate for any lack of "natural" spelling talent.

SUGGESTED CORRECTIVE STRATEGIES

In School

1. If your child has chronic spelling problems on spelling tests and/or written assignments, request that her hearing be evaluated by the school district audiologist or her pediatrician. If the tests indicate that your child does *not* have a hearing loss, she should be tested by the school psychologist, resource specialist, or reading specialist to identify a possible auditory discrimination or visual memory problem (see pages 19 and 326). You may need to assert your right to have her tested if your request is denied (see **Parents' Rights,** page 201), or you may choose to have her tested privately.

2. If your child has auditory discrimination deficits and is struggling to differentiate basic sounds such as *i* and *e, o* and *u,* and *p* and *b,* she will require specialized assistance. Ask if there is a teacher at the school trained in the *Lindamood Auditory Discrimination in Depth Program* (ADD) published by Developmental Learning Materials. (See **Parents' Rights,** page 201, if you are told your child does not qualify for help.) A wide range of other remedial materials specifically designed to develop auditory discrimination is available to schools; check teacher supply stores and bookstores.

3. If your child has visual memory problems, request that the resource teacher use materials specifically designed to develop these skills.

4. Ask if your child's school has any other materials specifically designed to improve spelling (see Resource List).

At Home

1. Children learn differently. The first step in improving your child's spelling skills is to help her discover her own most effective learning style. Is she a visual, auditory, or kinesthetic learner? To help you make this determination, take the following steps:

■ Ask your child's teacher for his or her opinion.

■ Observe how your child learns school and non-school-related material (e.g., a new dance step or a cooking procedure).

■ Ask your child which learning modality is easier.

■ If you and your child are unsure about how she learns best, experiment together. You might select three words that are unfamiliar to your child. First, ask her to learn the definition of one word by reading it silently several times. Then, you read the second word and its definition to her. Have her repeat the definition aloud several times. Finally, have her "act out" the definition of the third word (for example, have her pretend she is "despairing"). Wait a few minutes and give her a fun, nonstressful "quiz." Be careful not to appear judgmental or critical if she forgets words. Emphasize that the procedure is an experi-

ment. Through observation and feedback from your child, attempt to determine which learning modality is the most comfortable and successful for her.

■ Request that the resource specialist or school psychologist administer the *Learning Styles Inventory* published by Creative Learning Press, Inc.

■ Refer to *In Their Own Way* (see Resource List) for more information about learning styles.

Auditory learners typically prefer to repeat the spelling of words verbally. They should be encouraged to spell the words aloud. A tape recorder can be used for this verbal drilling.

Kinesthetic learners generally prefer to write the letters of words repetitively. They should be encouraged to trace words in the air using their entire arm and shoulder. For younger children writing spelling words on a cookie sheet containing Plasticine or tracing the letters gently on sandpaper can be effective.

Visual learners learn best by reading words repetitively and by practicing writing the words. For the reasons discussed in the introduction to this section, visual learners have the ability to see words in their minds, and this gives them a distinct advantage when they spell.

2. Whenever possible, encourage your child to capitalize on her preferred learning style. Some types of information, however, may be best learned by utilizing a particular modality. Spelling is a perfect example. Although the auditory learner should be encouraged to use a tape recorder and repeat words aloud, she may discover that this method does not produce the desired results. By urging her to develop her visualization skills, you are providing her with an additional learning resource. This resource could be invaluable when she is required to memorize large quantities of information. To help her develop her visualization skills, have her write each of her spelling words on individual index cards using colored pencils or felt pens. Tell her to select any color she wants. If she prefers, she can write the individual letters of the word in different colors. Have her hold the word slightly above eye level. The word should be held either slightly to the right or the left of the child's line of vision (see illustration, below).

Let your child experiment to determine which side produces the best results. (Looking up and to the right or left helps your child access and represent information visually, as the eyes naturally go upward and to the preferred side when information is being processed visually.) Have your child study the word until she thinks she knows it. Then have her close her eyes and see if she can still "see" the word in the colors she has chosen. If she can't, have her open her eyes and study the word again. Once she can see the word in her mind's eye, have her spell it aloud to you. Then have her write it. She can choose the same colors or dif-

ferent colors when she writes the word. Follow this procedure for five to ten words and then give a review spelling quiz. Encourage your child to close her eyes and visualize the words when taking the actual test in school or when writing a difficult word in a report. This technique can also be used for remembering number facts, definitions, and chemical formulas.

3. You might want to purchase spelling development materials that are generally available in teacher supply stores (see Resource List) for use at home.

STUDY BREAKS

Sparks fly in many families when the issue of study breaks is discussed. The confrontations can become especially heated when parents are convinced their child is taking too many breaks and their child is convinced that his repeated trips to the kitchen, his interludes on the phone, and his diversions with the TV and the stereo are not negatively affecting his studying and schoolwork.

Most parents believe that the quality of their child's studying must suffer if he cannot concentrate, sustain his effort, and eliminate distractions. They want their child to sit down and work conscientiously until he completes his homework. Although they can accept the occasional break, they do not want him to get up from his desk every five minutes.

Before chronic disagreements about study breaks can be resolved, parents must ask themselves four key questions:

- How much time should our child realistically be expected to study before taking a break?

- What underlying learning or concentration deficits could be causing our child to take excessive breaks?

- Is our child's work suffering because of too many breaks?

- How can we help our child improve his endurance?

Traditional parental attitudes about study breaks must be applied selectively when a child has a chronic concentration problem. A youngster who lacks effective impulse control will have difficulty focusing for more than a few moments on any subject that does not interest him (see **Attention Deficit Disorder,** page 5). Any object or stimulus in the environment can attract his attention. He might begin to play with a pencil, become engrossed in tapping his fingers on the table, drift off into a daydream, or attempt to participate in a conversation in another room (see **Distractions While Studying,** page 55). If he is hyperactive, he will fidget, repeatedly drop objects and retrieve them, and continually get up from or fall out of his chair. He will use any pretext to go into the kitchen for a snack, to make a gratuitous comment, to ask an irrelevant question, daydream, or wander into the TV room.

Youngsters with underlying learning problems are especially likely to interrupt their studying. This behavior is either a conscious or unconscious escape mechanism. Frustrated by the continual battle to decipher, comprehend, and complete their assignments, they grasp at any opportunity to stop working. Most of these children are not consciously aware that they are using interruptions to avoid work, and those who are aware may not be able to control their behavior. To struggling, demoralized children who lack skills and self-confidence, interrupting their studying can be a compelling temptation.

Children with poor study habits also work inefficiently when they do their homework. They are typically disorganized and uninvolved in the process. They rarely establish goals or priorities, and they have difficulty managing time (see page 308), planning ahead (see page 222), and preparing for tests (see page 225). These children are delighted to interrupt their homework as often as they can. (See **Distractions While Studying,** page 55, and **Passive Learning,** page 205.)

If you feel that your child is working below his potential and that his marginal performance is attributable to poor study habits and excessive study breaks, establishing firm and reasonable guidelines is vital. If your child is doing well in school despite a great many study breaks, he may function best with short bursts of intense studying, and the maxim "Don't fix it if it isn't broken" applies. To impose study break guidelines when there is no apparent need could precipitate an unnecessary showdown.

SUGGESTED CORRECTIVE STRATEGIES

At Home

1. How long children are able to sustain their concentration and study without a break varies according to the age of the child and the nature of the child's academic or study skills deficits. As a rule children with no underlying problems should be able to study for the following sustained periods:

grades 1–2: 10 minutes
grades 3–4: 15 minutes
grades 5–6: 20–25 minutes
grades 7–8: 25–30 minutes
high school: 30–50 minutes

These numbers are not chiseled in stone. Some second-graders can study for twenty minutes, and some sixth-graders can study for forty-five minutes without a break. If the work is particularly taxing, they may take more frequent breaks. Ask the teacher what she feels would be an appropriate study routine for your child based on her observations and experience. Your child's age, skills, and concentration span must be factored into the equation. Study time should be increased in small increments, and you should involve your child in establishing the guidelines and working toward meeting the standards agreed on. The guidelines should be realistic. Insisting that a seven-year-old study for thirty minutes without a break is as unfair as insisting that a twelve-year-old with attention deficit disorder or a learning disability study independently for thirty minutes without a break. Praise, acknowledgment, and incentives for more sustained effort should be integral components in the behavior modification process.

2. Explain to your child why you feel repeated study breaks can reduce his efficiency and undermine his concentration. Tell him that you want to set up an experiment for increasing the amount of study time between breaks. Your goal may be to have him study for ten minutes between breaks and in two- to five-minute increments per week slowly work up to twenty-five-minute study periods. Have him set

an egg timer for ten minutes and encourage him to work for this time period without a break. Set up an incentive program in which your child can earn points toward a prize or special treat when he can study for the agreed-on time without looking up. The next day, have your child set the time for eleven minutes. *Slowly* build to the defined goal of twenty-five minutes. To document improvement, keep track of changes in your child's school performance. The record should be an integral part of this experiment.

3. Hyperactive children and those with concentration problems will have difficulty meeting the standards described above. When working with your child on modifying poor study habits, remember that the way you communicate is pivotal. Your words can trigger cooperation and insight *or* resistance and resentment. Frontal attacks and disparaging comments ("Well, if you wouldn't get up every five minutes, maybe you could pass your next history test") are guaranteed to produce a negative reaction. The more strategic alternative is to examine the issues in a cooperative, nonemotionally charged, and nonaccusatory context and to develop a well-conceived plan that can help the child improve his concentration and study for more sustained periods. (For suggestions about how to help children who cannot concentrate, see **Attention Deficit Disorder,** page 5.)

STUDY BREAK RECORD

Amount of Time Between Study Breaks	Grades on Homework, Tests, and Reports

Repeatedly acknowledge and affirm your child for progress and express positive expectations that he can achieve his performance and study goals. (For more suggestions, see **Time Management,** page 308, **Smart Thinking,** page 275, **Passive Learning,** page 205, **Distractions While Studying,** page 55, **Planning Ahead,** page 222, **Procrastination,** page 235, **Disorganization,** page 46, **Inadequate Study Time,** page 116, and **Monitoring Homework,** page 185.)

STUDY SKILLS

The commonly held belief that intelligence is the primary factor that determines school success discounts the role of focused, applied effort and efficient study skills in the academic achievement equation. Although the capacity to grasp concepts, perceive relationships, and remember information can certainly facilitate learning and enhance school performance, a superior IQ does not guarantee achievement. Brilliant children may perform marginally in school while their less-than-brilliant classmates may do exceptionally well.

Achieving students share certain characteristics that set them apart from underachieving and nonachieving students. They are motivated, diligent, and self-disciplined. They define their goals, establish priorities, record assignments accurately, manage time efficiently, plan ahead, identify and recall important information, take good notes, engage themselves actively in what they are learning, organize materials, meet deadlines, check for errors, and anticipate what is likely to be on the next test. (See relevant entries for a more detailed examination of the specific components of good study skills and suggestions about how to help your child improve in these areas.)

Underachieving students have a very different modus operandi. Because most of these students learn passively, studying means little more than mindlessly turning the pages of their textbooks and notes. Their marginal involvement inevitably produces marginal mastery and marginal grades.

Although they may not openly admit it, many teachers consciously or unconsciously ascribe to the theory that the "cream rises to the top." They believe that bright, capable children will *naturally* discover how to study. Some youngsters, of course, do figure out on their own how to win in school. They join an elite, primarily middle-class "club" of motivated college- and career-oriented students. Countless other potentially capable children are excluded from this club because they never learn how to study effectively (see **Smart Thinking,** page 275). As a consequence, their academic and vocational advancement will suffer.

A child's school experiences cannot help affecting her assessment of her talents, intellect, and prospects. Positive experiences produce confidence and lofty expectations. Negative experiences usually cause a child to conclude that she is incompetent. This conclusion may be completely erroneous, but the child has little or no evidence to refute it.

Youngsters who are not winning in school can persevere, lower their expectations and aspirations, develop ego-protecting compensatory behaviors, or shut down. Most children choose the path of least resistance. If they are not winning in school, they will probably do everything in their power to avoid studying.

Children with the greatest need to study are usually the most resistant to it. Often described by their exasperated, despairing parents and teachers as unmotivated, lazy, irresponsible, and disorganized, these children prefer to delude themselves that by not trying they are not really failing. To protect themselves, they typically procrastinate, submit sloppy, incomplete, and late assignments, blame others, become helpless, resist help, and deny that they have any problems. Their nonadaptive behavior accentuates the very deficiencies they're trying to hide or deny.

Reason dictates that *every* child should be systematically taught how to study properly as an integral part of her educational process, and this instruction should be provided *before* counterproductive habits, attitudes, and behaviors become entrenched. Ideally, study skills should be taught in every elementary school, and students should be required to apply the skills in all subject areas. Mastery of the skills should be a precondition for advancement to junior high school, and students who cannot demonstrate mastery should be required to take an intensive remedial course before they are promoted. Students already in high school should be required to take a study skills class, and they too should be required to demonstrate mastery.

To assume that your child will naturally discover how to study and learn efficiently is risky. It is far safer to assume that she would benefit from being taught academic survival study skills. If she is already a good student, reviewing and practicing basic and advanced study skills cannot help making her an even better student.

SUGGESTED CORRECTIVE STRATEGIES

In School

1. To determine if your child has a study skills problem, ask his teacher to complete the study skills checklist on page 294.

2. If the teacher indicates that your child has study skills problems, ask her for suggestions about how your child can be taught the necessary skills

STUDY SKILLS CHECKLIST

Code: *0 = Never*　　*1 = Rarely*　　*2 = Sometimes*　　*3 = Often*　　*4 = Always*

This student:

Works independently　　　　　　　　　　　　　　　　　　　　_____

Is well organized　　　　　　　　　　　　　　　　　　　　　_____

Establishes short-term goals (e.g., an A on the next quiz)　　_____

Establishes long-term goals (e.g., a B+ in English for the
　　semester)　　　　　　　　　　　　　　　　　　　　　　_____

Establishes priorities　　　　　　　　　　　　　　　　　　　_____

Records homework assignments　　　　　　　　　　　　　　　_____

Plans ahead　　　　　　　　　　　　　　　　　　　　　　　_____

Manages time well　　　　　　　　　　　　　　　　　　　　　_____

Uses a study schedule　　　　　　　　　　　　　　　　　　　_____

Identifies important information when studying　　　　　　　_____

Remembers important information when taking tests　　　　　_____

Comprehends the assigned material when studying　　　　　　_____

Takes good notes from textbooks　　　　　　　　　　　　　　_____

Takes good notes from lectures　　　　　　　　　　　　　　　_____

Anticipates what is likely to be asked on tests　　　　　　　_____

Studies for ten minutes without a break (grades 1–2)　　　　_____

Studies for fifteen minutes without a break (grades 3–4)　　_____

Studies for twenty to twenty-five minutes without a break
　　(grades 5–6)　　　　　　　　　　　　　　　　　　　　_____

Studies for twenty-five to thirty minutes without a break
　　(grades 6–8)　　　　　　　　　　　　　　　　　　　　_____

Studies for thirty to fifty minutes without a break (grades 9–12)　_____

Reviews conscientiously for tests　　　　　　　　　　　　　　_____

Checks over assignments to find errors　　　　　　　　　　　_____

Has confidence in her academic skills　　　　　　　　　　　　_____

A pattern of 0s or 1s indicates your child has a significant study skills problem. Although a pattern of 2s is common in underachieving children, it should alert you to the need for closer monitoring of your child's study habits in school and at home. Use the checklist selectively with children in the lower grades of elementary school. Your child would not yet be expected to have mastered some of the study skills on the list. These skills, however, should be introduced as your child progresses into the upper grades.

in school, at home, or in an after-school study skills program. (Also refer to relevant entries—e.g., **Notetaking,** page 193, **Inadequate Study Time,** page 116, **Time Management,** page 308— for corrective strategies that address your child's specific study skills deficits.) Most children can significantly improve their study skills and academic performance with only a few hours of focused, intensive help. Parents who unite and demand that their schools provide systematic study skills instruction as an integral part of the curriculum generally discover that squeaky wheels do, in fact, get the grease. The noise, however, may have to be loud enough to disturb a complacent and often myopic educational bureaucracy!

At Home

1. If the checklist completed by your child's teacher indicates study skills deficits, make up a priority list of skills your child needs to master. For example, the teacher may have identified problems with disorganization, incomplete assignments, notetaking, and preparing for tests. Refer to these entries and use the appropriate suggested corrective strategies.

2. (ES) If your child is in grades 1–4, you may want to avoid potential problems by beginning to teach her good study skills *before* she may actually need them. Begin working with your child on goal setting, recording assignments, and planning ahead. Make the sessions short and fun. For example, you might actively involve your child in planning the next family vacation or her own birthday party. Help her establish priorities, make up lists, and create schedules (see relevant entries for suggestions).

3. Encourage your child to get in the habit of making up a checklist before beginning a major project such as a term paper or before beginning to study for a mid-term or final exam. She should list all of the things she needs to do and when she needs to complete each task. As she accomplishes the task, she should check it off. This process is a key component in the development of effective study habits.

STUDYING WITH FRIENDS

Studying with a friend or friends can be effective if students are serious and have clearly defined educational goals. Although the procedure is not a substitute for individual study, it can be helpful in preparing for tests because students can capitalize on each other's insights, learning strengths, and skills. They can identify key information, ask each other questions, help each other understand and memorize key facts and concepts, compare notes, and share the burden of outlining a chapter or developing a diagram that ties the information together.

Study groups have been used very effectively by law and business graduate students for decades, but many elementary and secondary school teachers have only recently discovered the method. Labeled *cooperative learning,* the practice of having students break up into small groups is becoming quite popular, and many teachers have made study groups an integral component of their instructional strategy.

If your child wants to study at home with a friend or friends, you will need to make a judgment call: is he sufficiently mature and motivated to profit from the procedure? You must also be alert to hidden agendas. Children who use study groups primarily to socialize defeat the intent of the process and will get little or no good from it.

SUGGESTED CORRECTIVE STRATEGIES

In School

1. If cooperative learning is not being used in your child's class and you believe it might be effective, you might discuss the issue with your child's teacher. Some teachers might consider this interference or an invasion of their territory; others may be resistant to any innovative teaching procedure. Be guided accordingly. If you sense resistance or resentment, back off. You might find it more strategic to discuss the matter with the principal.

At Home

1. Show your child how to use cooperative studying to prepare for a test. Pretend you are one of his classmates. Work together at identifying key information in his notes and textbook. Ask each other questions. Make up a practice test and discuss which information the teacher is likely to include on her test. Ask him if he would like to try the method with a carefully selected classmate who is serious about doing well in school. Discuss the temptation to get sidetracked and to talk about unrelated issues when friends study together. Brainstorm how to handle this temptation (e.g., a twenty-five-minute session followed by a ten-minute break for talking or for a snack). Observe portions of the session without being too obvious. (Be especially diplomatic and discreet when observing older students, who may be particularly resentful of any type of adult interference.) Discuss your observation, elicit feedback from your child, and brainstorm ideas for improving the procedure. If it is clear that your child is not yet sufficiently mature to study with a friend, discourage him from using the procedure for now.

2. When your child studies with a friend or friends, urge them to ask each other questions and to make up practice tests. The method will help them review and identify important information, encourage them to begin to think like teachers when they study, and improve their chances of anticipating what is likely to be on the real test (see **Test Anxiety**, page 304).

3. Urge your child to record and compare his test performance when he studies cooperatively and when he studies alone. The results should indicate whether or not group studying is effective for him.

TEACHER-CHILD CONFLICT

Teachers and children do not always get along. The friction, which can usually be traced to a child's misbehavior or lack of effort, may involve relatively minor issues such as talking in class or more serious issues such as cheating, fighting, or stealing. Specific behaviors that are all but certain to upset teachers include disruptiveness, irresponsibility, disrespect, hostility, dishonesty, profanity, aggressiveness, distractibility, resistance, hyperactivity, laziness, and excessive dependency on the teacher for assistance or supervision (see **Anger and Frustration,** page 1, **Behavior and Performance Guidelines,** page 26, **Negative Attitude Toward School,** page 188, **Learned Helplessness,** page 152, **Psychological Problems and Psychological Overlay,** page 239, **Disregard of Consequences,** page 50, and **Effort and Motivation,** page 63).

Smart and strategic students who understand the basic principles of cause and effect recognize that their teachers have the ultimate authority in the classroom and rarely place themselves in conflict with the power hierarchy. They recognize the facts of life: Students are generally blamed when there is conflict, and the teacher can enforce compliance (see **Smart Thinking,** page 275).

Not-so-smart children are either oblivious to the power hierarchy or are intent on testing the rules. They talk in class. They are tardy, act silly, distract other students, talk back, get into fights on the playground, or pass notes when the teacher's back is turned.

Teachers are not, however, always blameless. The assumption that every teacher is skilled, creative, caring, dynamic, insightful, tolerant, flexible, and nurturing is comforting but naive. Though there are many highly competent teachers who possess these admirable traits and do the best job possible under often less-than-perfect conditions, there are also those who are burned out, uninspiring, and intolerant of any child who requires extra effort, guidance, understanding, support, or patience. These teachers increase the probability of conflict in the classroom.

A teacher's reaction to misbehavior and conflict mirrors her values, attitudes, teaching philosophy, professional training, and feelings about children. Some teachers prioritize obedience, decorum, and course content. Others prioritize self-esteem, active learning, critical thinking, and creativity. They believe that when children enjoy learning and are affirmed for their accomplishments, they rarely misbehave.

Wise teachers can defuse most conflict by identifying the source of the problem and developing a strategy for resolving the underlying issues. If a child is talking in class, they will analyze the situation and do something constructive to correct it. They don't let minor problems become major conflicts which they win because they have the power and children have no power.

Some teachers lack this wisdom and insight. They wittingly or unwittingly create showdowns with students who may be misbehaving because they are insecure and lack self-esteem, self-confidence, and academic skills or because they have underlying emotional or family problems. Conflict is inevitable when teachers choose to perceive a student's nonadaptive behavior as a personal affront. Although there is no question that counterproductive behavior can disrupt the class, interfere with the teaching process, and trigger resentment, the issue is whether reprimands, punishment, and showdowns are the most effective way to deal with these problems.

Teachers are charged with the responsibility to develop their students' academic and thinking skills and to reinforce society's position on such issues as effort, diligence, and attention to detail. Teachers, however, are not surrogate parents or police officers, and it is not their responsibility to inculcate basic values and attitudes that should rightfully be taught at home. Nor are teachers trained psychotherapists who can be expected to "cure" children who are chronically out of control, manipulative, or disrespectful of authority. A society that expects its teachers to play these roles is going to be disillusioned.

The responsibility to be objective, reasonable, and, when appropriate, flexible and tolerant, however, does not preclude teachers from imposing punishment or from implementing firm and consistent behavior and academic standards when children misbehave. Each situation must be judged on its merits.

In most instances, teacher-child conflicts can be resolved when:

■ the problem or conflict is accurately defined

■ the underlying issues are identified

■ communication channels are intentionally opened

- parents and teachers work together
- the child is engaged in the process of finding solutions to the problem or conflict

Just as children who are preoccupied with defending themselves may not realize or deny that their attitudes and behaviors are causing conflict, teachers may also become so preoccupied with their own position that they too lose perspective. Once they begin to perceive the child as an enemy, intervention by parents or the school administrator is essential.

Although it is usually the student who alienates the teacher, sometimes this situation is reversed. When an entire class loses respect for a teacher, the disrespect is usually earned. Children who are yelled at continually or who perceive their teacher as unfair, inconsistent, or prejudiced often respond by misbehaving. If the teacher clearly prefers girls to boys, she can expect to antagonize the boys in her class. Misconduct may be the most accessible retaliatory weapon and may express the classes' collective sense of injustice.

Improved communication is the key to resolving conflict between a teacher and a child. Both must be willing to assess their respective positions, attitudes, and actions. Teachers who are convinced *their* way is the only correct way, and teachers who are inflexible, unwilling to analyze disagreements objectively, and resistant to altering their attitudes, preconceptions, or approach erect major barriers to communication. Teachers are clearly signaling their refusal to engage in the problem-solving process when they self-righteously proclaim "I've been teaching for twenty years, and I am not about to change my methods to accommodate your child. When he improves his behavior in my class, the conflict will be resolved."

If your child lacks the insight and communication skills to resolve his conflicts with his teacher, you will need to step into the breach and help him define the problems and the behaviors that may be causing the conflict, without necessarily making your child wrong. You must help him identify and understand the teacher's values and priorities and explore how he can make reasonable and expedient accommodations. You may also need to help the teacher understand the factors that are contributing to the problem without necessarily justifying your child's behavior. You must also make every effort to see the conflict from the teacher's perspective. If she has thirty other students in her class, managing your child may require so much of her time and effort that she may legitimately feel she is depriving her other students of their fair share.

By modeling how to resolve conflict, communicate effectively, and think strategically, you have an unparalleled opportunity to teach your child vital survival skills that will serve him throughout his life (see **Smart Thinking,** page 275). The child who learns how to deal successfully with people who are in authority and how to resolve conflict has acquired a powerful resource.

Should your attempts to help your child resolve the conflict with his teacher prove unsuccessful, you will need to consult with the school psychologist, counselor, and/or principal. Transferring your child to another class should be a last resort. Although this may resolve the immediate problem, it may be only a temporary solution. If your child is causing the problem by misbehaving and if the underlying issues are not identified and resolved, it is likely that he may find himself in conflict with his new teacher.

SUGGESTED CORRECTIVE STRATEGIES

In School

1. If your child is in conflict with his teacher, it is vital that you acquire as much specific information as possible. A well-focused parent-teacher conference will provide these data (see page 198). At this juncture you have two options: You can encourage your child to work out his problems with the teacher on his own (see suggestions below), or you can take an active role in the problem resolution. The extent of your involvement should reflect the nature of the conflict, your child's age, level of confidence, communication skills, and insight, and his teacher's attitude. If you decide to serve as a mediator or facilitator, you and the teacher must define the problem and underlying issues (see the DIBS method, page 233). Once the problem is defined and the causal factors are identified, you and the teacher can brainstorm solutions to the conflict. It may be appropriate for your child to attend this meeting with the teacher, or you may conclude it would be more appropriate for the initial conference to be held without your child present so that you and the teacher can talk more openly and frankly. Your attitude will play a major role in the outcome of the conference. If you are accusatory and hostile, the teacher is likely to be defensive, resistant, and resentful. If the teacher is uncooperative and unwilling to work with you despite your efforts to be diplomatic and objective, you will need to involve the principal in subsequent discussions.

2. (ES) If you believe your child's attitude or behavior is contributing to the conflict, you and the teacher should develop a behavior modification program to use in school and at home. The following checklist will provide daily feedback about your child's behavior, and the information can be used to make any discussions with the teacher or your child more substantive and meaningful.

3. Consult the school counselor or principal if you feel you need more suggestions about how to resolve the conflict between your child and his teacher. If you and the teacher are hav-

---

DAILY BEHAVIOR CHECKLIST

Code: *0 = Never* *1 = Rarely* *2 = Sometimes* *3 = Often* *4 = Always*

	MON.	TUES.	WED.	THURS.	FRI.
The student:					
Pays attention in class	___	___	___	___	___
Raises hand in class	___	___	___	___	___
Behaves on the playground	___	___	___	___	___
Follows instructions	___	___	___	___	___
Is respectful	___	___	___	___	___
Obeys the class rules	___	___	___	___	___
Works independently	___	___	___	___	___

This checklist can be altered and categories substituted that pinpoint specific issues that are producing friction in the classroom. You might give your child a reward if he achieves a targeted performance score for the week. The initial targeted score should be realistic and should be raised incrementally. Experiment with involving your child in the process of determining the behavior and attitudes included on the checklist.

ing difficulty communicating or working together and it becomes apparent that the conflict is not resolvable despite the efforts of the principal to mediate, you may need to request that your child be placed in another class.

At Home

1. Discuss with your child the feedback you received about the conflict from his teacher. Be prepared for him to deny his responsibility and blame the teacher entirely. Your job is not to take sides but to help your child identify the issues; understand the teacher's values, priorities, and concerns; and identify the attitudes and behaviors that the teacher feels are contributing to the conflict. Your child must accept that the teacher has the power in her classroom. Although he may feel the teacher is unfair (and you may concur), he must learn how to adapt to the reality of the existing power hierarchy. Helping him recognize and accept that life is not always fair is an important part of preparing him to deal with the real world. His ability to make the best of a bad situation is a vital survival skill. If, however, you honestly feel the teacher is unreasonable, intransigent, or prejudiced

and the situation is unresolvable, you will need to support your child in your dealings with the school.

2. Although you should urge your child to discuss the issues that are causing conflict (e.g., an unfair grade on a report or a test or the feeling that the teacher is embarrassing him in class) directly with the teacher, it is reasonable for your child to feel apprehensive about broaching these subjects and possibly having to confront an authority figure. Questioning and perhaps challenging an adult is likely to be an intimidating experience for a child. Helping create a plan that addresses the issues can be an invaluable learning experience. Refer to the DIBS method on page 233 for specific problem-identification and problem-solving techniques. Rehearsals can be invaluable in refining your child's technique and in developing his confidence. You might model how your child could broach the subject ("Mrs. Lantham, I would like to talk to you about how I feel when you criticize my handwriting in front of the class"). Have your child play the role of the teacher. Then switch roles. Be patient and affirming as your child struggles to express himself and perfect his communication skills.

TEST ANXIETY

The prospect of taking a test can produce apprehension for any student. For some, however, the anxiety can be so debilitating that it invalidates the test as an accurate measure of their knowledge and skills.

The excessively test-anxious child is often convinced in advance that he will do poorly. These catastrophic expectations tend to be self-fulfilling. The forebodings may begin days before the test and intensify as D day approaches. While waiting for the test to be handed out, a voice inside the child's head screams: "I know I won't be able to answer the questions!" Finally, he gets his copy of the test and quickly scans it. Overwhelmed by panic, he can see no relationship between the test questions and the material he studied so diligently. His brain shuts down. He forgets how to spell words he knew how to spell that morning at the breakfast table. He cannot remember how to multiply despite having done dozens of similar problems in class and for homework. He cannot recall important dates, math formulas, chemical symbols, vocabulary definitions, grammar rules, verb conjugations, or biology phyla. His worst nightmare becomes a reality.

Chronic and excessive test anxiety can usually be traced to one or more of the following factors:

- Poor preparation

- Poor skills

- Negative experiences with tests

- Negative associations with school and learning

- Low self-confidence

It is virtually impossible to assess accurately the skills of a child who is paralyzed by fear. Even moderate fear can undermine the validity of standardized (nationally normed) or teacher-designed tests (see **Understanding Diagnostic Test Results,** page 316).

Before your child can overcome his test anxiety, you must help him examine the source of his apprehension. An objective assessment of his academic skills and study skills is the first step in this process. If your child is convinced that he lacks the skills to complete or understand the assigned material, his test-taking fears are reasonable. His specific academic deficits must be corrected for his confidence to improve. (See suggestions below for specific corrective strategies that address the causes of test anxiety.)

If your child has poor study skills, his test-taking anxiety is also reasonable. He must obviously learn how to study and prepare for tests if he is ultimately to build his self-confidence and reduce his anxiety (see **Study Skills,** page 292, **Notetaking,** page 193, **Preparing for Tests,** page 225, **Smart Thinking,** page 275, **Problem Solving,** page 231, **Planning Ahead,** page 222, and **Identifying Important Information,** page 110).

When your child's fears cannot be attributed to specific underlying deficits, he may need to be taught basic relaxation techniques (see suggestions below). Systematic training in specific performance-improving techniques would also improve his confidence.

Once your child learns how to study more efficiently and strategically and how to relax before and during tests, his faith in himself and his abilities will improve. Success and self-confidence are the two most powerful antidotes for test anxiety. If, however, his fears persist despite your best efforts to help him, psychological counseling is advisable.

SUGGESTED CORRECTIVE STRATEGIES

In School

1. If your child is test-phobic and you suspect that his poor performance is linked to specific academic deficits, learning problems, or study skills deficits, request that he be evaluated by the school psychologist or resource specialist. If your suspicions are confirmed, your child will require learning assistance and/or study skills instruction before you can expect his test anxiety to diminish. (See **Learning Disabilities,** page 157, **Study Skills,** page 292, and **Parents' Rights,** page 201.)

2. (ES) If you suspect other children in the class may also be experiencing test anxiety, ask the teacher if she would be willing to give occasional practice tests. Providing test-phobic children with opportunities to take practice tests can significantly lower their anxiety level. The objective of these "dry runs" is to demonstrate that test taking need not trigger fear. Encouraging children to make up their *own* practice tests when they study will also reduce their stress and help them study more effectively. Practice tests that are intentionally designed not to be too difficult can provide a major boost to self-confidence. *Good teachers want their students to win in school, and they do everything in their power to improve the chances of success.* As students become more confident, skilled, and test-wise, their teachers can make the academic demands more stringent and the tests more challenging.

3. Request that the teacher show your child an effective test-taking system. A good system would include the following steps:

1. Take a few deep breaths with your eyes closed to calm your nerves.

2. Visualize yourself doing well on the test.

3. Quickly scan the entire test so that you know what is being covered.

4. Calculate approximately how much time you can spend on each question or each section of the test.

5. Answer the easiest questions first.

6. If an essay is required, make a very short and quick outline (a thumbnail outline) of what you want to include (see Essay Tests, page 67).

7. Be alert for "trick" questions that seem to be too easy.

8. If you feel butterflies while taking the test, close your eyes for a few seconds, breathe, feel yourself relax, and calmly remind yourself that you studied diligently and *know* the material.

9. If possible, allow time to check over your answers.

10. Write clearly and neatly so that your answers can be read.

Good test-taking strategies can play an instrumental role in reducing test phobias and improving performance.

At Home

1. Work with your child to design sample tests and quizzes that cover the material he is studying. After reading the material, ask each other questions. Once he understands how to ask probing questions about what he has studied, you can begin to write down test questions and make up a facsimile test. Each of you should take the test. Initially, these practice tests should be intentionally designed to allow your child to succeed. As his self-confidence improves, make up harder tests that parallel the types of tests he takes in school.

2. Practice basic anxiety-reducing relaxation techniques with your child. Have him close his eyes and become conscious of his breathing. Urge him to feel his chest expand and contract. Have him take two or three deep breaths (too many could cause him to hyperventilate). The entire process should not take longer than a minute. Urge him to use the technique before a test is handed out. He should not be self-conscious about using this relaxation method. No one in the class need know he is doing it.

3. Review the test-taking steps described above. Have your child study the procedural steps until he knows them. Then have him practice the procedure when he takes the practice tests you create together.

TIME MANAGEMENT

The ability to manage time is a critical component in the study skills equation. This capacity becomes increasingly important as children progress into the upper grades and the academic demands become more stringent. Students who manage time poorly don't allow enough time to prepare for tests, check over their math papers, and proofread their book reports (see **Disorganization,** page 46, **Procrastination,** page 235, **Attention to Details,** page 12, and **Smart Thinking,** page 275). They rarely establish goals and priorities (see pages 84 and 228), record assignments properly (see page 258), create a study strategy, organize materials, or meet deadlines. Their nonstrategic modus operandi inevitably produces continual crises. Ironically, those children with the greatest need to improve their planning skills are the ones who are most oblivious to their predicament.

Students who deny they have poor time management skills will be forced to confront reality in junior and senior high school. Their inability to plan ahead can make the challenge of completing a history term paper on time or studying for an algebra final overwhelming. Some students shut down. Others spin their wheels and lurch ahead spasmodically. Others become increasingly dependent on their parents.

With good instruction and sufficient practice your child can acquire effective planning skills. A key in converting her to a more efficient time management system is to show her a system for budgeting her time and to demonstrate how the system can make her life easier and allow her greater freedom to do what she wants to do. Once she sees the value of planning ahead, she will do so voluntarily.

SUGGESTED CORRECTIVE STRATEGIES

In School

1. (ES) If you suspect your child's entire class might benefit from formal instruction in time management, diplomatically suggest that the teacher consider including a segment on planning skills in the curriculum. For example, students might plan a class project and design a schedule that incorporates basic time management principles. Students would prioritize the steps (see page 228) and determine the projected time requirements for each step. These data could then be plotted into a flowchart.

At Home

1. Study the sample schedule below with your child. Explain that the schedule indicates how one student has chosen to use her time and make sure she gets her work done.

2. Help your child complete her own weekly schedule. This hands-on procedure is intended to demonstrate how she can budget the time necessary to complete her homework assignments and still have free time to herself. After you both agree on the approximate amount of homework time required on a typical school night, your child should decide when *she* wants to study (see **Inadequate Study Time,** page 116). This empowerment is important and can usually defuse the "I'm an oppressed child" resistance. Insist that your child main-

SAMPLE WEEKLY SCHEDULE					
TIME:	MONDAY	TUESDAY	WEDNESDAY	THURSDAY	FRIDAY
3:00–3:30	Free	Free	Free	Free	Free
3:30–4:00	Free	Free	Free	Free	Free
4:00–4:30	Study	Study	Study	Study	Study
4:30–5:00	Study	Study	Study	Study	Study
5:00–6:00	Free	Free	Free	Free	Free
6:00–6:45	Dinner	Dinner	Dinner	Dinner	Dinner
6:45–7:45	Study	Study	Study	Study	Study
7:45–9:00	Free	Free	Free	Free	Free
9:00–7:00	Sleep	Sleep	Sleep	Sleep	Sleep

tain the schedule for a minimum of two weeks. Discourage deviations and manipulations as these will defeat the intent of the scheduling process. If your child has agreed to study from 6:15 until 7:00, she should keep this commitment. Wanting to watch a TV show is an unacceptable excuse. After two weeks, allow your child to make adjustments in her schedule. Once she makes the adjustments, she must keep to the revised schedule for at least another two weeks.

MY WEEKLY SCHEDULE					
TIME:	MONDAY	TUESDAY	WEDNESDAY	THURSDAY	FRIDAY
3:00–3:30					
3:30–4:00					
4:00–4:30					
4:30–5:00					
5:00–5:30					
5:30–6:00					
6:00–6:30					
6:30–7:00					
7:00–7:30					
7:30–8:00					
8:00–8:30					
8:30–9:00					
*9:00–7:00					

* Adjust this time slot for older students.

3. Monitor your child to make sure she is keeping to her schedule. Discuss any problems that arise. Do not nag or give sermons about responsibility, as your child is likely to tune out admonitions and lectures. Have your child list the projects, chores, and assignments she needs to complete each week. You might want to set up a way to reward her if she completes these tasks on time. A Projects/Assignments Check-Off sheet could give points for completed work, which could be applied to winning a prize.

Household chores could also earn points. Your objective is to modify your child's counterproductive behavior. Remember to express positive expectations and to give lots of praise!

4. Do planning activities with your child. For example, you might have your child plan her own birthday party or a family project. Write down the target dates for completing each step. Figure out the amount of projected time that will be required to do each step.

UNDERACHIEVEMENT

At any given moment in classrooms throughout the United States, millions of students are working below their full potential. Approximately 1.8 million of these children have significant, specific, and identifiable learning deficits and are officially classified as learning disabled.* Millions of other children with less specific and more puzzling learning problems also work below their potential. These students are usually classified as underachievers (see **Atypical Learning Problems,** page 16).

Economics have forced many school districts to reserve their learning assistance programs for students with serious academic deficiencies. These children represent between 3 percent and 15 percent of the student population (depending on who is making the estimate). Underachieving children with hard-to-identify problems may represent an additional 40 percent of the student population. In most school districts marginally performing youngsters plod through twelve years of school without receiving substantive help. Legions of these poorly educated and, in some cases, emotionally scarred graduates arrive each year at the end of the educational production line vocationally unprepared to compete in a technologically advanced society.

The subtle, enigmatic, or intermittent deficits that cause underachievement may manifest themselves exclusively in one or two specific areas or in all academic subjects. One child may read aloud well but may have poor comprehension. Another child may read inaccurately but may miraculously have good comprehension. A third child may get decent grades in history, English, and science but may spell atrociously and do terribly in math. Despite the fact that these students are struggling academically, their problems are rarely considered serious enough to qualify them for learning assistance. These programs are reserved for children with more debilitating problems.

Some educators argue that children struggle in school because teachers are failing to develop effective and creative teaching strategies.† They contend that

---

* Gene L. Maeroff, *The School Smart Parent,* Times Books, 1989.

† Thomas Armstrong, *In Their Own Way,* Tarcher, 1987; and Gerald Coles, *The Learning Mystique,* Pantheon, 1987.

there would be no learning disabled and underachieving students if schools would develop individualized teaching strategies that capitalize on how each child learns best and if schools would improve curricula, enhance teacher training, raise the standards for tenure, and increase teacher salaries.

It is difficult to fault this logic. Motivated, dynamic, well-paid, well-trained, creative teachers could achieve better results in small classes of children with similar skills. The results would be even better if parents actively supported the educational process and monitored and encouraged their children at home. Unfortunately, these ideal conditions are the exception rather than the rule. Classrooms often contain thirty or more students representing a wide spectrum of abilities, cultures, and personalities. Active parental support of the educational process is becoming less and less common. Parents are increasingly preoccupied with earning a living, paying the rent or the mortgage, making the car payments, and keeping their family intact. Under these less-than-perfect conditions teachers must jury-rig their methodology, adjust their expectations, and impart skills and information to their students.

Because of the crisis in American education and the dismal academic abilities of many students, teachers are being asked to rethink their methods, objectives, and assumptions. They are also being asked to be more creative and to modify their teaching so that they can reach children who learn differently. Some teachers are receptive to this pressure to improve the educational delivery system. Others are quite resistant. After years on the academic front line they have become set in their ways, reactionary, and wary of educational fads that periodically sweep the country and then just as quickly disappear. They are also wary of outside consultants and experts in ivory towers and "think tanks" who critique them and make unsolicited suggestions about how they could teach better. A common reaction, stated or unstated, to the proposal that they develop new and creative curricula and individualize their teaching strategies is "No way! I'm already overworked, underpaid, and unappreciated."

The net effect of our less-than-perfect educational system is that underachievers often slip through gaping holes in the safety net. As they proceed through school, their subtle, unresolved learning deficits usually become increasingly problematic. By the time they reach high school, their "minor" deficiencies may have become major impediments.

Even under less-than-ideal conditions, your child must still get the job done. He must adjust to his teacher's standards, guidelines, and expectations, just as someday he must adjust to the demands of the competitive, imperfect world beyond the classroom. He must learn number facts, recognize verbs and adjectives, and know about Benjamin Franklin. He must learn to write legibly, spell correctly, comprehend what he is reading, and express his ideas. He must learn to solve algebraic equations and write grammatically correct Spanish sentences. If he cannot make these accommodations to the system, he will suffer.

Children are programmed by nature to achieve. This programming accounts for the bridges, the vaccines, novels, poetry, symphonies, new technology, and paintings that human beings build, discover, or create.

The thousands of hours your child spends in the classroom will have a profound impact on his expectations, self-image, self-confidence, and ultimate career choices. Although achievement, per se, does not guarantee happiness and emotional adjustment, chronic nonachievement and underachievement significantly increase the probability of unhappiness. By helping your child identify the roadblocks that are impeding his progress, by showing him how to solve problems and remove these barriers, and by providing guidance, emotional support, and quality control, you can play a key role in reducing the risk that he will remain an underachiever.

SUGGESTED CORRECTIVE STRATEGIES

In School

1. Before you can develop a strategy for helping your child, you must identify the specific deficits that are causing him to underachieve. To help you in this "detective work," refer to the Table of Contents. Check off the areas in which your child might be deficient and read the description of each problem area. If you feel that your child has a specific deficiency (e.g., sloppy assignments), discuss the issue with your child's teacher. If she concurs, explore how the suggested corrective strategies might be implemented in class.

2. If you suspect that your child may have a learning disability, ask his teacher(s) to complete the student evaluation form on page 160 (elementary school) or page 163 (junior and senior high school). If the teacher identifies a pattern of deficits that suggests a learning disability, refer to the appropriate suggestions on pages 162 and 165 and to other specific, relevant entries in this book.

At Home

1. Once you've identified specific problem areas, make a priority list of issues that can be addressed at home. Examine the suggested corrective strategies. Begin with only one problem (e.g., spelling, study skills, or time management). Don't attempt to remedy all of your child's deficits at once, as this would undoubtedly trigger resistance and resentment.

2. If you feel you cannot provide the learning assistance your child needs to work up to his full potential, consider hiring a tutor or an educational therapist. If you believe there are psychological issues that are impeding your child, you may need to consult a mental health professional (see **Psychological Problems and Psychological Overlay,** page 239).

UNDERSTANDING DIAGNOSTIC TEST RESULTS

The diagnostic tests given by school psychologists, resource specialists, speech therapists, and classroom teachers are designed to provide important information about a child's academic strengths and weaknesses. These data are a vital component in the process of developing an effective remediation strategy, targeting specific educational goals, and creating reasonable criteria for evaluating the efficacy of the learning assistance program (see **Individual Educational Program [IEP],** page 126).

Because there are so many different types of learning problems, educators and psychologists have developed a broad spectrum of diagnostic tests to identify specific academic and perceptual deficits. These tests range from quick screening assessments to comprehensive multifaceted evaluations. Most school districts use a fairly standardized package of highly accurate tests. The more precise the identification process, the more focused and effective the learning assistance program will be. (Unfortunately, the testing procedures are often far more effective than the actual remediation procedures!)

Testing procedures assess perceptual processing skills (how efficiently children decode auditory, visual, and kinesthetic sensory data), IQ, word recognition, vocabulary, reading comprehension, inferential reasoning, spelling, math conceptual and computational skills, visual and auditory memory, expressive language, visual-motor skills, and motor coordination. (See specific entries for more information about these learning skills and suggested remedial strategies.) Certain tests are administered by the school psychologist and others by the resource specialist or speech pathologist.

A brief glossary of common testing terms and educational jargon is presented below. These terms often appear on diagnostic test reports and may also be used during the IEP meeting.

Achievement Test: A test designed to measure how much your child has learned after instruction in specific content areas. These tests are usually standardized and nationally normed. ("Standardized Test" and "Norms" are defined on page 318.)

Aptitude: A natural ability, a capacity, or talent in a particular area such as music or mathematics. Aptitude is a specialized facility to master a particular skill.

Criterion-Referenced Test: A test, usually designed by a teacher or publisher, that measures a student's mastery of a specific subject he has studied. The scores are not standardized (nationally normed) but can provide the teacher and parent with useful information about what the child has and has not learned.

Diagnostic Test: A test that pinpoints your child's academic or perceptual strengths and weaknesses. The results are generally used to plan a learning assistance strategy specifically designed to correct the identified weaknesses.

Grade Equivalent: A ranking of test performance based on a raw score that statistically compares your child's correct answers with those of other children in the same grade. The score is expressed in terms of years and months (with nine months making up each school year). For example, a grade equivalent score (G.E.) of 2.8 means that a child's test performance compares with that of other children in the eighth month of second grade.

Intelligence Quotient (IQ): An index designed to predict academic success. The IQ test compares your child's performance (or learning potential) with that of other children of the same age. This comparison yields a statistically derived score called *IQ*. The score does not measure creativity, developed talent, or motivation. An IQ score between 85 and 115 is considered to be in the average range. A score between 70 and 85 is low average, while 115 to 130 is considered high average. A score below 70 indicates probable mental retardation, and a score above 130 indicates probable giftedness. These scores may vary slightly depending on the particular IQ test administered, and the scores can be influenced by rapport with the examiner and by emotional, cultural, and perceptual factors (see **IQ Test Scores,** page 130).

Mastery Test: See Criterion-Referenced Test.

Mean Score: The mathematical average of all students' test scores on a particular test. One half of the students taking the test score above the mean and one half score below.

Mental Age: A score on a mental abilities test that statistically compares your child's performance level to that of other children. The score distinguishes your child's chronological age from his mental age. For example, your child's chronological age may be 10–6 (ten years, six months), but the number of his correct answers on the test may compare with that of children whose chronological age is 11–4. His total correct answers produce a statistical mental age score that is six months above his chronological age. Your child would, thus, be considered to have higher than average intelligence.

Norms: A statistical frame of reference on a standardized test (see below) that enumerates the actual performance on the test by pupils of specific ages and in specific grades in school. Through the use of norms your child's score can be compared nationally to the scores of other students of the same age or in the same grade.

Percentile: A score that states a student's relative position within a defined group by ranking all students who have taken a test. A score at the fiftieth percentile is generally considered to be at grade level. A score at the fortieth percentile would be approximately one year below grade level, and a score at the sixtieth percentile would be approximately one year above grade level.

Power Test: An untimed test with items usually arranged in order of ascending difficulty that determines a student's level of performance in a particular subject area.

Raw Score: The total number of correct answers on a test.

Readiness Test: A test that measures your child's mastery of requisite skills before he proceeds to the next academic level. This test is typically used by kindergarten teachers to determine if your child is academically and developmentally prepared to function effectively in first grade.

Reliability: A statistical representation of how well a test consistently produces the same results.

Scaled Score: A ranking system, chosen by the publisher of a test, that is derived from the raw scores obtained by students taking the test. A different scale is established for each test. For example, one test might have a scale from one to nineteen while another might have a scale from one to seventy. To interpret a scaled score, you must know the mean score and the standard deviation for that test.

Standard Deviation: A measure of how much your child's score varies from the mean score of all the students taking the test.

Standard Score: A statistical ranking of your child's performance on a standardized test based on the raw score he achieved relative to the performance of a large sample of students of the same age and/or grade level.

Standardized Test: A test with specific and uniform instructions for administering, timing, and scoring that is given to large numbers of children at one time. The test statistically compares your child's performance with that of a large sample of students of the same age and/or grade level. On many tests local norms are also provided for comparing your child's scores with those of other children of the same socioeconomic background. The norms established by the standardization process are used by teachers and school psychologists to determine a child's relative level of performance and achievement.

Stanine: A statistical ranking of your child's performance on a standardized test on a scale of one through nine. The mean score is five, and a score from three to four is generally considered low average. A score from six to seven is considered high average. Frequently the results on a standardized test will be reported in both a stanine score and a percentile score. The higher the stanine score, the higher the percentile score will be.

Survey Test: A test that measures general achievement in an academic area. It is not as comprehensive or specific as a criterion-referenced test.

Validity: The accuracy with which a test measures what it was designed to measure.

SUGGESTED CORRECTIVE STRATEGIES

In School

1. Understanding your child's academic strengths and weaknesses, identifying underlying deficits, and concurring with the objectives of the learning assistance program and the choice of corrective methods are requisites to your playing a constructive, contributory role in the remediation process. The test results can guide you in selecting the most appropriate program for your child, in evaluating progress, in communicating with the classroom teacher and resource specialist, and in providing appropriate support and assistance at home.

It is crucial that the person evaluating your child take the time to explain carefully in comprehensible terms the test results and any technical data or jargon. If you are perplexed or if you have reservations, don't hesitate to ask questions and to express your concerns. You may need several explanations before you agree to the remediation strategy. Don't feel "dumb" if you need clarification. You're your child's primary advocate, and you must have information and insight if you are to fulfill this vital function. What happens at the IEP meeting when the results are discussed is extremely important (see **Individual Educational Program [IEP]**, page 126, **Understanding Diagnostic Test Results,** page 316, **Evaluating Special Education Programs,** page 70, **Communicating with the School,** page 35, **Conferencing with School Officials,** page 39, and **Parents' Rights,** page 201). Be prepared to assert your rights and your child's rights!

At Home

1. If you are dissatisfied with the testing procedures, the test interpretation, the proposed learning assistance strategy, or the denial of learning assistance services, you may want to consult a professional outside the school system. This person should be able to explain the test results, offer a "second opinion," and suggest alternative options for addressing your child's learning needs such as private learning assistance.

2. If you feel your child's educational needs are not being met, discuss your concerns with the school authorities. You may need to involve the superintendent if you do not get satisfaction at the local level. Consult the district's parents' rights manual (see page 201). In extreme cases you may need to hire a parent advocate to represent you (see **Individual Educational Program,** page 126). Advocates are educational or clinical psychologists or educational therapists who are knowledgeable about learning problems and well versed in educational law. Their function is to represent your child's and your family's interests during the planning stages of the remediation strategy. (See **Parents' Rights,** page 201.)

Your child's interests will be best served if you work with the school district constructively and cooperatively. Make every effort to be reasonable and to negotiate calmly if there is disagreement about the test interpretation, the proposed remediation strategy, or the educational services being offered or denied your child. An adversarial situation with possible legal action should be a last resort.

VERBAL EXPRESSION

Children are continually responding to stimuli received through their five senses (decoding) and selecting words to express their perceptions, feelings, and thoughts (encoding). Their choice of words and the quality of their expressive language skills are influenced by intelligence, natural language aptitude, home environment, and educational experiences (see **Vocabulary**, page 329, **Language Arts [Essays and Reports]**, page 141, and **Speech Disorders,** page 280, for a description of articulation and pronunciation problems).

Profound expressive language deficiencies are usually symptomatic of a condition called *dysphasia* or, in extreme cases, aphasia (total inability to use language). These neurologically based disorders erect major barriers to communication, and children afflicted with them require intensive language therapy. In some cases profound communication disorders may be linked to autism, a perplexing condition that causes children to become emotionally distant and noncommunicative.

Mildly inarticulate children have more subtle communication deficits. Although they, too, may require language therapy, most can usually improve their verbal skills dramatically if they simply receive guidance and feedback in school and at home. They must practice using language until they feel more comfortable and confident, and they must be constructively critiqued and repeatedly affirmed and acknowledged for progress. Even children with relatively minor communication problems can be extremely sensitive about their language deficiencies. Their struggle to express themselves can cause insecurity, feelings of inadequacy, and psychological vulnerability. The more significant the communication deficits, the more defensive they are likely to become. To protect themselves, they may resist discussing their feelings, thoughts, and observations. They may respond grudgingly to direct questions, answer in monosyllables, and avoid speaking in public. This reticence ironically calls attention to the very inadequacies they're trying to hide. Unless their specific language deficits (vocabulary, grammar, or organization of thoughts) are identified and treated, chronically noncommunicative children can become increasingly isolated from other children and even from their families. It is critical that these youngsters be evaluated by a speech pathologist to determine if language therapy and/or psychological counseling is required.

Some children who are actually extremely articulate in private conversation may be traumatized by the prospect of speaking in front of a group. These children are usually insecure and chronically shy. To overcome their fears, they must be gently coaxed to communicate and repeatedly affirmed and praised. Their parents and teachers must also make special efforts to convince them that they are not being judged critically. Allaying their fears and building their self-confidence will require time, patience, emotional support, and careful planning (see suggestions below).

Logic dictates that *all* children, and especially those with poor communication skills, be provided with repeated opportunities to express their ideas and feelings and must receive sensitive, supportive, and constructive feedback. Their parents should intentionally draw them into family discussions, and their teachers should encourage them to participate in class debates, give speeches and oral presentations, discuss current events, and summarize verbally what they've read in their textbooks (see suggestions below). Although these experiences will undoubtedly trigger anxiety, this anxiety must be overcome. Fearful children require extra coaching, rehearsals, encouragement, acknowledgment, praise, and instruction in basic relaxation and visualization techniques (see the suggested corrective strategies under **Test Anxiety,** page 304). A series of carefully orchestrated successes can be a powerful elixir for building self-confidence and a powerful antidote for stage fright.

Unless our society begins to prioritize the teaching of effective verbal skills, our high schools will continue to crank out graduates with a working vocabulary of 1,000 words. And these youngsters will continue to preface each inarticulate, noncogent statement they utter with the words *you know.*

SUGGESTED CORRECTIVE STRATEGIES

In School

1. Ask your child if he participates regularly in class discussions, verbal question-and-answer periods, and class debates and is required to give oral reports and speeches. If you conclude that he is not being provided with sufficient opportunities to develop his communication skills, discuss your concerns with the teacher or, if appropriate, the principal. Urge the school administration to set up programs specifically designed to help students develop communication skills. Attend school board meetings and express your concerns publicly.

2. If you believe your child has an expressive language problem, request that he be evaluated by the school speech pathologist. (Consult with your pediatrician for a second opinion.) If your child attends regular classes, his teacher may need to coax him gently to express his ideas and feelings in a non-stressful, noncompetitive context. If he is shy, reticent, or language-deficient, his teacher will need to be especially patient, nurturing, affirming, and supportive. Although opportunities to speak in front of other children should be orchestrated, the process of building your child's skills and self-confidence must proceed in small, carefully controlled increments. Your child, for example, might initially be asked to talk for only fifteen to thirty seconds about his vacation or a project he is doing. The teacher may need to help him, but she should not correct him in front of the other children, as this might cause embarrassment. Feedback should be given privately after class.

3. If your child's school doesn't have a debating club, suggest to the principal that one be established at each grade level. Opportunities to debate should also be created in the classroom. Acting out historical events from textbooks provides a wonderful opportunity for public speaking and for acquiring confidence. The students might assume the roles of King George and his advisers and generals. Other students could play the roles of George Washington and the Founding Fathers. A script could be written by the students. Each side would present and debate its respective position. The same process could be used to debate such issues as the use of insecticides and disarmament.

At Home

1. By creating opportunities for communication at home and providing constructive feedback, support, and criticism, you can play a vital role in developing your child's verbal skills. Practice can compensate for a lack of natural talent in almost any endeavor. The dinner table is an excellent place for family discussions about current events. Youngsters who participate in discussions and hear their parents express themselves almost invariably become more articulate than those who don't have these experiences. If your child responds to the question "What happened in school today?" by saying "Nothing," be more specific without sounding as if you are a detective grilling a suspect. You might say: "Tell me

what the teacher said about the field trip," or "How did you solve those fraction problems that were giving you trouble?" or "What are you going to cover in your science report?" There are two guiding principles for engaging shy, reticent, defensive children: Avoid making the discussions stressful and know when to stop.

2. Debate issues — offshore oil drilling, women reporters in men's locker rooms, etc.—with your child. Be careful not to overwhelm him with your superior communication skills, vocabulary, and knowledge. Newspaper articles can be a great catalyst for discussion. If your child is interested in sports, read aloud something from the sport's page. Your objective here is to develop *verbal* skills and not reading skills. Ask thought-provoking questions: "What do you think about this decision to fire the baseball manager?" Encourage him to organize his thoughts. If his ideas don't appear to be logical or sequential, you might respond: "I'm not sure I understand. Could you explain it again?" Use this approach sparingly, or you risk making your child defensive and impeding communication. Know when to listen and when to back off. Don't interrupt your child. Make the session fun and brief. Your child's attention span is shorter than yours. Let him know that you appreciate his ideas and acknowledge not only his progress but also his effort. Praise him when he makes a

good point and effectively communicates his position.

3. (ES) To develop your child's telephone communication skills (a vital asset!) call home and engage him in conversations. Ask him to describe everything that happened that day in school. For some children talking on the telephone and not seeing the face of the person they are speaking to poses a significant challenge. These children tend to "freeze" as soon as they pick up the phone.

4. Encourage your child to expand his vocabulary by intentionally using new words in her daily communication. Demonstrate how carefully chosen words can express ideas with precision (see **Vocabulary,** page 329).

5. Periodically set aside time after a TV show for a family discussion. The discussion could be about issues in an episode of *The Cosby Show* or *The Simpsons,* or any movie, network special, or sitcom. Encourage your child to express his ideas and feelings. Use discretion in presenting an opposing viewpoint. You goal is to stimulate, not stifle, communication and the exchange of ideas.

6. If your child has chronic expressive language difficulties or does not make progress after you use the preceding strategies, consult with your pediatrician. A neurological examination and a comprehensive assessment by a private speech and language specialist may be advisable. Psychological counseling may also be advisable if your child is highly fearful about expressing himself.

VISUAL MEMORY

Teachers expect their students to assimilate prodigious amounts of written information. Youngsters with good visual retention have a distinct advantage in classes where teachers emphasize the retention of facts and details.

Good visual memory skills are a particularly valuable resource when children spell. The child who can "see" words in his mind is invariably a better speller than the student who tries to sound out words or who tries to apply the rules of spelling and phonics (see **Spelling Problems,** page 283, and **Nonphonetic Words,** page 191). The capacity to imprint a mental picture of words can significantly reduce errors and is especially useful when spelling words that are commonly mispronounced (*prerogative*), nonphonetic (*allegiance, through,* and *bought*), or foreign (*sergeant* and *lieutenant*).

Having good visual memory skills can be an asset in virtually every subject area. The child who can see the date when the Declaration of Independence was signed, the formula for sulfuric acid, the conjugation of the French word *savoir,* or the formula for determining the circumference of a circle will generally have little difficulty recalling information.

There are, of course, other ways to learn and recall information. Auditory learners prefer to imprint spoken or subvocalized information in their minds (see **Auditory Memory,** page 22). This ability to remember auditorially can be especially useful when teachers lecture. As a general rule, however, visual imprinting is a more effective tool for memorizing the large quantities of factual data written in textbooks, in notes, and on the chalkboard.

Good visual memory skills do not necessarily guarantee good reading comprehension. A child may be able to remember and regurgitate facts, but she may not understand the facts or be able to apply them (see **Reading Comprehension,** page 250). The child, however, will usually do well on multiple-choice and true/false tests that stress details (see **Memorizing Information,** page 182).

Although rote memorization has a place in the educational process, a primary emphasis on memorization discourages critical thinking. The cerebral

RPMs required to answer the question "When was the cotton jenny invented and who invented it?" are considerably fewer than those required to answer the question "Discuss the long-term effects of the Industrial Revolution on our present culture and cite specific inventions that have affected the American life-style and economy." (See **Critical Thinking,** page 42.)

Students forget information that is poorly understood, not reinforced by discussion and application, and/or perceived as irrelevant. Most children who are required to memorize the names of the bones in the hand will forget this information soon after taking a test. Their long-term retention usually increases significantly if they assemble a model of the hand (kinesthetic learning), draw diagrams (visual learning), discuss and describe the information verbally (auditory), and interact with other students in a cooperative learning experience. When multisensory learning is reinforced by having students intentionally create visual pictures in their minds, their recall will be even better.

Smart students capitalize on their natural and preferred learning style. If they are required to memorize a great many facts, dates, names, or formulas, they use those learning modalities that will facilitate recalling this subject matter (see **Smart Thinking,** page 275, **Spelling Problems,** page 283, and **Study Skills,** page 292). This pragmatism distinguishes the achieving student from the non-achieving and underachieving student.

With instruction and practice your child can improve her visual memory skills and can learn how to use her eyes like the lens of a camera and her brain like the film inside the camera. Her ability to imprint visual pictures is an invaluable resource that will serve her throughout her life.

SUGGESTED CORRECTIVE STRATEGIES

In School

1. If you suspect that your child has visual memory deficits, request that she be evaluated by the Child Study Team (see page 111 for definition), school psychologist, or resource specialist. Highly accurate tests can be used to substantiate any findings. If deficits are found, request that the resource specialist provide remedial assistance. If help is denied, consult the district's parents' rights manual, which spells out the official guidelines for participation in the resource program (see **Parents' Rights,** page 201).

2. Ask about the wide range of materials that classroom teachers and resource specialists can use to improve visual memory skills.

At Home

1. Urge your child to create visual pictures whenever she needs to memorize information. Encourage her to close her eyes and "see" in her mind a definition of a word she needs to memorize or the conjugation of a Spanish verb. Suggest that she see the letters or numbers in her favorite color or colors. When studying, have her hold the paper above eye level and look up (this facilitates visual accessing). For specific techniques that develop visualization skills, refer to the suggested corrective strategies under **Spelling Problems,** page 283.

2. If your child's preferred learning mode is auditory or kinesthetic/ tactile, encourage her to capitalize on her natural abilities. For example, have her act out the definition of a word or trace the letters of a word in the air using her whole arm. Have her use Scrabble squares to form words. Turn over the squares and write numbers and scientific symbols on them. Have her create the scientific notation for sulfuric acid (H_2SO_4). Urge her to be creative. But also encourage her to use the visualization techniques described above to reinforce her preferred learning modality and to help her memorize material that may not lend itself to her preferred learning modality.

3. Go to your local teacher supply store and ask to see materials specifically designed to develop visual memory skills.

VOCABULARY

Effective communication demands a precise vocabulary. Yet each year legions of bright, potentially capable teenagers graduate from high school with woefully inadequate vocabularies thanks to a society and an educational system that place little value on good communication skills.

The traditional method for developing children's vocabulary skills is at best uninspiring and at worst mind-numbing. Teachers typically assign a list of new words each week and require their students to look up and memorize the definitions. Children are then instructed to use the words in sentences or paragraphs and are given weekly vocabulary tests to measure their mastery. Once they have "learned" the words, they are seldom reviewed, and students are rarely required to use them again. The outcome is predictable: The meaning of the words is quickly forgotten.

The "memorize/use in a sentence/take a test" ritual leeches the joy children could derive from participating dynamically in the process of enriching their vocabularies. Children who learn words mechanically cannot possibly experience the beauty, precision, and potential of the English language.

There are, of course, exceptional teachers who do a first-rate job of developing vocabulary skills. Their enthusiasm for language is contagious and seductive. They inspire their students to improve their vocabulary and communication skills. Unfortunately, most teachers approach vocabulary development as a painful chore, and their students respond accordingly.

In many school districts the primary concern of administrators, teachers, parents, and school boards is to improve students' scores on reading and vocabulary tests. In an annual ritual the test performance of local schools is compared to that of schools in other districts and states. These test results have become the major criterion for measuring the efficacy of local educational programs, and because of the political implications, many teachers are overtly or covertly pressured to "teach to the tests." In the frenzy to raise scores the issue of retention and application of language skills is often overlooked.

Listening to children communicate confirms that most youngsters actually use very few words to express their thoughts and feelings. The typical high school graduate has a working vocabulary of perhaps 2,000 words. In daily communication a youngster may use fewer than 1,000 words. (Two of the most common of these words are *you know.*) Our beleaguered educational system cannot be held exclusively responsible for this sad state of affairs. Insufficient encouragement and opportunities to use communication skills at home and negative social pressures frequently deter children from developing their verbal skills. In our society, and especially in certain teenage subcultures, having and using a good vocabulary are equated with pretentiousness, and youngsters are often reluctant to use "big" words for fear of social rejection. Even educated adults may hesitate to use precise vocabulary because they do not want to be considered pedantic or superior.

Language mastery requires continual practice and application both in school *and* at home (see **Verbal Expression,** page 321). Children who hear their parents use language effectively around the dinner table, who are encouraged to express their feelings, perceptions, and ideas, and who are acknowledged and affirmed for developing their communication skills and expanding their vocabulary invariably become more articulate than children who are permitted to coast through life with a working vocabulary of 1,000 words. With sufficient practice your child's expressive language and vocabulary skills can improve dramatically.

SUGGESTED CORRECTIVE STRATEGIES

In School

1. If you suspect that your child is not acquiring good vocabulary skills, express your concerns to the teacher. Ask if there are any creative materials or methods that might be used to help your child (and other students) develop these skills. Materials specifically designed with this objective in mind are included in the Resource List at the back of the book.

2. (J/HS) If you have concerns about the vocabulary development methods used in your child's class, ask the teacher to describe the program and its objectives. Diplomatically express your concerns, being careful not to make the teacher feel he is being attacked or denigrated.

At Home

1. Establish a family tradition of looking up in the dictionary and introducing one interesting new word each day. By using the dictionary and demonstrating your appreciation for language, you cannot help "infecting" your child with your enthusiasm. Be supportive of his use of new words and effusively affirm and acknowledge his progress. Everyone should try using the word at least twice during dinner. Make the process fun. You might say: "In the movie we rented yesterday, one of the lawyers said, 'I'm not your adversary.' What do you think *adversary* means? Let's look it up. I'll use the word in a sentence. Now you make up a sentence." Make the procedure a family ritual and try to introduce a new word every day. Keep a dictionary handy. Purchase one that is written specifically for children your child's age. Reviewing previously used words could be a game or contest. ("For one point, can you remember the definition of *adversary,* and for an extra point, can you use it in a sentence?") Learning the definitions of new words is only a small part of the mastery process. The litmus test is the ability and desire to use new words in conversation. Remember, your child will probably require many exposures and a great deal of practice before he will be able to remember and use newly learned words with facility.

2. Purchase from your local bookstore or teacher supply house vocabulary development workbooks, games, or flash cards appropriate for your child's grade level (see Resource List).

3. Play word games with your child. Make two copies of a list of twenty-five words and their definitions. You can pick the words yourself or use a vocabulary development book. Have your child look at the words and definitions on his list while you say: "I'm thinking of a word that means hardworking. It begins with the letters *in* and ends with the letter *s.*" Your child would get one point for figuring out the word *industrious* and a bonus point for using the word in a sentence. (The points could be used for winning a prize.) Now have your child take a turn. He gives the clues, and you figure out the word and use it in a sentence. Don't make the words too difficult. Intentionally use the new words in conversation during the week and urge your child to use them. Vocabulary materials you might want to examine are included in the Resource List at the back of the book.

4. See **Verbal Expression**, page 321, for additional strategies to develop your child's language and vocabulary skills.

WORKING INDEPENDENTLY

In fourth grade a major shift occurs in the classroom: teachers expect students to work with increasing independence. Those children who require constant supervision are destined to have significant academic difficulties in junior and senior high school.

Parents alarmed by their child's lack of independence may attempt to compensate by becoming excessively involved in monitoring his work and in helping him with his assignments (see **Monitoring Homework,** page 185). Their intentions may be noble, but these parents are unwittingly discouraging the development of self-sufficiency. Overly protected, continually rescued children may misconstrue their parents' motives and conclude that their parents *want* them to remain dependent. In some cases this perception may be accurate, for some parents actually do have an unconscious need to create and perpetuate a symbiotic relationship with their child (see **Learned Helplessness,** page 152).

The emotional and vocational consequences of excessive dependence can be catastrophic. Children addicted to having their parents serve as on-call academic paramedics will be tempted to call for help whenever they encounter any challenge or problem. Being continually assisted, protected, nagged, cajoled, and consoled may become a primary payoff. The dependence guarantees attention and sympathy. Once a child becomes firmly ensconced in this comfort zone, he will often vigorously resist all attempts to help him become self-sufficient.

Children with learning difficulties are at the greatest risk for becoming dependent on their parents and teachers. If they are falling further and further behind because they are not receiving learning assistance or because they are not responding positively to the assistance, they will either give up or need constant parental support.

The parents of a learning disabled child are faced with an obvious dilemma. They realize their child needs help, but they also realize that if they provide too much help he could become overly needy. Extricating themselves from the "dependence loop" requires careful planning and the willpower to resist rescuing their child every time he encounters a glitch (see suggested strategies).

A powerful natural instinct impels parents to protect a weak and vulnerable child. If you suspect that this protective instinct is excessive and not in your child's best interests or if you suspect that you might be unwittingly encouraging your child's dependence, you must be willing to examine objectively your own psychological needs and hidden agenda. A red flag should go up if you realize you are continually using the pronouns *we* and *our.* ("*We* have a spelling test tomorrow, or *we* have to do *our* math problems.")

A child's "security blanket" must be withdrawn in carefully planned, incremental stages. Removing the support system too abruptly could trigger anxiety, resentment, insecurity, resistance, and shutdown.

SUGGESTED CORRECTIVE STRATEGIES

In School

1. If you observe that your child is having difficulty working independently, the following step-by-step procedure will help you develop a strategy for correcting the situation.

1. Ask the teacher, school psychologist, and resource specialist to help you realistically assess your child's current academic skills and needs.

2. Make certain that necessary remedial assistance is provided in school or in a private after-school program (see Parents' Rights, page 201).

3. Adjust your expectations and performance guidelines to your child's skill level (see Behavior and Performance Guidelines, page 26).

4. Request that the teacher adjust the difficulty of her assignments to your child's current skill level.

5. Request that the teacher and/ or resource specialist provide guidance about the type and extent of assistance you should furnish at home (e.g., should you proofread his book reports?).

6. Objectively examine your child's behavior and modify your responses to manipulative behavior.

2. If your child is receiving extra assistance and has become overly dependent, discuss this issue with the teacher and/or resource specialist. Define specific, realistic academic and behavioral objectives that take into consideration his current academic skill levels. You may decide that after he does several sample math problems and clearly understands the concepts he will be expected to complete the remaining problems without any help. This "weaning" process may cause your child some anxiety initially, but it is vital to preparing him to deal with the real world, where he cannot expect

someone to be there to hold his hand. If he makes "silly" mistakes because his teacher is not continually monitoring his work, he will simply have to redo the work.

3. If your child can do the work that is assigned but insists on being helped by his teacher, suggest that she deflect his request. She might say: "I believe you can do this on your own. I will evaluate the work after you hand it in, and if you don't understand something, we can go over it together." If your child continually asks "Is this right?" she might respond "What do you think?" The teacher's refusal to be manipulated may make your child unhappy, but modifying his self-defeating behavior is far more critical than his grade on an assignment.

At Home

1. For academically needy children some at-home help will undoubtedly be necessary. You must strike a balance between appropriate and excessive help. Consult your child's teacher, resource specialist, and/or school psychologist for suggestions about how best to provide assistance. Progress reports and periodic conferences are vital. You may also want to consult an independent educational therapist or psychologist for ideas about how to help your child catch up and modify nonadaptive behaviors.

2. (J/HS) Helping academically deficient junior and senior high school students can be quite difficult for parents, especially when the material requires skills you have not practiced in twenty-five years. You may need to hire a tutor to help your child with homework and studying. Discuss your concerns about excessive dependence with the tutor. Even a highly skillful tutor can be manipulated into providing too much help.

3. Be realistic and patient. Dependence habits cannot be changed overnight. If your child continually requests help, and you're convinced he can do the work, you might respond: "I believe you know how to do this on your own. I'm willing to check it over after you've completed it." If he makes spelling mistakes, you could check the lines where errors are found and have him find the errors himself. If he can't, so be it. Being rescued is habit-forming! Helping him become more self-sufficient is, in the long run, far more important than correcting every one of his spelling mistakes.

4. Discuss with your child your concerns about the need to be able to work independently and brainstorm together how he could begin to do more work on his own. You might say: "Now that you understand how to do these problems, how much of this math assignment can you do without any help?" If he is reluctant to work on his own, propose an experiment and create a system for rewarding him for independence (e.g., "If you can do all these yourself, we'll go out for an ice cream cone").

5. If your child is struggling to do his work because he lacks important skills, you will have to make a judgment call about how much help to provide. If his skills are very poor, consider hiring a qualified tutor. The tutor should be able to assess his skills and determine the true extent of his needs.

RESOURCE LIST

ALTERNATIVE TEACHING STRATEGIES
(see **Atypical Learning Problems, Keeping Up with the Class, Communicating with the School, Negative Attitude Toward School, Teacher-Child Conflict, Passive Learning**)

Armstrong, Thomas. *In Their Own Way.* Los Angeles: Jeremy P. Tarcher, 1987.

Coles, Gerald. *The Learning Mystique.* New York: Pantheon, 1987.

Gardener, Howard. *Frames of Mind.* New York: Basic Books, 1983.

Jensen, Eric. *Student Success Secrets.* Hauppauge, N.Y.: Barron, 1989.

Jensen, Eric. *You Can Succeed.* Hauppauge, N.Y.: Barron, 1989.

Maeroff, Gene L. *The School Smart Parent.* New York: Times Books, 1989.

GRAMMAR
(also see **Punctuation, Phonics**)

Auld, Janice L. *Cut & Paste Phonics* (gr. 1–3). Belmont, CA: Fearon Teacher Aids, 1985.

Burch, Marilyn. *Phonics Seatwork* (gr. 1–2). Belmont, CA: Fearon Teacher Aids, 1985.

Criscuolo, Nicholas. *Boost Skills with Practice* (gr. 3–6). Belmont, CA: Fearon Teacher Aids, 1987.

Criscuolo, Nicholas. *Brush Up on the Basics* (gr. 2–5). Belmont, CA: Fearon Teacher Aids, 1987.

Freeman, Sara. *Nouns, Verbs & Adjectives* (gr. 1–2). Palo Verdes Estates, CA: Frank Schaffer Pubs., 1990.

Hoeber, Margaret. *Nouns, Verbs & Adjectives* (gr. 2–3). Palo Verdes Estates, CA: Frank Schaffer Pubs., 1990.

Knoblock, Kathleen. *Compounds & Contractions* (gr. 2). Palo Verdes Estates, CA: Frank Schaffer Pubs., 1987.

Laird, Stanley. *Hands-on Grammar* (gr. 4–12). Belmont, CA: Fearon Teacher Aids, 1978.

Manhard, Stephen. *The Goof-Proofer* (all grades). New York: Collier Books, 1985.

Rodgers, Molly, and Linda M. Zimmer. *Grammar* (gr. 5–7 & up). Columbus: Essential Learning Products, 1990.

Shiotsu, Vicky. *Compounds & Contractions* (gr. 1). Palo Verdes Estates, CA: Frank Schaffer Pubs., 1987.

Games and Learning Activities

"Capitalization & Punctuation Activity Cards" (gr. 1–2). Palo Verdes Estates, CA: Frank Schaffer Pubs.

"Punctuation Bingo" (gr. 1–6). St. Paul: Trend Enterprises.

"Punctuation Patterns" (gr. 1–3). Baltimore: Media Materials.

LANGUAGE ARTS

(also see **Essay Tests**)

Akers, Deborah, and Von McInnis. _Writing Power Plus_ (gr. 1–6). Belmont, CA: Fearon Teacher Aids, 1986.

Corbett, Paula. _Fantasy Fling_ (gr. 5–8). Santa Barbara, CA: Learning Works, 1984.

Dean, John F. _Writing Well_ (gr. 5 & up). Belmont, CA: Fearon Teacher Aids, 1985.

Evans, Marilyn. _Guided Report Writing_ (gr. 3–6). Monterey, CA: Evan-Moor Corp., 1987.

Hamilton, Sally. _Spin Your Wheels_ (gr. 4–6). Santa Barbara, CA: Learning Works, 1982.

Johnson, Eric. _You Are the Editor_ (gr. 5 & up). Belmont, CA: Fearon Teacher Aids, 1981.

May, Robert R., & Sarah P. Cerny. _Power Writing_ (elem.–Jr. high). Mount Laurel, NJ: Learn Inc., 1979.

Robertson, Debbie. _Blast Off with Book Reports_ (gr. 3–8). Carthage, IL: Good Apple, 1985.

Wentrcek, Ginger. _Leaping Lizards Language Arts_ (gr. 2–4). Belmont, CA: Fearon Teacher Aids, 1986.

LEARNING THE ALPHABET

(see **Auditory Discrimination, Spelling Problems, Visual Memory, Phonics**)

Coudron, Jill. _Alphabet Activities_ (pre-k–gr. 3). Belmont, CA: Fearon Teacher Aids, 1952.

Coudron, Jill. _Alphabet Fun and Games_ (pre-k–gr. 3). Belmont, CA: Fearon Teacher Aids, 1984.

Coudron, Jill. _Alphabet Puppets_ (gr. k–3). Belmont, CA: Fearon Teacher Aids, 1979.

Coudron, Jill. _Alphabet Stories_ (pre-k–gr. 3). Belmont, CA: Fearon Teacher Aids, 1982.

Foust, Sylvia. _Beginning Book of Letters and Consonant Sounds_ (gr. k–2). Belmont, CA: Fearon Teacher Aids, 1986.

Foust, Sylvia. _Beginning Book of Vowel Sounds_ (gr. k–2). Belmont, CA: Fearon Teacher Aids, 1986.

Gruber, Barbara. *Alphabetizing Activities* (gr. 1–2). Palo Verdes Estates, CA: Frank Schaffer Pubs., 1988.

Tauber, Annette. *Alphabet* (pre-k). Palo Verdes Estates, CA: Frank Schaffer Pubs., 1987.

Tauber, Annette. *Alphabet Dot-to-Dot* (pre-k–k). Palo Verdes Estates, CA: Frank Schaffer Pubs., 1987.

Games and Learning Activities

"Basic Word Skills Activity Cards" (age 4–7). Palo Verdes Estates, CA: Frank Schaffer Pubs.

"Bearamores Go to the Big City" (gr. pre-k–1). Baltimore: Media Materials.

"Bearamores Learn Letter Sounds" (gr. pre-k). Baltimore: Media Materials.

"Beginning Sounds" (gr. k–2). Baltimore: Media Materials.

"Easy Blends and Digraphs" (age 4–7). Palo Verdes Estates, CA: Frank Schaffer Pubs.

"Easy Consonants" (age 4–7). Palo Verdes Estates, CA: Frank Schaffer Pubs.

"Easy Picture Word Opposites" (age 4–7). Palo Verdes Estates, CA: Frank Schaffer Pubs.

"Easy Picture Words—Sets" (age 4–7). Palo Verdes Estates, CA: Frank Schaffer Pubs.

"Easy Sight Words" (age 4–7). Palo Verdes Estates, CA: Frank Schaffer Pubs.

"Easy Special Vowels" (age 4–7). Palo Verdes Estates, CA: Frank Schaffer Pubs.

"Easy Vowels" (age 4–7). Palo Verdes Estates, CA: Frank Schaffer Pubs.

"Phonetic Quizmo" (gr. 1–4). Baltimore: Media Materials.

"Picture Word Bingo" (age 4–7). Palo Verdes Estates, CA: Frank Schaffer Pubs.

"Short and Long Vowel—Do-Mi-No-Es" (age 4–7). Palo Verdes Estates, CA: Frank Schaffer Pubs.

"Sight Word Bingo" (age 4–7). Palo Verdes Estates, CA: Frank Schaffer Pubs.

"You Can Read Phonetic Drillcards" (gr. k–3). Baltimore: Media Materials.

LEARNING DISABILITIES

(also see **Attention Deficit Disorder, Atypical Learning Problems, Dyslexia, Mainstreaming and Special Day Classes, Parents' Rights, Understanding Diagnostic Test Results, Reading Comprehension**)

Greene, Lawrence J. *Kids Who Underachieve.* New York: Simon & Schuster, 1986.

Greene, Lawrence J. *Learning Disabilities and Your Child.* New York: Fawcett, 1987.

Dias, Peggy. *Diamonds in the Rough.* E. Aurora, NY: Slosson Educational Pubs., 1989.

Henzl, Elizabeth M. *Visual Aural Discrimination* (gr. 1–12). Novato, CA: Ann Arbor Pubs., 1973.

Justus, Fred. *Visual Discrimination* (gr. 1–2). Jonesboro, AR: ESP, 1979.

Levinson, Harold, M.D. *Smart but Feeling Dumb*. New York: Warner Bk, 1988.

Levinson, Harold, M.D. *A Solution to the Riddle of Dyslexia*. New York: Springer-Verlag, 1983.

Love, Maria. *20 Decoding Games*. (gr. 1–3). Belmont, CA: Fearon Teacher Aids, 1982.

Osman, Betty B. *Learning Disabilities—A Family Affair*. New York: Warner, 1985.

Taylor, John. *Helping Your Hyperactive Child*. Rocklin, CA: Prima Publishing, 1990.

Valett, Robert E. *The Remediation of Learning Disabilities*. Belmont, CA: David S. Lake, 1978.

MATH

Fisk, Sally. *Primary Fractions* (gr. 1–3). St. Louis: Millikin Pubs., 1984.

Herlihy, Ruth. *Math Workbook: Drill & Practice* (gr. 1–6). St. Louis: Millikin Pubs., 1980.

Herlihy, Ruth. *Decimals Workbook: Drill & Practice* (gr. 5–7). St. Louis, Millikin Pubs., 1980.

Howell, Will C. *Grid and Bear It* (gr. 1–3). Belmont, CA: Fearon Teacher Aids, 1989.

Howell, Will C. *Grid and Graph It* (gr. 4–6). Belmont, CA: Fearon Teacher Aids, 1987.

Kirkpatrick, Vicky. *Addition/Subtraction with Regrouping* (nongraded). St. Louis: Millikin Pubs., 1984.

Nance, Beverly. *Beginning Algebra* (gr. 6–8). St. Louis: Millikin Pubs., 1989.

Panchyshyn, Robert, and Eula Ewing Moore. *Developing Key Concepts for Solving Word Problems* (gr. 3–4). Baldwin, NY: Barnell Loft, 1989.

Parson, Judith N. *Math-A-Dot* (gr. 1–5). Belmont, CA: Fearon Teacher Aids, 1974.

Parson, Judith N. *Math-A-Draw* (gr. 1–5). Belmont, CA: Fearon Teacher Aids, 1983.

Ryan, John J. *Developing Key Concepts in Math*. Baldwin, NY: Barnell Loft, 1986.

Vervoort, Gerardus, and Dale J. Mason. *Advanced Calculator Math* (gr. 7–10). Belmont, CA: Fearon Teacher Aids, 1980.

Vervoort, Gerardus, and Dale J. Mason. *Beginning Calculator Math* (gr. 5–7). Belmont, CA: Fearon Teacher Aids, 1980.

Vervoort, Gerardus, and Dale J. Mason. *Intermediate Calculator Math* (gr. 6–8). Belmont, CA: Fearon Teacher Aids, 1980.

Games and Learning Activities

"Addition, Multiplication, Division, Subtraction Flash Cards" (gr. 1–5). St. Paul: Trend Enterprises.
"Arithmetic Quizmo" (gr. 1–7). Baltimore: Media Materials.
"Castles & Keys" (gr. 1–3 or 4–6). Baltimore: Media Materials.
"Count Your Change" (gr. 1–4). Baltimore: Media Materials.
"Divisor Countdown" (gr. 5–7, reading level 4.0). Baltimore: Media Materials.
"Flannel Board Cut-Outs" (gr. k–1). Baltimore: Media Materials.
"Fractions Are Easy as Pie" (gr. 2–6). Baltimore: Media Materials.
"Fraction Discs" (gr. 4–6). Baltimore: Media Materials.
"Geometric Shapes" (gr. pre-k–3). Baltimore: Media Materials.
"Learning Multiplication Facts" (gr. 1–3). Baltimore: Media Materials.
"Make Your Own Flash Cards" (gr. pre-k as needed). St. Paul: Trend Enterprises.
"Math Lotto" (gr. k–3). Baltimore: Media Materials.
"Menu Madness" (gr. 4–8, reading level 3.0). Baltimore: Media Materials.
"Mark on Wipe off Math Cards" (gr. k–4). Baltimore: Media Materials.
"Numbers 0–25 Flash Cards" (gr. pre-k–1). St. Paul: Trend Enterprises.
"Numbers 0–100 Flash Cards" (gr. k–1). St. Paul: Trend Enterprises.
"Prime Factor Scramble" (gr. 5–7, reading level 4.0). Baltimore: Media Materials.
"Prime Number Checkers" (gr. 5–7, reading level 4.0). Baltimore: Media Materials.
"Tangram & Pattern Cards" (gr. 3–adult). Baltimore: Media Materials.
"Tell Time Quizmo" (gr. 1–4). Baltimore: Media Materials.
"Telling Time" (gr. 1–3). St. Paul: Trend Enterprises.
"Tigo Game" (gr. 4 & up). Baltimore: Media Materials.
"Toy Money" (gr. k–4). Baltimore: Media Materials.

PHONICS

(see **Auditory Discrimination, Dyslexia, Nonphonetic Words, Reading Aloud, Spelling Problems, Visual Memory**)

Dolch, Edward W., and Marguerite P. Dolch. *Dolch Proper Word Lists,* Sets I & II, Allen, TX: Developmental Learning Materials, 1987.
Greene, Lawrence J. *Key Word Inventory.* San Jose, CA: Developmental Learning Products, 1981.

Games and Learning Activities

Auditory Discrimination
"Sounds Lotto" (gr. pre-k–1). Baltimore: Media Materials.

Visual Discrimination

"Creature Factory" (ages 4–9). Dominguez Hill, CA: Educational Insights.

"Mix & Match Bears" (gr. pre-k–2). Baltimore: Media Materials.

"Play Scenes Lotto" (gr. pre-k–3). Baltimore: Media Materials.

"Teddy Bear Search" (gr. pre-k–1). Baltimore: Media Materials.

READING COMPREHENSION

(also see **Auditory Memory**)

Bell, Nanci. *Visualizing & Verbalizing for Language Comprehension & Thinking* (all ages). Baldwin, NY: Lowell & Lynwood, 1978.

Boning, Richard A. Multiple Skills Series (gr. 1–6). Baldwin, NY: Lowell & Lynwood, 1978.

Boning, Richard A. Specific Skill Series: *Detecting the Sequence* (gr. 2–12). Baldwin, NY: Barnell Loft, 1977.

Boning, Richard A. Specific Skill Series: *Drawing Conclusions* (gr. 2–12). Baldwin, NY: Barnell Loft, 1977.

Boning, Richard A. Specific Skill Series: *Getting the Facts* (gr. 2–12). Baldwin, NY: Barnell Loft, 1977.

Boning, Richard A. Specific Skill Series: *Getting the Main Idea* (gr. 2–12). Baldwin, NY: Barnell Loft, 1977.

Boning, Richard A. Specific Skill Series: *Locating the Answer* (gr. 2–12). Baldwin, NY: Barnell Loft, 1977.

Boning, Richard A. Specific Skill Series: *Using the Context* (gr. 2–12). Baldwin, NY: Barnell Loft, 1977.

Boning, Richard A., Charles R. Boning, and John F. Higgins. *Interactive Reading Program—Clues to Cloze* (gr. 1–6). Baldwin, NY: Barnell Loft, 1989.

Ceaser, L. D. *The Big Book of Comprehension Capers* (gr. 1–3). Belmont, CA: Fearon Teacher Aids, 1986.

Ceaser, L. D. Comprehension Capers Series: *Intent on Inferences* (gr. 4–6). Belmont, CA: Fearon Teacher Aids, 1986.

Ceaser, L. D. Comprehension Capers Series: *Main Ideas Maneuvers* (gr. 1–3). Belmont, CA: Fearon Teacher Aids, 1986.

Ceaser, L. D. Comprehension Capers Series: *Making Inferences* (gr. 1–3). Belmont, CA: Fearon Teacher Aids, 1986.

Liddle, William. *Reading for Concepts*. New York: McGraw-Hill, 1977.

Love, Marla. *20 Reading Comprehension Games* (gr. 4–6). Belmont, CA: Fearon Teacher Aids, 1977.

Wittenberg, Willima H. *Identifying Inferences* (gr. k–12). Baldwin, NY: Barnell Loft, 1986.

SPELLING

(also see **Handwriting**)

Abbatino, Vincent. *Spellbound* (gr. 1–6). New York: Vantage, 1990.

Barr, Linda. *Spelling & Writing* (gr. 1–4). Columbus: American Education, 1991.

Feinstein, George W. *Programmed Spelling Demons* (gr. 1–6). Englewood Cliffs, NJ: Prentice-Hall, 1984.

Kottmeyer, William, and Audrey Claus. *Basic Goals in Spelling* (gr. 5–8). New York: McGraw-Hill, 1984.

Wittenberg, William. *Diagnostic & Prescriptive Spelling Program* (gr. 2–8). Baldwin, NY: Barnell Loft, 1980.

STUDY SKILLS

(also see **Smart Thinking, Preparing for Tests, Inadequate Study Time, Note-taking, Conferencing with School Officials, Critical Thinking, Goals, Performance on Standardized Tests, Priorities**)

Flippo, Rona. *Test Wise* (gr. 11–college). Belmont, CA: Fearon Teacher Aids, 1988.

Greene, Lawrence J., and Leigh Jones Bamman. *Getting Smarter* (gr. 6–12). Belmont, CA: Fearon Teacher Aids, 1985.

Greene, Lawrence J. *Smarter Kids*. New York: Fawcett Crest, 1987.

Herman Ohme. *Learn How to Learn* (gr. 9–college). Palo Alto: California Educational Plan, 1986.

THINKING

(see **Critical Thinking, Logic, Smart Thinking**)

Anderson, Valerie, and Carl Bereiter. *Thinking Games 1 & 2* (gr. 4–7). Fearon Teacher Aids, 1980.

Black, Howard, and Sandra Black. *Building Thinking Skills II* (gr. 4–7). Pacific Grove, CA: Midwest Publications, 1987.

Gregorich, Barbara. *Logical Logic* (gr. 7–12). Santa Barbara: The Learning Works, 1985.

Greene, Lawrence J. *Smarter Kids*. New York: Fawcett Crest, 1987.

Harnader, Anita. *Critical Thinking* (gr. 4–7). Pacific Grove, CA: Midwest Publications, 1976.

Hopkins, Lee Bennett, and Annett Shapiro. *Creative Activities for the Gifted Child* (gr. 1–6). Belmont, CA: Fearon Teacher Aids, 1969.

Karnes, Merle B. *Primary Thinking Skills* (gr. k–2). Pacific Grove, CA: Midwest Publications, 1987.

Meredith, Paul, and Leslie Landin. *100 Activities for Gifted Children* (gr. 1–6). Belmont, CA: Fearon Teacher Aids, 1957.

Pavlich, V., and E. Rosenast. *Do Something Different* (gr. 4–7).Belmont, CA: Fearon Teacher Aids, 1987.

Post, Beverly, and Sandra Eads. *Digging into Logic* (gr. 5–8). Belmont, CA: Fearon Teacher Aids, 1987.

Post, Beverly, and Sandra Eads. *Logic Anyone?* (gr. 5–8). Belmont, CA: Fearon Teacher Aids, 1982.

Post, Beverly, and Sandra Eads. *Logic Anyone? Workbook* (gr. 5–8). Belmont, CA: Fearon Teacher Aids, 1982.

Prizzi, Elaine, and Jeanne Hoffman. *Re: Thinking* (gr. 5 & up). Belmont, CA: Fearon Teacher Aids, 1989.

Schoenfield, Mark, and Jeannette Rosenblatt. *Adventure with Logic* (gr. 5–7). Belmont, CA: Fearon Teacher Aids, 1985.

Schoenfield, Mark, and Jeannette Rosenblatt. *Discovering Logic* (gr. 4–6). Belmont, CA: Fearon Teacher Aids, 1985.

Schoenfield, Mark, and Jeannette Rosenblatt. *Playing with Logic* (gr. 3–5). Belmont, CA: Fearon Teacher Aids, 1985.

Symonds, Martha. *Think Big* (gr. 4–6). Santa Barbara: The Learning Works, 1977.

Williams, Wayne. *More Quizzles* (gr. 5 & up). Palo Alto: Dale Seymour Pubs., 1984.

Williams, Wayne. *Quizzles* (gr. 5 & up). Palo Alto: Dale Seymour Pubs., 1982.

Games and Learning Activities

"Critical Thinking Activity Cards" (gr. 2–3). Palo Verdes Estates, CA: Frank Schaffer Publications.

"Four-Scene Sequence Cards" (gr. pre-k–3). Baltimore: Media Materials.

"Pick Pairs Game" (gr. pre-k–3). Baltimore: Media Materials.

"Sequencing Activity Cards" (gr. 1–2). Palo Verdes Estates, CA: Frank Schaffer Publications.

"Smart Choices" (gr. 6 & up): St. Paul: Trend Enterprises.

"Space Race" (age 3–6). Palo Verdes Estates, CA: Frank Schaffer Publications.

"Three-Scene Sequence Posters" (gr. pre-k–3). Baltimore: Media Materials.

VOCABULARY

(also see **Verbal Expression**)

Allman, Barbara. *Vocabulary Building* (gr. 1). Palo Verdes Estates, CA: Frank Schaffer Pubs., 1987.

Criscuolo, Nicholas, and Barry E. Herman. *Fun with Words* (gr. 2–5). Belmont, CA: Fearon Teacher Aids, 1988.

Gill, Nancy. *Vocabulary Boosters* (gr. 4 & up). Belmont, CA: Fearon Teacher Aids, 1985.

Glicksberg, Joy Brumby. *Crosswords for Language Arts* (gr. 1–5). Belmont, CA: Fearon Teacher Aids, 1985.

Heymsfeld, Carla. *Digging into Language* (gr. 4 & up). Belmont, CA: Fearon Teacher Aids, 1983.

Knoblock, Kathleen. *Basic Word Vocabulary* (gr. 1–2). Palo Verdes Estates, CA: Frank Schaffer Pubs., 1989.

Love, Marla. *20 Word Structure Games* (gr. 2–5). Belmont, CA: Fearon Teacher Aids, 1983.

Marshall, Kim. The Kim Marshall Series: *Vocabulary* (gr. 5–6). Cambridge, MA: Educators Publishing Service, 1981.

Mueser, Anne Marie, and John Alan Mueser. *Practicing Vocabulary in Context* (gr. 2–8). New York: Random House, 1989.

Muncy, Patricia Tyler. *Word Puzzles* (gr. 4–6). Belmont, CA: Fearon Teacher Aids, 1974.

Robinson, Joan. The Roots of Language Series: Word Building (gr. 4–9). Belmont, CA: Fearon Teacher Aids, 1980.

Robinson, Joan. The Roots of Language Series: *Word Wise* (gr. 4–9). Belmont, CA: Fearon Teacher Aids, 1989.

Runjamin, Rosemary E. *New Dimensions in Dictionary Practice: Creative Lesson for Reinforcement and Enrichment* (gr. 4–6). Belmont, CA: Fearon Teacher Aids, 1987.

Wentrcek, Ginger. *Dandy Dictionary Skills: Motivating Work Sheets and Dictionary Practice* (gr. 2–4). Belmont, CA: Fearon Teacher Aids, 1986.

Games and Learning Activities

"Economo Word Builder" (gr. k–3). Baltimore: Media Materials.

"Sentence Builder" (gr. 1–3). Baltimore: Media Materials.

"Vocabulary Quizmo" (gr. 5–8). Baltimore: Media Materials.